# *HOAX*

# HOAX

*The Inside Story of the*
*Howard Hughes – Clifford Irving Affair*

STEPHEN FAY

LEWIS CHESTER

MAGNUS LINKLATER

*New York* | *The Viking Press*

First published in 1972 by The Viking Press, Inc.
625 Madison Avenue, New York, N.Y. 10022

Published simultaneously in Canada by
The Macmillan Company of Canada Limited

SBN 670-37430-x

Library of Congress catalog card number: 72-76797

Printed in U.S.A.

ACKNOWLEDGMENT
Regent Music Corp.: From "Managua, Nicaragua" by Albert Gamse and
Irving Fields.
Copyright 1946 by Regent Music Corp.

# Contents

*A C T  V*  **The Ladies Are Revealed**

*A C T  V I*  **Consternation in the Marketplace**

*A C T  V I I*  **The Monarch Flees His Palace**

*A C T  V I I I*  **The Jester Loses His Bells**

*(Illustrations follow page 150)*

# Preface

For the first two months of 1972, the hoax perpetrated by a little-known novelist, Clifford Irving, on the billionaire Howard Hughes attracted more attention in American newspapers than the Vietnam war or the impending presidential election. It was an ephemeral story which ended as suddenly as it had begun, but its significance is already the subject of some substantial generalizations. There are pro- and anti-hoax factions who debate with a sometimes startling disregard for specifics. To take one example, Clifford Irving was hailed in a New York underground paper as the architect of "one of the most imaginative revolutionary acts of the season. In what seems to be a masterly orchestrated game of sequential logic, he exposed the system's affinity [*sic*] for gullible stupidity. His ripoff has class."

At the other extreme are those who regard the hoax as a straightforward criminal fraud which came unstuck. Neither explanation, it seems to us, comes close to the real point. Yet it was an intriguing affair, illuminating some of the best and worst features of the American spirit and deserving of more than instant mythology.

While the public drama was unfolding both the principals gave it personal review notices. For Clifford Irving, it was "right out of the worst detective story you ever read," but it made Howard Hughes wish he was back in the motion picture business because, as he put it, "I don't remember any script as wild or as stretching the imagination as this yarn has turned out to be."

In trying to describe what actually happened, we have been helped by many people. Most spoke to us on the record, and their names are in the text. The narrative, however, has one special feature which we should mention here; it is one in which journalists are participants as well as observers. We are conscious of the fact that many of our American friends were better equipped to write this book than ourselves, but we had the time and they did not. They never appeared to begrudge us this luxury and were unfailingly kind and helpful to us. Among those to whom we are especially grateful are Frank McCulloch and William Lambert of *Time* magazine, John Goldman of the *Los Angeles Times,* and Bob Thomas of the Associated Press. But the greatest debt we owe is to James Phelan, the most ardent and able Hughes-watcher of them all, and the reporter who ultimately exploded the hoax.

We also have some debts to friends we left behind. It was a fast-moving story and at times it was hard to discern exactly where it was. At one stage we obtained a lead that the singing baroness, Nina Van Pallandt, a key figure in the hoax, had departed New York for London, and we cabled a young reporter suggesting that he might land the big interview on our behalf. Back came the reply:

THANK YOU FOR EXCELLENT OPPORTUNITY TO MAKE MY NAME IN BIG-TIME JOURNALISM. THIS IS THE MOST WONDERFUL BREAK—AND WITH A LUSCIOUS DANE, AND COUNTESS TO BOOT. THERE'S JUST ONE PROBLEM. NINA IS NOT IN ENGLAND, SHE IS IN NEW YORK WHERE YOU ARE SUPPOSED TO BE. . . .

As is often the case in prefaces to books written by *Sunday Times* reporters, we must single out our Paris correspondent, Anthony Terry. Not only did he travel regularly to Zurich and Ibiza on our behalf, but his reports were always of a quality that improved both our morale and our prose. We were, as we have come to take almost for granted, consistently and cheerfully looked after in the New York office of the *Sunday Times* by Laurie Zimmerman, Sheila Robinette, Mildred Temple, Lois Bidel, Akhtar Hussein, Joe Petta, Fred Crawford, and Robert Ducas.

In the London office of the *Sunday Times,* Frank Giles and James Evans calmed us in times of crisis. As did Harold Evans, the paper's editor, who begat the idea for this book and let us concentrate on the subject for rather longer than most editors would allow.

STEPHEN FAY

LEWIS CHESTER

MAGNUS LINKLATER

*New York City*
*April 1972*

# ACT I

## Excitement in the Marketplace

# The Elusive,
# Often Painful Truth

What we have here is a failure to communicate.

Donn Pearce, *Cool Hand Luke*

At 6 p.m. on Tuesday, December 7, 1971, the McGraw-Hill Book Company in New York released a 550-word news item. With the decorum customary in the publishing trade, it was delivered by hand to the wire services, the major metropolitan newspapers, and the television networks. The release contained the kind of story that any news editor could recognize as big. After fifteen years in self-imposed purdah, Howard Robard Hughes, billionaire, aviator, movie mogul, real-estate magnate, airline boss, gaming *supremo*, litigator, womanizer, and ecologist, a man who had often been described as "a dozen personalities rolled into one," was about to tell all. McGraw-Hill had his autobiography. Exclusive.

The release could afford understatement, and the policy of restraint, privately agreed in advance by those on the inside, was reflected in its contents. It told how Mr. Hughes, who would be sixty-six on Christmas Eve, had spent much of the past year developing his memoirs with an American author called Clifford Irving. The two men were said to have had almost a hundred sessions together "in various motel rooms and parked cars throughout the Western Hemisphere." At these sessions Irving had tape-recorded the reminiscences of the great man.

A hardcover edition of the total memoir, which ran to 230,000 words, would be published by McGraw-Hill on March 27, 1972. The price paid for this remarkable acquisition was not mentioned, but a figure of $300,000 was rumored; the rumor was less than half right. *Life* magazine, which had obtained serial rights, would carry three 10,000-word installments from the book, and a separate article by Mr. Irving telling the remarkable story of how the interviews had been conducted. The release went on to outline Mr. Hughes's reasons for breaking cover at this late stage of the game. It quoted what was said to be an extract from his preface to the book:

> I believe that more lies have been printed and told about me than about any living man—therefore it was my purpose to write a book which would set the record straight and restore the balance. . . .
>
> Biographies about me have been published before—all of them misleading and childish. I am certain that in the future more lies and rubbish will appear. The words in this book—other than some of the questions which provoked them—are my own spoken words. The thoughts, opinions and recollections, the descriptions of events and personalities, are my own. I have not permitted them to be emasculated or polished, because I realized, after the many interviews had been completed and transcribed, that this was as close as I could get to the elusive, often painful truth.
>
> I have lived a full life and, perhaps, what may seem a strange life—even to myself. I refuse to apologize, although I am willing now to explain as best I can. Call this autobiography. Call it my memoirs. Call it what you please. It is the story of my life in my own words.

Mr. Hughes, according to the release, paid tribute to his assistant on this massive enterprise. He had chosen Mr. Irving "because of his sympathy, discernment, discretion and, as I learned, his integrity as a human being."

There was little information about this paragon of ghosts. Mr. Irving, the release stated, was the author of several books, among them *The Losers* and *The Thirty-eighth Floor*. Oddly, it failed to mention his most recent and best-selling work, *Fake!*, a study of Irving's close friend, the master art forger Elmyr de Hory.

The omission was all the more curious since it was claimed later that *Fake!* was the book which had inspired Hughes to adopt Irving as his Boswell. Perhaps it was thought that mention of this intriguing detail would insert a regrettable hint of doubt in the public mind. There was, in the publishers' minds, no doubt whatsoever; so why invite problems? But journalists the world over are suspicious animals, and American journalists are more suspicious than most, especially about a Hughes story.

Howard Hughes had not been interviewed or photographed by any pressman since 1958. This had not prevented people from writing about him. There was a lively market for material speculating on Hughes's condition and whereabouts, but there had been nothing that any journalist could describe as "hard" information. There was even a body of opinion which suggested that he might be dead.

Every journalist with any experience of the Hughes organization knew that the obvious way to check the story— speak with the man himself—was quite simply impossible. Some, with the faith of atheists trying to get in touch with the Holy Ghost, did make calls to the Britannia Beach Hotel, Nassau, where Hughes was known to have rented the entire ninth floor for the past year. They got the old stonewall reply: "We don't have a Mr. Hughes registered here." Another long-distance call wasted.

More experienced hands did not even bother with this charade. They called up the time-honored Hughes public-relations firm, Carl Byoir and Associates. They had two options: Richard Hannah, in Los Angeles, who had handled the Hughes account for twenty-two years, or the Carl Byoir man in Las Vegas, Arelo Sederburg. Around 2:30 p.m. (Vegas and L.A. are three hours behind New York) both had jammed switchboards. And both were deeply confused.

All that Hannah or Sederburg could say was that they had no information, but both found the whole idea of a Hughes autobiography basically incredible. Could they deny the McGraw-Hill story? No, not at that stage, but they suggested that it be treated with extreme caution. Call back for clarification. Another half-hour went by, and Hannah and Sederburg became more assertive. Inquiring newsmen were told, "The Hughes Tool Company denies the existence of a Hughes autobiography."

This was an advance on "no comment" but scarcely the world's most convincing rebuttal. If there were no autobiography, then why not issue a denial in the name of Howard Hughes himself? The best efforts of the Carl Byoir men only succeeded in opening up a new area of speculation: Either Hughes had sanctioned his memoirs or he hadn't—the answer to this proposition could not be delegated.

In Las Vegas there were people who thought they knew why Hughes Tool had moved so quickly. McGraw-Hill's announcement of the autobiography coincided with the most delicate phase in negotiations over Hughes's $150-million gambling empire. After a prolonged wrangle, the Hughes Tool Company had finally persuaded the Nevada Gaming Control Board to consider a simplified management structure that would involve the issue of gaming licenses to Chester Davis, the company's general counsel, and other company officials.

Nevada law lays down that applications for gaming licenses must be supported in person by the owner of the gaming interests: by law, therefore, Howard Hughes ought to have appeared in Nevada to sanction Davis's applications, and for the past year Nevada's recently elected Governor, Mike O'Callaghan, and the new young Gaming Control Board Chairman, Bill Hannifin, had been taking a tough line and insisting that Howard Hughes could not be an exception to the law. It was only with the gravest reservations that they had, in November, agreed to consider a possible compromise —a handwritten letter from Hughes, authenticated by fingerprints. And they had accepted this formula on the grounds that Hughes found the prospect of a personal confrontation "traumatic."

When, therefore, on December 7, they heard that Hughes was apparently hale enough to travel round the continent talking his head off to an unknown author, the Nevada authorities were distinctly not amused.

Hannifin immediately contacted the Las Vegas law firm of Foley, Morse and Wadsworth, which represented Chester Davis, and told it to pass on a message to him. If the reports were true, the message went, Hughes and Hughes Tool had clearly breached faith with the Nevada authorities. The Gaming Board might find itself obliged to take a new view of the applications. The implication was clear: if Hughes Tool valued its Nevada interests, it would either have to explode the story of the autobiography or do a lot of explaining.

Back in New York, the Hughes Tool denial left the McGraw-Hill and *Life* executives conspicuously unmoved. Ralph Graves, *Life*'s managing editor, who had handled the magazine's interest in the Irving book, was telephoned that evening by an excited colleague with news of the denial.

"Well," said Graves coolly, "what did you expect?"

In a curious way the prompt thumbs-down by Hughes Tool buttressed the book's credibility. Irving had made it clear to his publishers that Hughes had told nobody in the higher echelons of his organization about his autobiography; not Chester Davis, or even Frank W. (Bill) Gay, the company's senior vice-president. So, since none of them knew about it, it was natural that they should deny the existence of an autobiography, particularly when there might be good business reasons for not wanting to see it published. Besides, nobody in the Hughes organization ever lost status by denying the authenticity of works about him. His distaste for publicity—good or bad—was legendary. The directors of Hughes Tool, Graves thought, were simply operating on well-trusted reflexes. They did not know the inside story.

Earlier that day, Graves had held court on the twenty-ninth floor of the Time-Life building, where he brought the middle-rank executives of the magazine into his confidence. The assembled crowd overflowed from his office into the corridor and listened with rapt attention. Up to this point only a tiny group of senior Time-Life executives had been "in" on the Irving-Hughes negotiations. *Life* had been in rocky financial shape for some years; it needed a big coup. This, Graves implied, was it.

At the meeting, Graves went much further than the official McGraw-Hill release in explaining the authenticity of the product. He read out a three-paragraph excerpt from a handwritten letter which Hughes had allegedly written to the publishers. It sanctioned publication of his memoirs. There was an awed silence before one executive, scarcely able to credit the magazine's luck, asked the obvious question.

"How do we know the letter's not a forgery?"

Graves fielded that one with easy aplomb. "No question. It's authentic all right. We've had it checked by an expert."

Over at McGraw-Hill, Ted Weber, the vice-president in charge of information, had left his office before news of the Hughes Tool denial came through. He took his usual train home, the 5 p.m. from Grand Central to Fairfield, Connecticut, with an unclouded conscience. When he arrived at 7 p.m., his wife met him on the doorstep with a sheaf of messages from the wire services and the networks asking for McGraw-Hill's observations on the tool company denial. He was a bit surprised but not shocked. As he put it later, "This was the way you expected the Hughes people to behave, whether the book was genuine or not." He referred all the calls to McGraw-Hill's trade-book spokesman and settled down for a quiet supper.

As the evening wore on, two publishing executives began to take most of the calls from newsmen bouncing back for comments on the denial. For McGraw-Hill, Albert Leventhal, the general-books vice-president, put the record straight. Leventhal told *The New York Times,* "We have gone to considerable efforts to ascertain that this is indeed the Hughes autobiography. And we believe what we say is correct." *Life* magazine's Donald M. Wilson, vice-president for corporate and public affairs, was even more crushing. "We never dealt with the Hughes Tool Company. It doesn't surprise us that they know nothing of this, since Mr. Hughes was totally secretive about the project." To another inquirer he said, "Oh, we're absolutely positive. Look, we're dealing with people like McGraw-Hill, and, you know, we're not exactly a movie magazine! This is Time, Inc., and McGraw-Hill talking. We've checked this thing out. We have proof."

Apart from Howard Hughes, there was another leading character conspicuous by his absence on launching day— Clifford Irving. Journalists asking about him and his whereabouts obtained very small change. He was a novelist, aged forty-one, who lived in Spain and was under contract to McGraw-Hill. He was not available for interviews at present. The reason for not unveiling the hero of the enterprise on this proud day was to emerge later. He was away on a delicate mission. Irving had told a few select McGraw-Hill executives that he must on no account be disturbed, as he would be in Florida, bracing Mr. Howard Hughes himself for the shock of the public announcement of his memoirs, handing over a check to him for $350,000, and getting Hughes to sign the Preface. He surfaced back at the publishers' a few days later, with signature and without check. Irving always delivered on his promises to McGraw-Hill.

Yet despite the elusiveness of the two principals, there was no doubt about who had won the battle of assertion on Day One. Against the cryptic and apparently self-serving denial by Hughes Tool there was the massive assertion of confidence by the largest publishing company in the world. Next morning *The New York Times'* story, by its publications specialist, Henry Raymont, ran for a full six paragraphs before making any mention of the denial. The *Life* and McGraw-Hill dismissals of it were given much greater prominence.

On the West Coast, the *Los Angeles Times* carried substantially the same story, though it did upgrade the tool company's denial to the fourth paragraph and quoted a friend of Irving's in Beverly Hills. The friend said, "I've been getting postcards from him [Irving] this past year from all sorts of funny places." It seemed to confirm Irving's claims to a series of meetings "throughout the Western Hemisphere." Most other newspapers showed a similar inclination to accept McGraw-Hill's claim.

The public balance of credibility was to remain undisturbed for another thirty-one days, and then the shift was only marginal. It took sixty-seven days before McGraw-Hill and *Life* were obliged to admit that what had once seemed the publishing coup of the generation was in fact the literary hoax of the century. By this time, the apparently simple problem of establishing whether a living person had or had not written his autobiography had involved an unrivaled assembly of investigative talent—public, private, and journalistic. But the final accolade for the world's greatest freewheeling fantasy came even later. On February 18, 1972, the New York *Daily News* underlined the effect of the hoax on media priorities with two headlines on its front page. The first, in bold banner style, gave information about a change of address by a private citizen: HUGHES MOVES TO NICARAGUA. The second, lower down, in a smaller and less compelling type face, announced that the President of the United States had started on the most important diplomatic mission since the last world war: "Nixon in Hawaii on China Trip" and, smaller still: "His 'Journey for Peace' Begins."

But we are running ahead of our story. It is time to go back to square one: a small offshore Spanish island called Ibiza, in the soft and clement winter of 1970.

# ACT II

## The Jester Discovers a Monarch

# Making It

It is a simple life that gives you a sense
of your own awareness.

Clifford Irving

On Sunday afternoons during the winter months a band
plays on the main square of Ibiza town. It is not a large
band—about a dozen musicians dressed in blue uniform,
wielding elderly cornets, a horn or two, and the odd clarinet.
They play marches, a waltz, some light Spanish airs; and
while the timing leaves something to be desired and they are
not always entirely in tune, their appearance on the square
is undoubtedly a high point in the day.

The afternoon strollers, mostly local Spanish people enjoying the warm winter sun, gather round to admire the
fierce concentration of the conductor and the agility of the
percussion man as he switches from drum to tambourine to
castanets and back to drum again.

The reaction of the people outside the long cafés on the
other side of the square is rather different. They have been
sitting in groups around the little glass-topped tables drinking gins or Cinzanos, and the noise of the band is an un-
welcome distraction. They lean forward to carry on their
obviously important conversations, irritated by the interrup-

tion. They are not local people, though it is clear, from their permanent tans and the nonchalance of their instructions to the waiter, that they have been around on the island for some time. They speak German or English, French or Italian, and they talk about art and literature and each other. Their most intense conversations appear to revolve around the latter.

Ibiza's colony of expatriates is typical of half a dozen similar outposts strung at various points across the western Mediterranean. It is peopled by the idle rich, retreating from cold weather, unsympathetic governments, and penal tax systems in order to sample once again the pleasures of the simple life; and by painters, writers, sculptors, poets, and sensitive journalists fleeing a world of avaricious (or uninterested) publishers, materialistic gallery-owners, and brutish editors . . . in order to sample once again the pleasures of the simple life. They began homing in on Ibiza about twenty years ago to nurture their various talents under the sun and watch them flower, unfettered by the pressures of money or the men who handle it.

The two groups mingle together without embarrassment in a flexible and relatively classless society, which is relaxed, unpompous, and unhurried. To the fleeting visitor it might seem to be a charming existence, and, indeed, he would meet with no lack of assurance from the inhabitants themselves that this was the perfect life.

A little more research, however, might reveal a few serious flaws in the idyl. The retreat to the simple life, for instance, has not been as absolute as it appears. The charming old farmhouses and the picturesque cottages in which most members of the colony live are certainly built in the simple local style, but there is nothing peasant-like about those simply indispensable refrigerators and the television sets which follow as soon as the *ghastly* inefficiency of the local electricity company allows. And of course no one can *really* afford to forsake forever the pleasures of an occasional trip back to London or Paris or New York. These journeys to the flesh-pots are in fact a necessity, considering the nature of the work in which much of the colony is involved; its products have little relevance to the local economy. When a book is completed or a set of paintings collected together, it has to be dangled in front of a publisher or a gallery-owner. The more productive expatriate Ibizans practice a curious kind of imperialism in reverse, exploiting the much despised industrial world to maintain the simple life in the style to which they have become accustomed. Ambivalence is a built-in social attitude.

There is another flaw. The atmosphere on the island, apparently so conducive to free expression, does not always encourage a high rate of productivity. Much of the conversation at the café tables revolves around the *next* novel, the *next* picture, the *next* poem, the *next* article, and there is often a serious time lag before the work in question actually appears. It is much easier to while away a warm afternoon sampling the local *vino* and discussing the agonies of creation than to face those agonies head-on. Those who do paint and sell their pictures or finish and sell their novels are therefore the object of some awe and not a little envy.

The winter of 1970 was, even for Ibiza, a mild one. It was also rather boring. There seemed to be no scandals, no serious vendettas, no flagrant affairs to gossip about. The tourist season just ended had thrown up more of those dreadful British tourists on their package holidays than ever before, and the hippies were getting beyond a joke, but that was no longer worth discussion. The steam had even gone out of the de Hory affair now that Clifford Irving's book had been published and the initial controversy had abated.

Elmyr de Hory, in better days, had been the focus of the island's attention. A dapper, exotic Hungarian of indeterminate background, he had rocked Ibiza with the revelation that he was the forger of countless pictures supposedly by such artists as Matisse, Modigliani, Renoir, and Chagall, which sold for millions of dollars across Europe and America.

The affair had escalated into bitter quarrels between de Hory and art dealers Fernand Legros and Real Lessard, in which everyone on the island had naturally taken sides. Add the fact that all three were given to theatrically violent gestures, and there was incident enough to feed the gossipers a diet of almost unbearable richness. Clifford Irving, with a novelist's eye for drama, had stepped in to take advantage of the situation and had persuaded de Hory that his story would be an eminently marketable property. He had held out the possibility of making "anything from $50,000 to $1,000,000" on the project and had assured de Hory not only that he would be free of legal problems but that he would get half the profits. There had, however, been bitter quarrels between the two almost from the outset, about Elmyr's editorial control (or lack of it) and Irving's expenses on the job. The book, when it finally emerged, was greeted with modest reviews and uninspiring sales. What is more, it prompted a spectacular libel suit for $55 million by the outraged Fernand Legros.

But at the outset, in 1968 and early 1969, it had all been rather jolly. At one stage an independent French film company had visited Ibiza to film the great forger and his literary promoter in their natural habitat. De Hory obliged the cameramen by knocking off a fast Picasso and boasting of a past "original" which had been unloaded on to an art dealer for $100,000. Irving was invited to explain the significance of it all. He said he was profoundly impressed by de Hory's attention to significant detail—he would "put a little coffee stain on a Modigliani to make it look really as if Modigliani had done it in some Paris café." Such painstaking work had rich rewards. Irving related how he had taken two Matisses and one Modigliani (all, in fact, de Horys) to the Museum of Modern Art in New York, spun some cock-and-bull story about inheriting them from an aunt in France, and asked: could they, conceivably, be genuine? The Museum decided that they were.

De Hory, Irving felt, was much misunderstood. "If you

were to put it to him that he had taken advantage of the world, that he had cheated people, he would be horrified." The man himself was both "charming and lovable," but he was more than that. He was an example for all mankind. Irving assumed a serious expression for the benefit of potential owners. "All the world loves to see the experts and the Establishment made a fool of, and everyone likes to feel that those who set themselves up as experts are really just as gullible as anyone else. Elmyr, as the great art faker of the twentieth century, becomes a modern folk hero for the rest of us."

While this portentous nonsense was being uttered, a squirrel monkey took occasional peeks over Irving's shoulder. Most expatriate Ibizans thought Irving was being both funny and wise: he had neatly encapsulated two strands in the islanders' subconscious: a contempt for the modern world and a yearning to be recognized by it. Nobody, not even Clifford Irving, realized that he was shaping up as Ibiza's second "modern folk hero."

With the de Hory affair behind him, Irving, in the winter of 1970, was toying with the plot structure for his fifth novel. It was going to be called *The Man in the Mink Collar.*

Clifford Irving was the quintessential Ibizan, straddling easily the narrow dividing line between the upper crust and the artists. He was six feet four inches tall, loose-limbed, dark-haired, with a warm smile that managed to put most people immediately at their ease. His charm was a cultivated asset, enhanced by his relaxed clothes (no one had ever seen him wearing a tie), by the pipe he smoked with some diffidence, and by a habit which was enormously appreciated on Ibiza, of listening with apparent enjoyment to other people's conversations. He was as much at home with the more raffish elements of Ibizan society, as they drifted from bar to bar through a long night of ferocious drinking, as he was in the drawing rooms of the island's jet set, outplaying its members at poker or backgammon, drinking their Scotch, impressing them with his knowledge of the rich people and the rich life

they had left behind them. There was often a suspicion, however, that even after ten years on the island Clifford Irving
had not entirely settled down to the easy life and that his
ambitions were harder and deeper than was usual amongst
Ibizans. He obviously resented bitterly his lack of success as
a writer and made no secret of wanting the kind of acclaim
from the outside world that would finally outweigh it. But a
lifetime spent in search of rich rewards had brought, so far,
only an ever-lengthening list of failures.

The search goes back to the early years in New York, where
Clifford Michael Irving was born on November 5, 1930, an
only child. The family was Jewish, but not aggressively so.
Clifford's mother, Dorothy, was never very close to him. His
father, however, was a strong and dominant influence. Jay
Irving was a cartoonist, successful in his day as a designer of
magazine covers and the creator of a cartoon strip called
*Pottsy,* featuring the trials and tribulations of a stout and
jovial policeman, which ran for years in the Sunday *News.*

He was a big man with a hobby, which he himself described
as "a passion," of collecting mementos of policemen. The six-
room apartment on West End Avenue was crammed with bil-
lies, nightsticks, shields, helmets, and uniforms dating back
three hundred years. One of them had belonged to his father,
Abraham Lincoln Irving. His admiration for policemen was
equaled only by his pride in his son, Cliff, about whom he was
prepared to talk for hours on end. Clifford Irving's "Jewish
mother" was his father.

Jay had determined views about his son's future. He
wanted him to achieve the success and respect which he had
never quite achieved himself, and he wanted him to be his
own master. There was never, it seems, any precise idea in his
mind as to how Clifford was going to achieve this, but it
would probably be in movies or by writing. It was not an
unhappy background, but the remoteness, the lack of overt
affection, which was part of Jay's character was one of the
salient traits Clifford Irving inherited from his father.

As a schoolboy Clifford was popular, his work in class enough to get by on. He was tall, good-looking, and, as he progressed into his teens, increasingly attractive to the opposite sex. In 1947 he graduated from the High School of Music and Art with a reputation as a keen football player and an incipient ladies' man. The only record remaining in the class yearbook, however, is a harmless jingle predicting that Clifford would become Secretary of the Treasury. It goes:

> Cliff, at six foot two, you'll see,
> Maestro of our Treasury.

It was not the most accurate of predictions, though Clifford was extremely keen on making money.

He went on that same year to Cornell University, where the seeds of his literary ambition were sown and the first signs of a limited nonconformity emerged. A small clique of fledgling writers, of which Irving was part, began to get together to hold long and animated discussions about such revolutionary topics as the limitations of American cultural standards, the restrictions imposed on the artist by society, the blows for literary freedom that a writer ought to strike. They talked about the novels, the poems, the short stories they intended to write in order to pierce the fabric of the establishment. It was heady stuff, a bit like Ibiza's *Kaffeeklatsch,* with youthful enthusiasm taking the place of the Cinzanos.

Like most young writers of the day, they admired Hemingway as a cultural hero, but there is little evidence that for Clifford Irving he was more than an initial influence. Only one of Irving's subsequent novels owes much to Hemingway's style. Although there is a superficial resemblance between the life styles of the two, it was seldom translated into words. Irving's ambitions seemed to be concerned more with the role of the writer than with writing for its own sake.

Socially, however, Irving and his friends were a. success. They were considered outspoken, colorful, daringly disrespectful of their elders, and Irving was a ringleader. "He was the closest thing we had then to a hippie," recalled one starry-eyed contemporary. It sounds romantic, but, as one studies photographs of Irving in those days, with his close-cropped curly hair and neatly arranged collar and tie, it is just a little difficult to imagine.

Academically his career was unremarkable, but his extra-curricular activities sparkled. President of the Pi Lambda Phi fraternity in his senior year, he married, at the age of twenty, the most glamorous girl on the campus, Nina Wilcox. A classmate described them as "the golden couple," and when Clifford stayed on to take a course in creative writing, Nina introduced him to anti-war politics in the aftermath of Korea. For a time he was even quite interested in the subject.

The marriage lasted barely two years. It ended effectively when Clifford Irving's wanderlust took over and he left Nina behind at Cornell. He began traveling across America, working first as a copy boy in New York, then as a machine hand in Detroit, later as a Fuller brush salesman. He was at the same time writing his first novel, to be called *On a Darkling Plain,* and he took the manuscript with him on his first visit to Europe, where he moved about from Stockholm to Vienna, the Mediterranean, London, Amsterdam, Spain. The book is, like most first novels, heavily autobiographical, with characters drawn from his Cornell days. It was also not immediately salable and went to eight publishers before finally finding a home with Putnam in 1956. The financial rewards were negligible.

Unlike most first novelists, however, he quickly produced a second book. This one was a depressing story, though skillfully told, called *The Losers.* Irving, who had by this time discovered the Balearic Islands, had been to discuss the book with Robert Graves, on the island of Majorca, and had returned triumphantly to tell everyone that Graves had described it as "the best short novel I have read in twenty years." Graves does not remember saying this. When asked his opinion of Irving, he recalls only discussing the novel with him, and giving him some advice about how it could be improved.

In 1958 Irving married again. Claire Lydon was an English girl whom he had met on the island of Ibiza, and he took her with him to California. It was not a successful marriage. Irving was unfaithful, Claire was unhappy, and the relationship was drifting toward disaster when an accident of horrifying suddenness cut it short. Driving with the wife of a novelist friend—Dennis Murphy—Claire was killed, along with her companion, when the car plowed off the road near Monterey.

The blow came at a critical stage in Irving's career. He had written two novels, neither of them particularly successful; he had momentarily exhausted his desire for travel; and his personal life seemed to be dogged by disaster. Tentatively, he began work on a new book, couched in a very different style, which represented an obvious attempt to break out of the mold. A tough, low-key Western called *The Valley,* it set out to describe the impact of a domineering father on his favorite son. As Irving progressed with it he grew more confident of its possibilities, and when it was completed in 1960 he submitted it to the prestigious firm of McGraw-Hill in New York, which accepted it for publication. Irving returned to California in better heart and with a new girl friend.

California in 1961 was the lodestar of the literary Beat scene, and Irving decided to try the temperature of Venice West, the Beat capital, at the instigation of Fay Brooke, a beautiful English girl who had been a fashion model and wanted to be a poet. But while Fay was received with open arms by the old-timers in Venice, Clifford met with a cooler reception. For one thing, as *The Valley* began to make him some money for the first time, he appeared to be devoting as much time to cultivating rich Hollywood producers as he did to sitting at the feet of Venice gurus, smoking pot and drinking in the counterculture. He even slipped off for an occasional visit to the capitalist gambling hells of Las Vegas.

Lawrence Lipton, one of the movement's architects, was

contemptuous of Irving's failure to "make the Venice West Beat scene in any honest and meaningful way." He derided his reputation as a nonconformist and said sarcastically, "He never bought himself a beret." The Irvings (Fay had become the third Mrs. Irving by this time) rented Lipton's apartment, and she became an ardent disciple of the new poetry. But Clifford did not appear to take Lipton and his friends as seriously as they would have liked; this may have inspired the article which Lipton later wrote about him in the Los Angeles *Free Press*.

> He was giving up on prosecraft [Lipton said]. His attempts at Beat writing had been unsuccessful. He was too inhibited, too secretive with himself to achieve a truly communicative style. He was beginning to hang around with writers of *non-books,* books which are based on pre-sold, pre-publicized material, on interviews, research, tape-recordings. It was the easy way. It had led others to fame and fortune. The Hollywood name for it was a "pre-sold property," something that had publicity already going for it, that made no demands on the author for inventive plot, or character development.

Irving, however, was rapidly becoming as disillusioned with the Hollywood moguls as he was with Lipton and his crowd. Surrounding him was all the gilt and glitter of rich California. It was no problem for a young man of charm and good appearance to mingle easily with the rich, even if he did live out in the slums of Venice West. He was invited to Hollywood dinner parties where producers and scriptwriters moaned about their taxes and their $2000-a-week incomes. Money seemed to be as easily available as the eager starlets who hung around the studios, but somehow the jobs that were discussed so airily and generously over the dinner table never quite materialized in the form of hard offers the next day. Irving watched as men whom he considered to have mediocre talent and mediocre ideas wrote themselves contracts worth thousands of dollars for unoriginal projects and unoriginal movies. There was a system for quick success, but he himself never found the key.

The trouble was that Clifford Irving, as a writer, was unable to distinguish himself, even in mediocre company. The basic qualities that make a good novelist—curiosity, observation, and the ability to work hard at his craft—seemed to be lacking. Perhaps the first person to begin to realize this was Fay Irving, and her feelings on the subject came tumbling out one evening after a dinner party at which one of the guests was not only an observer but a meticulous recorder of his observations—the novelist Irving Wallace.

Wallace kept a notebook in which he wrote down personal details of people he met. If they interested him, he would record what they said and how they behaved, and some of them might even end up as characters in his novels. He had met the Irvings from time to time. He liked Clifford, but he was *interested* in Fay. "I like magnificent, intelligent, slightly damaged women for models and she possibly could be one," he noted at the time. As she talked to Wallace about herself, Fay began to analyze her relations with Clifford. She was disappointed in him—as a man and as a writer. Self-absorbed, selfish, he seemed to have no real consideration for others, to have experienced no love for anyone, and therefore to be incapable of receiving it. And it was just these characteristics that made him an uninteresting writer. He was lazy, preferred to write off the top of his head rather than carrying out any inquiring research about people or things outside his immediate range of experience. No amount of skilled writing could cover up the shallowness of that observation.

Wallace wrote later in his journal that Fay had said, "I suggested to Cliff that he make a doctor or a lawyer character, but he said I know nothing about a doctor or a lawyer. I said you should do research to get into their skins but he wouldn't."

Wallace was reminded of his acquaintance with the Irvings some years later when Clifford brought out his fourth novel.

It was called *The Thirty-eighth Floor* and was about an American Negro who becomes Acting Secretary-General of the UN. The theme and one or two of the characters bore a remarkable resemblance to Irving Wallace's novel *The Man,* a best-seller published eighteen months earlier, about a Negro who becomes President of the United States. So struck was Wallace by the similarities that he intended to write to Clifford, poking some fun at him. But the novel flopped badly, and Wallace felt it would be too cruel a point to make.

Another friend at this time, Robert Kirsch, book reviewer for the *Los Angeles Times,* watched in consternation as Irving's confidence in himself began to crumble. Irving was drinking more, and he took much of his frustration out on Fay. But through it all he retained a tight control, in public, at least. No one ever saw him give way amongst friends to rage or despair. There was only a growing bitterness.

One evening the Irvings invited Kirsch to dinner together with a friend, Dennis Murphy, and his wife. It was not an easy occasion, for some reason, and after dinner everyone sitting around in the shabby living room seemed to be on edge. Then Irving and Murphy began to quarrel. In low, tense, and strangely cryptic language they began to argue over something that had happened on Ibiza some time before. Kirsch was unable to make out what it was, but gradually it became clear that the row was going to turn violent. Suddenly Murphy leaped on Irving and began to grapple with him. It was no ordinary brawl. Murphy was in a black rage as he tried to wrestle Irving to the ground. Kirsch ordered the women out of the room and started to intervene. But Irving, tall and immensely powerful, had seized Murphy by the wrists and was holding him back. His face was pale and set, and there was no emotion in it as Murphy struggled impotently at the end of that iron grip. Just as suddenly as it had begun, the fight was over.

"Irving was struggling as much to control his feelings as he was to control Murphy," said Kirsch. "It was like a man playing an intense and controlled game of poker rather than a man fighting for his life." Kirsch was not to see that expression on Irving's face again until he met him ten years later on Ibiza, when the struggle was a very different one.

By the summer of 1962 Irving had finished with California, in spite of a job teaching creative writing at UCLA Extension school, which Kirsch had found to tide him over the previous winter. Late that year, together with Fay and their young son, Josh, he left for Ibiza and what Lipton described in his article as "that Lost Legion of expatriate pseudo-intellectual jet-set poseurs."

If Irving's confidence in himself was hurt, Ibiza was certainly the place to go for recuperation. The colony looks after its own. If you abide by the rules, there is always someone to reach out a helping hand when the money really begins to run short or the outside world turns its coldest shoulder. More than one hard-pressed Ibizan writer has had cause to be grateful for the charity or sympathy of those more successful than himself, and Irving, when he was in the money, had been a giver. Generosity is one of the better qualities of Ibizan life.

As the bruises began to heal in the warm Mediterranean sun, Irving settled into more easygoing ways; there was a long, five-year gap between the publication of *The Valley* and the appearance of his next book. His closest friends on the island were now less frequently the writers and artists along the cafés and more often the Ibizan upper class. People like the Albertinis.

Gerald and Laurel Albertini were the kind with whom Irving could feel at ease—physically, because they were extremely rich, and mentally, because they offered no great challenge to his ego. They expected nothing from him except his company, and he did not need to sell them his talents as a scriptwriter or his ideas for a movie. Gerald was a retired playboy. At the age of twenty-one he had inherited $8,500,-000 from the Reynolds-Albertini American railroad fortune, though he himself was English-born and -bred. For the next eight years, in the late 1950s and early 1960s, he had gambled on the tracks and the tables, thrown extravagant parties, bought expensive racehorses. He was the toast of the London gossip columns in the days when gossip meant gossip and the vagaries of the rich and famous were its lifeblood. The columnists recorded Albertini's punch-ups and reproduced his betting slips with the zeroes running off the edge of the paper. They simpered over his marriage to the beautiful widow of his best friend, killed in the romantic Mille Miglia road race, and they nudged each other over the gilded stag party that preceded it. They dubbed him Gerry "Golden Boy" Albertini. Others, less impressed, called him a high-class bread-roll-thrower. In 1963, however, the pace began to tell on Gerry and his fortune, and he retired without fanfare to Ibiza. It was quiet, true, but he still managed to slip back for the really important race meetings at Epsom and Goodwood, and the supplies kept on coming through with reasonable regularity from Harrod's and Fortnum's, so life was tolerable, if just a little tedious. And above the little village of San Antonio he renovated and redecorated one of the most impressive mansions on Ibiza, looking out over the bay and furnished inside like an English stately home. Here, of an evening, Clifford Irving would relieve him of large slices of money at poker, and he would sometimes win them back at backgammon.

Among his other friends on the island Irving was admired as a skilled chess-player and an outdoor man who could serve his turn on the local basketball team. He would take an annual trip to the States to watch the Superbowl in January. He was also, now as ever, the object of a deeper kind of admiration from the opposite sex. There is an unfair proportion of beautiful women on Ibiza, not only in the summer, when the beaches are crowded with sun-worshiping secretaries for whom male attention is right at the top of the holiday agenda, but within the colony itself, amongst the painters and the poets. As often as not there is a clutch of film stars, a divorcée

or two, perhaps even a few bored wives in holiday villas.
There was also a beautiful Danish singer who owned a house
on the island—the Baroness Nina Van Pallandt.

In 1965 Clifford and Fay were finally divorced. Some of
Irving's friends ascribed the breakdown to his coldness, but
this quality does not seem to have been an insurmountable
barrier to the many women he met. His success in the sexual
field, according to those best in a position to record it, sprang
from a certain kind of lazy charm combined with that fatal
quality evinced by a man who appears to have suffered much
and who needs the sympathy and understanding that only a
woman can supply. But his coolness and the insensitivity he
often showed in the later stages of a relationship meant that
many of his liaisons were short-lived.

His marriage to Edith Sommer, an artist on Ibiza, in 1967,
had a more permanent look to it than the first three. She was,
for one thing, just as clever as he was and quite determined
that the marriage was going to be an equal partnership. She
could, and frequently did, point out his shortcomings in
public and upbraid him for his failings as a husband and,
later, as a father. Those present would note that Clifford listened calmly, a trifle embarrassed, but not unduly upset. It
seemed to be good for him.

Edith was in her thirties, slim, attractive, with streaked
light blond hair falling to her shoulders, and capable hands.
She was the daughter of a Swiss businessman who had left
her a comfortable yearly income, and she had been divorced
from her first husband, who was German and whom Edith
claims she found unbearably stuffy, though they remained
friends. She was a serious painter of abstracts, one of the half-
dozen artists on the island who appeared to have some talent,
and she had received encouragement and a little mild spon-
sorship from Elmyr de Hory, who was, of course, something
of an expert in appreciating good paintings. Those on Ibiza
who liked her said that she was the best thing that had ever

happened to Cliff and that he simply didn't appreciate her. Others thought that she gave him a tough time.

She was certainly not an enthusiastic *Hausfrau*. She hated cooking and left most of the domestic chores to the Spanish couple who ran the house and looked after the children. The Irvings ate out in Ibiza more often than not. Edith dressed as casually as Clifford, but she was vainer about her appearance. Her clothes were blouses and jeans, but they were expensive and carefully chosen. Her hair usually looked tousled but had probably taken half an hour to arrange. Her moods were unpredictable: she could be silent and sullen or gay and mischievous for no apparent reason. And she was very possessive about Cliff. Her more malicious friends said that she had set out to stalk Clifford from the moment she set eyes on him.

Together the Irvings built onto the three-hundred-year-old farmhouse she had bought, until it had fifteen cluttered rooms, suitably modernized à la mode Ibiza. By that winter of 1970 they had two charming sons—Ned, whom they called Nedsky, and Barnaby. They also owned a black mongrel dog and three cars. Clifford had produced another novel and *Fake!* and had been rewarded in December 1969 with a remarkable contract, which guaranteed him a total advance payment of $150,000 against royalties for his next three books. He had already received half of it, and at last his life appeared to be set on a steady course.

Those who knew him well, however, were not so sure. They detected a re-emergence of that restless quality which had once been such a dominant trait. There were several reasons, they thought. *Fake!,* on which he had pinned such hopes, had not been the runaway success he had been counting on, and in spite of the fact that Fernand Legros's $55-million lawsuit had frozen the royalties, de Hory was beginning to ask pertinent questions about his share of the proceeds. Two subsequent books, *Spy* and *Battle of Jerusalem,* neither published by McGraw-Hill, had failed to make an impact, though the latter, an account of the Six-Day-War, had evoked suggestions from Israel that Mr. Irving had relied too heavily on his imagination in describing certain scenes. Edith was becoming suspicious about Clifford's feelings toward Nina, the Danish baroness, and—like quite a number of people on Ibiza that winter—Clifford was feeling bored and inactive and old and unfulfilled. He had just celebrated his fortieth birthday and he didn't seem to like the view on the other side of the watershed.

None of which could explain why, toward the end of December, he became so anxious to see more of his old friend Dick Suskind. Dick was a solid, dependable character who had once lived on Ibiza and had been a close companion. Irving had borrowed money from him on one or two occasions. But since he had left to live on the larger island of Majorca, where he could get a better education for his children, the two had not met with any frequency and there seemed no immediate reason for the sudden amity. Nevertheless the craggy, lumbering figure of Richard Raphael Suskind ("built like an avalanche with a gargoyle on top," as one admirer put it) became familiar around the Irving house in the succeeding weeks and months, while Clifford Irving was an equally frequent passenger on the Iberian DC-9 that ferried between Ibiza and Palma, Majorca's capital.

Suskind was a writer of speedily produced nonfiction. His books had included one on anarchy, one on the Moslem Empire (for the "young adult" market), a history of Richard the Lionhearted, and one on the Crusades. One of these—his history of the Crusades—leaned fairly heavily on Sir Steven Runciman's classic three-volume masterpiece on the subject but gave no acknowledgment to Runciman. One reviewer who noticed the parallels and the lack of attribution was Robert Kirsch of the *Los Angeles Times*. Suskind later admitted to Kirsch that there should have been a bibliography.

Suskind had wanted originally to be a singer, and he had attended both the Juilliard School in New York and the Conservatory of Music in Paris in 1947. But the demand for heldentenors was rock-bottom at the time, and after trying to sing, write, and act bit parts in movies, mainly in Italy, he had given up the notion. A ludicrous spell in the Israeli Army in 1948, in which he claims to have sung Neapolitan songs for the troops, finally convinced him that neither the army nor singing was a profitable employment, and he applied for a discharge. This was followed by a spell as a merchant seaman, a university term at Columbia in his home town of New York, and a period during which he helped to edit an adventure magazine for men.

But in 1960 he began to put down roots on Ibiza, and by the time he moved over to Majorca he had secured a safe if unspectacular reputation in potted history. There was little to tempt him away from it. Unless, of course, there was the chance of a really spectacular book. . . .

The Albertinis and the Baroness Van Pallandt were among the first Ibizans to discover early in 1971 that Irving and Suskind were onto something very spectacular indeed. The word went around Ibiza, under many an oath of secrecy, about what it was: Clifford Irving was close to his literary breakthrough. There were no details as yet, but it seemed that he had established a unique relationship with a twentieth-century Croesus called Howard Hughes, and this was being parlayed into a great publishing coup. Expatriate Ibiza had something important to gossip about again, a rock-solid half-truth.

Awareness of the half that was wrong was confined to the Irvings and Richard Suskind. But they were not about to tell even their closest friends that Howard Hughes didn't know a thing about it.

# The Unaccountable Man

Hot and cold running money piped in from
an inexhaustible reservoir. But money was
never free. Like any other commodity,
it had to be paid for.

Ross Macdonald, *The Galton Case*

The idea of perpetrating a hoax on Howard Hughes was not
especially novel. His style of life, or existence, invited it.

In any open society there is an uneasy friction between the
right of privacy and the right of free inquiry. When it comes
down to cases, they are not always compatible. Even so, the
American system, in its wisdom, has tended to narrow its
definition of "privacy" when the exploits and intentions of
great and powerful men are involved. The theory behind
this attitude is fundamentally democratic: those who have the
means to influence the lives of others should be subject to
the scrutiny of those who do not have such power. Like many
theories, however, it does not always work in practice. In the
case of Howard Hughes it scarcely worked at all.

Since the mid-1950s, the problem of how to render Howard
Hughes accountable at the bar of public opinion, or indeed
anywhere else, had been basically irresolvable. Yet Hughes's
last recorded contact with the media was an attempt, back

in 1958, to suppress a *Fortune* magazine series about his business empire. He wrote complaining about *Fortune's* standards of accuracy and cited as an example a recent article which described Paul Getty as "the richest man in the world." Hughes knew for a fact that this was not so; he was richer than Getty. At that time Hughes wholly owned Hughes Tool, far and away the largest supplier of oil and mineral drilling bits in the world. Over 75 per cent of drilling operations in the non-Communist world used the Hughes bit. He was the sole trustee of the Howard Hughes Medical Institute in Miami, which received all the profits of Hughes Aircraft. Hughes Aircraft was already the major supplier of electronics equipment to the United States defense establishment and was rapidly pushing into the Space Age. Hughes owned vast swatches of real estate in California, Arizona, Texas, and Nevada. He was also the majority shareholder in the world's second biggest international airline, Trans World Airlines. His fortune was variously estimated between $1.3 billion and $2 billion.

Hughes apparently thought he could take into the wilderness the respect due to a hermit with the power and prerogatives of a billionaire. For a while he managed it, but the fundamental incongruity of the enterprise began to surface. Throughout the 1960s, magazines would assign star reporters to "get the Howard Hughes interview." None achieved the impossible, but many came back with bizarre stories about the quest. The magazines ran them as funnies. Wallace Turner of *The New York Times* observed, "It is easier for a camel to go through the eye of a needle than for a poor reporter to enter into the kingdom of Howard."

A whole new journalistic specialty grew up, devoted to Hughesiana. Members of this loosely knit group called themselves Hughes-watchers, though many of them had never seen the man himself. Their skill was to develop a range of contacts inside the Hughes organization and from these sources come up with an interpretation of what the boss was thinking. It was a game, but a lucrative one. The market for Hughes articles had, if anything, become more inflated since his disappearance than it had been when his rather pedestrian utterances could be obtained on the record. In journalism, as everywhere else, there are laws of supply and demand.

Yet none of this could satisfy the appetite for authentic detail. It did not answer the basic questions of what Hughes looked like and how he lived. On these topics there was literally no information, but the less scrupulous Hughes-watchers felt free to let the imagination run riot. "True" stories about the wealthy anchorite had him sporting a navel-length beard and finger- and toenail development of six to eight inches. His favorite footgear was said to be a pair of Kleenex boxes. In the spring of 1969, *Esquire* magazine established a new level of irreverence. The cover of its March issue displayed what were ostensibly the first photographs of Howard Hughes since 1957. A blown-up strip of 16mm. film showed him dressed in a white bathrobe, speaking on the telephone, while a comely brunette companion emerged from a swimming pool nearby. The next frames had him spotting the cameraman and dispatching a security man to exact retribution. The gleeful headline read: "Howard Hughes: We see you! We see you!" Readers subsequently learned that the cover was *Esquire*'s idea of a joke. The pictures were fakes.

From bogus pictures of Hughes it was a logical step to bogus words by him. There was already a ready, willing, and more than slightly impatient market for the Hughes revelations. The prospect of an authentic Howard Hughes book had been dangled like a golden carrot over the New York publishing world for the better part of twenty years. It was the Hughesmen's way of deterring *others* from writing biographies about him. For a long time it was a highly effective strategy, but even publishers find it hard to be fooled all the time. Back in the late 1960s a few "unauthorized" biographies began to slip by Hughes's elaborate defenses, and the first private jokes were cracked about when the official biography or autobiography would finally arrive—like never. Still, hopes of such a magnificent property could never die.

It was, all agreed, the story of a life worth waiting for. You could take your pick from his early roles, and each was worth a volume in itself.

*The Gilded Child.* Howard Hughes was born on Christmas Eve, 1905, into a festive family. His father, "Big" Howard Hughes, was in the original mould of the buccaneering Texas oilmen who made and lost fortunes with an easy indifference. Shortly after young Howard arrived, Hughes Senior began making the big, imperishable fortune. His Houston home had all the infectious optimism and bonhomie then current among the Texas *nouveau riche.*

As a youth Hughes received the equivocal benefits of being the only child of a rich, generous father: good schools but rather too many of them, and plenty of spending money. He was not spectacularly gregarious himself, though he excelled in athletics and mathematics and got by in most other subjects. His most profound interest was in tinkering with cars and others forms of machinery; he found them complex but agreeably consistent. When he was sixteen, his gentle and retiring mother died, and his father introduced him to the new and fantastic world of Hollywood, where Big Howard, game to the last, became the dashing escort of the silent movie queen Mae Murray—"the girl with the bee-stung lips." He died shortly afterward, leaving his son saddled with some early symptoms of the deafness hereditary in the family, but otherwise very comfortably situated.

It was an exuberant upbringing, but not without its peculiar form of stress. Years later, in one of his few bouts of self-revelation, Hughes spoke of it with some passion to the writer Dwight Whitney. "He [my father] never suggested that I do something; he just told me. He shoved things down my throat and I had to like it. But he had a hail-fellow-well-met quality that I never had. He was a terrifically loved man.

I am not. I don't have the ability to win people the way he did. I suppose I'm not like other men. Most of them like to study people. I'm not nearly as interested in people as I should be, I guess. What I am tremendously interested in is science. . . ."

But if Hughes could not quite comprehend the subtlety of human beings, he had definite ideas about the need to impress them. He developed an engine of ambition that was never idle. Dudley Sharp, one of his few close boyhood friends in Houston (they tinkered with the same machines), made the most acute analysis of this drive.

"He seemed," said Sharp, "to have an absolute mania for proving himself. He didn't want to stay in Houston in his father's shadow. I think he even disliked bearing his father's name. He wanted to get out and find something he wanted to do. He didn't know exactly what, but nothing was going to stop him."

*The Teen-Age Litigator.* Orphaned at the age of eighteen, Hughes found himself owning the major part of the Hughes Tool Company, worth a cool $10 million, and, more important, United States Patent Numbers 930,758, and 930,759 for rock-drilling bits. It was not enough. Hughes technically was still a minor and as such unable to enter into business contracts. He went to court, had himself declared competent to run the business, and bought out the other stockholders in Hughes Tool. The courtroom experiences stood him in good stead in fighting off would-be infringers of the patents. His father had, with some assistance, invented an unmatchable oil-drilling bit with 166 cutting edges, and a strategy for keeping its benefits in the family. A Hughes bit is always rented, never sold outright. Howard Hughes was once asked whether he was the beneficiary of a monopoly position. "Of course not," he replied. "People who want to drill for oil and not use the Hughes bit can always use a pick and shovel."

*The Movie Mogul.* Aged twenty-one, Hughes moved to Hollywood to make his mark. He was persuaded to produce a movie, called *Swell Hogan,* about the love life of a Bowery bum. It proved to be of such deathless awfulness that no member of the viewing public was allowed to see it. Young Hughes was determined to do better. He did so with a succession of triumphs of money over taste. The world owes *Hell's Angels, Scarface,* and *The Outlaw* to the inventive energies of Howard Hughes. On *The Outlaw* set, with Jane Russell in close-up, Hughes managed to fire off a line that lived long after the movie: "We're not getting enough production out of Jane's breasts."

*The Ladies' Man.* Hughes married a nice Houston girl called Ella Rice when he was nineteen. After his move to Hollywood he spent very little time with her, and they were divorced four years later. He had another mark to make as an ace ladies' man and went on to court more lovely women than some of us have had hot dinners. Being tall, six foot three, dark, and handsome as a movie star, he had eminent qualifications but he was hampered by a basic shyness in approach. The problem was surmounted by his enormous powers of delegation. His movie talent scouts would often make the first connection on his behalf by inviting the lady of his choice to dinner. Hughes would arrive later and take up the running. Hughes never had any fixed abode, but he did for some years maintain five mansions around Beverly Hills on the Hughes Tool account. They were often used as residences for young ladies being groomed for stardom in Hughes's film enterprises; many never got beyond the grooming stage.

The list of famous ladies who were seen decorating his arm down the years included Billie Dove, Katharine Hepburn, Ida Lupino (who received as a gift from Hughes "the finest pair of binoculars anyone ever saw"), Olivia de Havilland, Faith Domergue, Ginger Rogers (who greatly admired Hughes's dancing), Mona Freeman, Loretta Young (who went with Hughes to a jazz joint where he made a special request for a waltz; the band played a waltz), Terry Moore, Lana Turner, Ava Gardner (who clouted Hughes over the head with a bronze statue), Linda Darnell, Mitzi Gaynor, Yvonne DeCarlo (who recalls that Hughes taught her how to land a plane and how to take off, but nothing about the flying in between), and Jean Peters, who became Hughes's second wife in 1957. Hughes had always said he would find time to marry again when he was fifty. He was a year behind schedule with Miss Peters. He never had any children.

*The Golfer.* Among Hughes's ambitions was the desire to become the greatest golfer in the world. He worked hard at it and reduced his handicap to a commendable 2 before giving up the ambition.

*The Aviator.* During the 1930s Hughes took time off from his movie enterprises to break a number of aviation records. In 1938, after two years of careful planning, he flew around the world in record time. In New York he received the traditional ticker-tape welcome reserved for the hero of the day. The garbage department recorded that it had to collect 1800 tons of trash after his triumphal procession down Broadway —200 more tons than was received by Lindbergh.

After he had captivated New York, Hughes made one of his rare visits back to his home town for a celebration banquet. A speaker said, "Howard Hughes has overcome one of the most deadening of handicaps, great wealth in youth, and we in Houston understand that."

*The Daredevil.* Hughes had a special relationship with his airplanes. He set up an aircraft division of Hughes Tool in California and insisted on his right to be the test pilot. He was sometimes criticized for this by the more responsible organs of business opinion. *Fortune* groaned: "He tinkers with his planes rather than attending to broad matters of company policy, as if his deepest satisfaction came from serving as a superconscientious test pilot and mechanic." It was, however, the most appealing side of his life—the one area where he made himself truly accountable and took risks with himself. Some of the risks were hair-raising. Hughes was involved in four airplane crashes. The last and most serious was in 1946, when he was testing the XF-11 and was forced to crash-land it next to a Los Angeles country club. He suffered concussion, burns, and a severe chest injury, and for a time his life was in the balance. He grew his mustache after the crash because the burns made shaving painful.

*The Lucky Devil.* Orthodox businessmen could never quite understand how he did it. Hughes never attended board meetings of the companies he controlled, and some of his enterprises, such as the RKO film studios and Trans World Airlines, were hotbeds of factionalism. Yet Hughes eventually sold RKO in 1955 for a tidy profit and TWA in 1966 for a world record profit of almost $500 million. Some said it was luck. Shrewder spirits felt it might be that Hughes was one of the few men in the world who could afford to wait— and sell out at the top.

*The Master of Understatement.* In 1936 Jack Frye, president of Transcontinental and Western Air, Inc., was desperate for investment funds. He was friendly with Hughes and decided to ask him for the necessary capital.

"How much capital?" asked Hughes cautiously.

"Fifteen million dollars."

"Great God, Jack, don't you realize that's a small fortune?"

*The Master Builder.* In 1941 the aircraft division became Hughes Aircraft. Hughes anticipated American involvement in the war and a big production schedule for what had originally been no more than a small offshoot of Hughes Tool. In 1942 he thrust upon the fledgling aircraft company the task of outmaneuvering the German U-boat threat by building an air freighter of such size that essential cargoes could be carried by air. This was called the Hercules, and its tough design problems were not licked until the war was over, and then not absolutely. Various cruel jokes were made about the craft, which was made of wood because of the shortage of other strategic materials. Some called it the "Flying Lumberyard," some called it the "Flying Coffin," but most called it the "Spruce Goose." Practically everybody said it would never fly. They were wrong. Hughes levered it off the water for a mile-long inaugural flight in 1947 before placing it in mothballs in a hangar at Long Beach, California. It was (and still remains) the largest airplane in the world. Hughes was sensitive about criticism of the Spruce Goose.

*The Master Moneymaker.* At an early age Hughes had expressed a desire to become the richest man in the world. Some people, including Hughes, say he became it. It was never clear in people's minds whether the credit was due to Hughes himself or to Noah Dietrich, the man who had become Hughes's accountant when he took control of Hughes Tool and who guided the destiny of the entire empire for over thirty years. Its fabulous growth has been attributed to "80 per cent Noah Dietrich's genius and 20 per cent Howard Hughes's gambling blood." Dietrich certainly had exceptionally strong business nerves and needed them. He got into the habit of making most strategic decisions himself and informing Hughes afterward. The times when Hughes took a personal hand in major decisions did not always turn out happily. At one point in the late 1950s, Hughes found that TWA was behind other major airlines in the changeover from turboprop to jet aircraft. After a long period of indecision he began placing his orders. The contracts piled up on Dietrich's desk, and one day he totaled the orders. When Hughes next called, he was ready with his question.

"Howard, where are we going to find this 497 million dollars?"

"What 497 million dollars?" asked Hughes.

"The 497 million for the jets."

"I'm not paying any 497 million dollars for jets."

"OK, Howard. But I got all the figures here. Let me just send them around to you."

"You can send me any goddam thing you like, Noah. But I haven't committed any 497 million bucks."

Dietrich sent the detailed analysis of the jet contracts

round to Hughes and received another call from his boss two days later. "Noah," said Hughes, "where are we going to find 497 million dollars?"

The real secret of Hughes's success as a moneymaker was his possession of the right invention at the right time. As drilling operations expanded around the world, the Hughes Tool plant in Houston became more lucrative than the deepest oil well. In an eight-year period after World War II its profits averaged $35 million a year. With this great pool of wealth at his disposal, Hughes could afford to prospect in his areas of real interest—movies, airplanes, and courtship. But the important thing was to look after the money tree down in Houston. Dietrich made a priority of keeping it carefully pruned and watered. Estimates of the number of times Hughes himself visited the Houston plant after 1930 vary between one and five.

*The Managerial Monster.* The parts of his empire to which Hughes paid most personal attention were almost invariably in confusion. *Fortune* magazine once described Hughes as "The Spook of American Capitalism" and gave some of the reasons why: "Suspicious and withdrawn, elusive to the point of being almost invisible, he is loath to give anything up, loath to admit error. . . . There is one other aspect of his character about which his former associates are agreed: he abhors making a decision." In the late 1940s, for example, Hughes spent 85 per cent of his working time on the problems of RKO studios. Under his management the number of RKO employees dropped from 2000 to 500 in four years. Meanwhile other parts of his empire, such as Hughes Tool and Hughes Aircraft, which had moved out of aircraft production and into electronics, were prospering enormously.

When, in the early 1950s, Hughes turned more of his attention to Hughes Aircraft, he almost started a riot. The sophisticated electronics boffins wanted a greater degree of independence and were denounced by Hughes as "Communistic." The chief subversive was an eminent war veteran,

General Harold L. George, who ran the Culver City plant of Hughes Aircraft in California.

General George's proposal for a reorganized company structure incurred Hughes's wrath. "You are proposing to take from me the rights to manage my own property. I'll burn the plant down first."

"You are accomplishing the same result without matches," replied General George.

*The Tax Man's Enemy.* Hughes had a fixed idea that what he had belonged to nobody else, especially not to the government. Noah Dietrich was ever conscious of the need to divert Hughes dollars from the federal pocket. Dietrich knew the Internal Revenue Code like the palm of his hand and advised Hughes accordingly. When IRS agents were looking at company books, they were exceptionally critical of such matters as overdepreciation of machinery, but, on the other hand, they rarely paid much attention to land values, which are not depreciable. Over the years Hughes enterprises made a habit of purchasing enormous areas of real estate for the alleged purposes of plant expansion, which did not always take place. Hughes as a result paid very little tax. The story, however, had a curious denouement. Dietrich, in the twilight of his career, became resentful of the fact that the income tax on his own salary (a useful $500,000 per annum) was ten times more than that paid by his boss. In 1957 he asked Hughes for a true recognition of his genius, stock options in Hughes Tool. Hughes refused on the grounds that this would "dilute" his ownership. They parted company, on mediocre terms.

*The Hunter.* Hughes had a limited but powerful reputation as a marksman. He would sometimes spend afternoons on his yacht, sitting in a deck chair and picking off seagulls with a .22 rifle. One day the skipper of the yacht asked Hughes what he had against seagulls. "I'm not having any of those goddam birds shitting on my boat," Hughes replied.

*The Unconscious Humorist.* Hughes had a habit of assuming that any idea which came his way, no matter how vestigial, instantly became his property. It was an attitude that led to some strange confrontations. Early in his movie career, while shooting *Hell's Angels,* he had occasion to upbraid a rival movie director, Howard Hawks, who also happened to be making an aviation picture. Hughes gave it to Hawks straight. "You have a scene in your picture where the pilot gets hit by a bullet and then vomits blood. That's my scene. I already have it in my picture and I insist you take it out of your picture."

Some years later Hawks was involved in an even more bewildering example of Hughes's proprietarial instinct. As he was working on a Western called *Red River,* Hawks received a deputation from Hughes's lawyers. They informed him that Hughes intended to sue because Hawks had a character in the film saying, "Draw your gun." Hughes alleged this had been stolen from the script of his own Western epic, *The Outlaw.* In the interests of a quiet life, Hawks dropped "Draw your gun" from his script but was not allowed to forget it. Other fun-loving directors took up the theme, and Hawks received a series of telegrams along the lines: "Please be advised that I own the rights to 'They went thataway,'" "You are forbidden to use the line 'Cut 'em off at the pass,'" and "The words 'Howdy, ma'am' may not be used without permission."

Howard Hughes could laugh at a joke—usually of the scatological variety—but there is no record of his being able to treat himself other than seriously. He himself hardly ever told jokes. In more than thirty years, Noah Dietrich could recall his boss telling only one obscurely humorous story. It went like this:

A man went to a very fancy English party. He was an old chap who carried an ear trumpet so he could hear the conversations. The hostess introduced him to one of the lady guests. "This is Mrs. Hefflefinger."

"What's that you say?" the old man asked.

"I said, this is Mrs. Hefflefinger."

"I can't hear you!" the man said, straining at his trumpet.

"THIS IS MRS. HEFFLEFINGER!"

"I don't understand," said the man. "It sounds like you're saying 'Hefflefinger.' "

*The Anti-Establishmentarian.* In 1947 Hughes was hauled before the Senate's Special Committee Investigating National Defense. The question of the day was why Hughes, who had been advanced a sizable number of federal millions for airplane production during the war, had never actually produced a combat airplane. The question, Hughes felt, was somewhat unfair, as his companies had made their contribution: the Hughes Tool aviation division had evolved a chute-feed system for 20mm. cannon that gave rear gunners an infinitely better chance of survival. But at the same time it was true that none of Hughes's flying machines had actually flown in the war. Hughes's ideas had been too far ahead of the "state of the art." It was not really his fault that the war had not lasted long enough to catch up with them. Hughes, in short, felt persecuted. As the hearings ground on, they reached into more and more bizarre areas. They focused ultimately on a Hughes employee called Johnny Meyer who had a gift for laying on female talent for potential government contractors. The committee could not leave Johnny Meyer alone, and after hearing his personal testimony twice they felt the need to call on him again. Hughes, testifying at the time, was asked whether he would be kind enough to "locate" Meyer for a third session. Not unreasonably fed up by this time, he immortalized himself with the reply, "No, I don't think I will."

*The Anti-Communist.* The "red menace" was one of the few public issues ever to excite Hughes, and at the height of the McCarthy era he even gave a speech about it. In 1951 he made a special contribution to the anti-Communist backlash in Hollywood by closing down the RKO studios for three months. The lockout broke the back of support for Paul

Jarrica, an RKO writer who had been fired by Hughes for refusing to testify before the House Un-American Activities Committee. Later, when the great comedian Charlie Chaplin was tarred with suspicion of leftish leanings, Hughes promoted a ban of Chaplin's film *Limelight* on the RKO theater circuit.

*The Allergic Defendant.* Hughes had an ambivalent attitude to the law. He used it with great frequency to defend his own interests and, in consequence, developed considerable knowledge in the areas of patent and corporation law. The courtroom drama, however, was something that he felt was best left to others. He himself was never keen on making an appearance, particularly in the capacity of a defendant. He would go to great expense to avoid it. The story is told of how an aide diligently researched the problem of how to persuade Hughes to make a modest concession in this area. He wanted Hughes to respond to a court order that required him to sign his name to a document in connection with an antitrust suit against Trans World Airlines. He explained the situation carefully to Hughes.

"You'll come to the building by car," said the aide, "walk five steps to an elevator, go up, walk five steps across the hall, go in a room where the judge will watch you sign your name, and then go back down and out of the building."

"How much will it cost if I don't do it?" asked Hughes.

"Maybe twenty million," was the reply.

"That's the bottom," said Hughes. "What's the top?"

"A hundred million."

"I don't think I can do it," said Hughes and turned to the next item of business.

*The Simple Man.* In his youth Hughes was a neat and elegant dresser. Later in life he became more functional, wandering around in a rumpled shirt, slacks, and sneakers. There are no sartorial standards for billionaires. His approach to food was similar. The thought that food might be a celebration never seems to have crossed his mind. He was particular about it but only in a nutritional sense, the engine needing high octane gasoline. He ate a lot of fruit and fresh vegetables. His dinner menu was always the same: steak, medium rare, salad, and peas. He was fascinated by cars, but those he used for business purposes lacked pretension. In one of his last public statements he told a reporter, "There is nothing mysterious about me. I have no taste for expensive clothes. Clothes are something to wear and automobiles are for transportation. If they merely cover me up and get me there, that's sufficient. In a Chevrolet, I can go where I want without being noticed. I can drive up to the curb without getting 'Hail the Conquering Hero.' "

*The Secret Man.* Hughes was a night person and tended to ring up his subordinates in the wee small hours. At such times they had to be ready with the right answers and questions because Hughes never showed up in more formal areas of business communication—such as board meetings. Hughes was convinced that his rivals were trying to "bug" his every move (sometimes they were) and took elaborate precautions to head off eavesdroppers, both personal and electronic. He held business conferences in parked cars and the cockpits of parked airplanes.

After the war he set up an elaborate communications "switchboard" at 7000 Romaine Street in Los Angeles, through which all messages to Hughes had to be channeled, wherever he was in the world. The same establishment maintained twenty Chevrolets with twenty individual drivers, for security purposes. All had to be available at a moment's notice. Hughes reckoned that even his worst enemies would be unequal to the task of bugging twenty cars and subverting twenty drivers. Bill Gay, a Mormon who later became the senior vice-president of Hughes Tool, had the job of finding incorruptible chauffeurs; many of them were Mormons.

*The Sanitized Man.* Hughes rarely shook hands with anyone. He was afraid of contamination, and the germ phobia got worse as he got older. In the interests of antisepsis, business documents were conveyed to him by couriers with white cotton gloves. He developed a habit of wiping doorknobs with his handkerchief.

*The Well-heeled Hermit.* The slide into invisibility was a gradual process. In 1954 Hughes gave his last on-the-record interview. Two years later he began to fade from visibility with his own staff by issuing a memo instructing all executives, except Dietrich, not to call him. He would telephone them, if necessary. In 1957, shortly before their rupture, he told Dietrich, "Don't raise new problems when I call you, but confine yourself to subjects I bring up." In 1958 he gave his last press interview, on an off-the-record basis. After that —complete silence from the man himself. In the meantime his business interests continued to prosper. Hughes Aircraft actually overtook Hughes Tool as the flagship of his empire, making major contributions in the fields of missilery, satellite communications, and aerospace. Hughes equipment helped put man on the moon.

Apart from TWA, Hughes still kept, under his remote control, enterprises of crucial importance to the industrial life and security of the nation. They broadcast their achievements, but they, like Hughes himself, were not in any real sense accountable. As wholly owned interests, they were not even obliged to publish annual accounts. There were no shareholders to mollify—well, only one. Hughes himself was a one-man shareholders' meeting in continuous private session, responsible only to himself. How he discharged that responsibility was unknown to the world, though he apparently had little or no contact with the management of Hughes Tool or Hughes Aircraft.

His movements were rumored with some precision, but except for a small private entourage and his wife he was never seen by anyone. For a time he lived in California; then he lived in Boston; and after a while he moved to Las Vegas.

There were many speculations about Hughes's reasons for this self-imposed seclusion:

He wanted to live in a private germ-free world.

He was embarrassed about his increasing deafness.

He was paralyzed.

He wanted privacy for his second marriage.

He wanted to avoid tiresome litigants trying to sue him.

He was afraid of being kidnaped and held for ransom.

He was working on secret plans to resuscitate the Spruce Goose.

He was finally overcome by shyness.

Hughes himself never gave any reason. It may have been a combination of them all, or something quite different. But it seemed in the 1950s that the engine of his personal ambition had finally run down. Perhaps he had run out of areas in which he needed to outperform his father.

Then, in the late 1960s, Hughes-watchers began to piece together evidence that Hughes was once again taking a personal interest, in the latest and most bizarre addition to his empire, the gaming operation in Las Vegas. It was an interest that was to provide raw material for his final embarrassment.

Any publisher would be animated by the prospect of getting the authoritative life story of such a man. It had everything—achievement, great mounds of money, mystery, paradox, sex, and singularity—and it was ultimately inexplicable: Was he, in the breathy opinion of Yvonne De Carlo, "a genius," or what Gore Vidal has described as "an honest-to-God American shit"? The construction of his literary monument would seem to demand a great tragic (or perhaps comic) talent. But all Howard Hughes got was Clifford Irving. The combination, as we shall see, was not entirely accidental.

# High Stakes in Las Vegas

For somehow this is tyranny's disease,
to trust no friends.

Aeschylus, *The Suppliants*

In December 1970, Clifford Irving perceived a way of supplying the Manhattan publishing world with its greatest literary coup. The inspiration did not come out of a clear blue Ibizan sky. As it happened, Irving's idea started to germinate at a time when the Hughes empire was undergoing a violent internal convulsion. There was no coincidence about these two phenomena—the hoax had an umbilical relationship with the power struggle inside the Hughes organization.

Irving had always been interested in Howard Hughes. He had slight but intriguing family connections with the man. His father, Jay Irving, claimed acquaintance with the young Hughes and shared his affection for Las Vegas. An aunt, Jay Irving's sister, had dinner with Hughes three times in California in the 1940s and was involved in a fun-loving abduction to Las Vegas in the company of a girl for whom, as she put it, "Hughes had the hots." The convulsion in Hughes's organization took place, appropriately enough, in Las Vegas.

Intimations of this struggle, climaxed by an embarrassingly well-covered court action, filtered into American newspapers from December 2 onward. They were read with great avidity in Irving's Ibizan home, for the story they revealed was deeply relevant to the next stage in his literary career; they provided the first real insights into Hughes's weird life style in almost twenty years. The revelations were the by-product of a collision between the two most powerful personalities in Hughes's empire—Robert Maheu and Chester Davis. Both were to play important parts in the development of the hoax.

The irony of it was that Hughes could not have wished for two more devoted servants. Chester Davis was on record with the most passionate defense of Hughes's right to invisibility: "Howard Hughes is brilliant and unusual. He knows what he's doing. He has very good reasons for what he does and for what he does not do. If he doesn't want to see somebody, why the hell should he?" Maheu was even more adulatory. He once told an *Esquire* reporter, "It's a constant challenge to work for a man with such great foresight and thoroughness and who perhaps enjoys the sole enviable title of never having been proven wrong by history." History had news for Mr. Maheu.

Although they represented different strands in the Hughes empire, Maheu and Davis had a lot in common. Both came from relatively poor backgrounds, both were self-made, both had deep reserves of resource and cunning, and, most important of all, both were rough customers in a power struggle. When, after years of cautious friendship and some mutual respect, they were obliged to contest each other, the chips really flew, with unfortunate consequences for their beloved chief.

Robert Aime Maheu was born in 1918 in Waterville, Maine, the son of a French-Canadian worker. He grew up looking like a policeman—large, amiable, and slightly ominous—and became something more grand, an FBI agent. During World War II he worked in counterespionage. On his departure from the agency in 1947, J. Edgar Hoover was said by Maheu's ardent spokesmen to have dashed a tear from his

eye. In the early 1950s, after running through a number of
jobs, Maheu started "a problem-solving organization" called
Robert A. Maheu Associates and staffed it with ex-FBI agents,
former IRS men, and lobbyists. It was based in Washington,
where industrial intelligence can be obtained at the highest level. Maheu was an intimate of senators, governors,
and the barons of big business and big trade unions. He had
a special talent for dovetailing interests and providing the
kind of lubrication that keeps the industrial state in motion
without too much public embarrassment. His clients included
the Greek shipowner Stavros Niarchos, the steelworkers'
union, and, of course, Hughes Tool.

Like most graduates of J. Edgar Hoover's training school,
he was deeply anti-Communist. His commitment in this area
gave rise to a suspicion that Robert A. Maheu Associates was
a CIA front. The Washington columnist Jack Anderson once
printed a story alleging that Maheu was involved in a plot
to assassinate Fidel Castro, with a Mafia gunman as the "button man." Maheu modestly offered "no comment" on the
story and has been no-commenting on it ever since. Nobody
has ever been able to decide whether this was because the
story was true or because Maheu was reluctant to kill a useful
legend. He is a man who cherishes a "reputation."

It was Maheu's anti-Communism that first caught the eye
of Howard Hughes. Maheu's first jobs on his account, in the
mid-1950s, were mainly confined to the discovery of "pinkos"
in Hughes's organization. Maheu took to the Hughesian am-
bience like a duck to a duckpond. The world of intrigue has
its own special fascination, and the private sector which
Maheu entered was in many respects more fascinating than
the public one he had left. The Hughes empire, based as it
was (and is) on the whim of an unseen autocrat, merited comparison with the court of the Medicis. In 1961 Maheu dropped
all his other interests, moved to Los Angeles, and started to
work exclusively for Howard Hughes. By this time he had
established himself as much more than a simple "red-catcher"

and was deep into Hughes's concept of "civic and community relations." Part of this work involved disbursing contributions to political candidates who seemed in sympathy with Hughes's interests.

In 1965, Maheu's main rival in the executive status race, Bill Gay, trod on a commercial banana skin. Gay, who had had a wraithlike rise as the architect of Hughes's personal security apparatus, established a subdivision of the empire called Hughes Dynamics. The new outfit was designed to loosen IBM's hold on the computer market, but IBM remained conspicuously unmoved. Hughes retained Gay's services but downgraded his counsel. He subsequently wrote a memo to Maheu instructing him "not to permit [Gay] to be privy to our affairs."

Maheu finally moved up to the number-one position in 1966, when Hughes started a new expansionist policy in Nevada. Both Hughes and Maheu moved to Las Vegas. Hughes installed himself in conditions of maximum security on the ninth-floor penthouse of the Desert Inn, which he promptly bought. Maheu was given company quarters nearby in a specially constructed $500,000 residence which became known as "Little Caesar's Palace." He was designated the exclusive spokesman for Howard Hughes and given the title Chief Executive, Hughes Nevada Operations.

Hughes, at the time, had an enviable problem. He had just realized his $500 million profit on TWA and was not anxious to enrich the tax man. His aversion to the claims of the Internal Revenue Service had not abated over the years. The TWA windfall, however, confronted him with a major difficulty: reinvested in stocks and securities, it would be subject to a high level of tax as "passive" income. Las Vegas beckoned with an "active" potential.

Vegas was undergoing one of the most testing periods in its short but action-packed history. Casino gambling, the staple industry that Bugsy Siegel had founded back in the 1940s before his abrupt departure on the losing end of a gangland shoot-out, was in trouble with the feds. Vegas had long been a convenient watering place for the Mafia. Casino gambling provided a useful machine for "washing" money obtained in more nefarious operations. It seemed, however, that the government was finally going to do something about it. The inevitable consequence was a lot of bad publicity, for Mafia and non-Mafia interests alike, and many casino- and hotel-owners were thinking of selling. All of which suited Hughes fine; he had a lot of buying to do. Nevada's Governor Paul Laxalt, alive to the potential of a new image, was ecstatic at the prospect. Hughes money power would, he felt, efface the old legends of criminality and give Vegas "the good housekeeping seal of approval."

Over the next four years Maheu contrived the investment of 300 of Hughes's millions in the Nevada area; they went into real estate, aviation, mining, and, most heavily of all, hotels and casinos on the Las Vegas Strip. Maheu was paid $10,000 a week but got little time to spend it. Apart from organizing the spending spree, he was involved on many other fronts: fending off antitrust suits, persuading the Gaming Board to issue licenses without seeing the casino owner, playing tennis with Governor Laxalt, relating tales of his FBI years for his boss (Hughes was fascinated by Maheu's counterespionage experience), and playing the part of his master's voice against nuclear testing in Nevada by the Atomic Energy Commission. The word was that Hughes planned to "buy" Nevada and turn it into a model new frontier, fun-loving but pollution-free. In Las Vegas, Hughes was known as The Man; with 8000 people on his payroll, he became far and away the largest employer in town. By 1970 The Man had added the Silver Slipper, the Frontier, the Sands, the Castaways, and the Landmark Hotel to his portfolio of casinos. As the Nevada operation grew, Maheu was in daily, sometimes hourly, communication with Hughes—by telephone and memorandum, though never by personal meeting (in seventeen years of collaboration, Maheu never actually met Hughes face to face).

Hughes in Las Vegas had refined his personal insulation equipment. The only men allowed into his presence were a hand-picked palace guard of five people. They had no specific executive roles in any of his companies. Their job quite simply was to act as body slaves and to screen Hughes's contacts with the outside world, which included all the directors in Hughes Tool and Hughes Aircraft. Hughes had achieved a degree of human inviolability that eludes even absolute monarchs: he dictated the composition of his own peer group. (Even absolute monarchs sometimes have to meet people outside their courts, such as ambassadors and occasional peasant leaders.)

The court that Hughes assembled reflected the obsession of his declining years. It contained no jester but it had one overwhelming characteristic: it was very clean. Three out of the five courtiers were stanch brethren of the Church of Jesus Christ of Latter-Day Saints. Mormons had special qualifications for the work: as men who did not smoke or drink and who kept their hair cropped short, they lacked allure for most forms of bacterial life. Most of them were graduates of Bill Gay's original school for incorruptible Chevrolet drivers.

Maheu, who both drank and smoked and had a reputation as a gourmet, was never entirely comfortable with the clean-limbed palace guard. He was proud of his membership in the old dining society La Confrerie de la Chaine des Rotisseurs. Despite these un-Hughes-like interests, Maheu continued to rise in the esteem of Hughes himself. His eminence, however, did arouse resentment in other outposts of the empire. The razzmatazz of the Vegas operation was not altogether congenial to the more image-conscious top brass in Hughes Tool and Hughes Aircraft, and old favorites of Hughes were disturbed at Maheu's near monopoly of the monarch's business ear.

Hughes, meanwhile, leaned more heavily on Maheu in areas that did not specifically concern Nevada. One of these was the thorny and still outstanding matter of a $145-million suit against Howard Hughes by TWA. Maheu became involved and made one enemy too many. The man who had been handling the TWA litigation up to that stage was Chester Davis, and Davis, unlike Bill Gay, was not given to suffering in silence.

Chester Davis was born Caesar Simon in Rome on October 14, 1910. His mother was an Italian and his father was French-Algerian. When his father died, his mother emigrated with her young family to the United States, where she met and married Chester Davis, Sr. The son of her first marriage was formally naturalized as an American citizen in 1935. He was then twenty-five, a graduate of Harvard Law School, and already set on a legal career. By the mid-1950s he was a partner in the august New York firm of Simpson, Thacher & Bartlett and well established as a rumbustious courtroom character. When, as sometimes happened, a ruling went against him, he had a forceful habit of going back to his desk, leaning over his law books to see what outrage had been committed, and scratching his backside for the delectation of the court.

He had married well, into one of the founding families of the Ferry-Morse Seed Company, though the connection led to some mildly embarrassing litigation. He ceased to participate in a trust as a result of legal action taken by other trustees, members of the Ferry family. They argued that he had failed to show enough interest in the trust's affairs; Davis did not contest the assertion.

By the early 1960s, however, Davis had other, and much bigger, fish to fry. He was the partner at Simpson, Thacher assigned to its biggest case—Hughes's defense of a suit brought by disgruntled TWA investors. By the time it arrived on his desk it was already in slightly tarnished condition and the subject of much public speculation. A journalist called James Phelan, one of the early Hughes-watchers, wrote about the early phase of combat in the following terms:

So many people were looking for Howard Hughes that at times Southern California resembled the chase ballet in *High Button Shoes*. The pursuit had its origin in a massive legal battle between Eastern financial interests and the billionaire Western owner over control of Trans World Airlines.

The Easterners engaged a posse of private investigators to serve Hughes with various court orders and writs, and Hughes promptly deployed a counterintelligence force to frustrate them. The drama of this war, enhanced by the intriguing fact that Hughes had not been seen in public for years, attracted a group of writers and photographers for national magazines. As the safari progressed, it was joined by a crowd of spear-carriers, including a Los Angeles lawyer who specialized in suing Hughes, the way some lawyers confine their practice to maritime law.

The "Easterners," who were comprised of a consortium of money houses that had sunk their funds into TWA, never succeeded in serving a subpoena on Hughes, but they did manage, by a variety of maneuvers, to get the case into court. The case was for damages of $137,500,000 to compensate for Hughes's "mismanagement" of TWA: the argument was that Hughes, as a result of his fussy incapacity to make up his mind, had inflicted TWA with a severe jet-lag problem.

The courts, mainly as a result of Hughes's cavalier refusal to appear, began to bear down hard on the plaintiff's side. Chester Davis was assigned the role of leading the Hughes salvage operation—without, of course, involving Howard Hughes.

There was one slight hitch before he could get down to the job. On checking around he discovered a conflict of interest within his firm: it handled some business for parties on the other side of the action. Davis solved the problem by setting up his own law firm and became, in practice, an almost full-time Hughesman.

As such he rose to dizzying heights and, among other

things, carved out a specialized role as Hughes's legal protector against the prying efforts of would-be biographers. Davis had a manner that could unman the more nervously inclined Manhattan publishers. He was an acknowledged asset to the Hughes operation except in one area: the TWA suit which had brought him into Hughes's orbit continued to go abysmally. The case dragged on disastrously even after Hughes sold his TWA stock in 1966.

In April 1970, TWA was awarded a default judgment for the full amount plus $7,500,000 for TWA's lawyers and interest at 6 per cent, about $9,000,000 annually, until the total was paid. Hughes would appeal, of course, but a new strategy obviously had to be devised. Maheu was given the task of finding it.

Maheu turned the problem over to three law firms, including that of Clark Clifford, the former Secretary of Defense in the Johnson administration. Their collective wisdom came up with the suggestion of an intriguing subtlety. They recommended that Davis's name be removed from the appellate proceedings. The argument could then be made that Hughes was not adequately represented at earlier stages of the case. As Hughes himself could do no wrong, there had to be another fall guy. Davis was available.

When Davis heard the news he was less than thrilled and sent a bitter complaint to Maheu. On November 10, 1970, Maheu, thoroughly riled and confident in the authority bestowed on him by The Man himself, responded with a long teletype:

TO DATE YOU HAVE LOST THIS CASE AT EVERY LEVEL WITH CATA-STROPHICALLY ADVERSE FINANCIAL AND OTHER INJURY TO THE DEFENDANT. . . . I DEEPLY RESENT YOUR PRESUMPTUOUS REQUEST THAT I "CEASE INTERFERENCE WITH COUNSEL IN CHARGE AND RE-SPONSIBLE FOR THE CASE." THERE HAS BEEN NO INTERFERENCE ON MY PART OTHER THAN TAKING STEPS TO ACCORD OTHER COUNSEL AN OPPORTUNITY TO SALVAGE A CASE WHICH YOU HAVE TRAG-ICALLY LOST.

At this point Hughes was going through one of his intense incommunicado periods. No calls to him were allowed. The story given out by the palace guard was that he had been unwell for some weeks and would be out of touch. When Davis became awkward, Maheu sent up a memo to the penthouse, outlining the views of the three law firms he had consulted. He later claimed that it was never delivered to Hughes.

On November 14 the unseen Howard Hughes turned 180 degrees and gave authority for Maheu to be ditched. He did it by signing a disputed proxy, witnessed and notarized by two of his palace guard, Howard Eckersley and Levar Myler. The final draft of the document had been prepared in Chester Davis's New York office and transmitted to Eckersley on the day it was signed. It gave management control of Hughes Nevada Operations to Chester Davis, Bill Gay, and another tool company vice-president, Raymond Holliday—or any two of the three.

A few days later Hughes left Las Vegas secretly with his palace guard and flew to the Bahamas. On December 2, the *Las Vegas Sun* carried an exclusive story about Hughes's mysterious departure, and the weird intrigue began to surface publicly. Two days later Davis announced to a legal friend of Maheu's that he had a proxy that cooked Maheu's goose, and told him to pass on the word: "Maheu resigns by sundown or he's fired."

Maheu passed back an impolite suggestion about what Davis could do with his ultimatum, whereupon Davis, with Bill Gay in tow, descended on Las Vegas with a small army of auditors and set up battle headquarters in the Sands Hotel. It proved a rollicking confrontation. Each protagonist was thoroughly convinced that he had the authority of Hughes himself—a man neither had actually seen—to fire the other. "If you're up there, you son-of-a-bitch," Davis announced to a suspected Maheu bugging device in the ceiling of his hotel suite, "you're going to jail." Across the Strip in the Frontier, where the indigenous forces were located, Maheu was telling all hands that he reacted very strongly to "muscle." "No son-of-a-bitch is going to run me out of my own town."

The press, unaccustomed as it was to getting even the time of day out of the Hughes organization, was trying to fathom what it was all about. There was a big story here, but nobody had much in the way of clues as to what it was. Reporters found Maheu pleasant but elusive; he was going the rounds of the Hughes casinos, drumming up his own loyalist support. Davis—well, Davis had a genial side, but it was one he rarely showed to the media.

On the evening of December 5, Wallace Turner, a *New York Times* man on the West Coast and the paper's Hughes expert, got Davis on the phone with a request for information. His notes showed a conversation on the following lines:

"Mr. Davis, I wanted to ask if you have any comment on the things Mr. Maheu has been saying about you and your behavior in Las Vegas."

"It's just bullshit."

"But Mr. Davis, we can't put 'bullshit' in *The New York Times.*"

"Why not? You do it every day."

"No, I don't mean it in that sense. I mean it's a term we can't print."

"Oh, would you like it better if I said his remarks are utter nonsense?"

Wallace Turner wrote a story on the following day, quoting Davis as saying that Maheu's remarks were "utter nonsense."

Maheu, meanwhile, was making a number of strategic moves. First, he secured a temporary restraining order against entry into Hughes's casinos by the Davis-Gay forces. Second, he dispatched two gumshoes to Nassau in the Bahamas to try to find out Hughes's circumstances. They were unlucky in this mission, but the expedition gave rise to rumors, emanating from the Davis camp, that Maheu was setting up a kidnap operation. Meanwhile, even more ominous rumors began to circulate about the health and safety of Hughes himself. In Las Vegas a sheriff's party, saying it had information of foul play, broke into the Hughes penthouse, searched it, but found nothing. Hughes's Nevada lawyer, Tom Bell, called a press conference to put on record his belief that Hughes would not willingly leave Nevada "without notifying his personal attorney." He wondered aloud whether Hughes was still alive.

Maheu, still leaving nothing to chance, made a move with important long-term consequences. In his office at the Frontier he kept copies of all his private memos to and from Hughes, many of them handwritten. He decided to have them taken to a place of safety, "to protect them."

At some point they collided with a photo-copying machine and started circulating in the unsanctified hands of journalists, among them Hank Greenspun, the publisher of the *Las Vegas Sun,* who is now said to be the owner of "the largest private collection of Hughes documents in captivity." Extracts from the memos began to surface in the media and made compulsive reading for a public starved of authentic Hughesiana for almost twenty years.

One of them, written in 1968, dealt with the theme of civil rights agitation and its relevance to employment policies in the Hughes Nevada operation:

> . . . Now, Bob, I have never made my views plain on this subject. And I certainly would not say these things in public. However, I can summarize my attitude about employing more Negroes very simply—I think it is a wonderful idea for somebody else, somewhere else.
>
> I know this is not a very praiseworthy point of view, but I feel Negroes have already made enough progress to last the next 100 years, and there is such a thing as overdoing it.

Another memorandum sketched out a proposed strategy for opposing the AEC's nuclear-testing program in 1968. Hughes felt they should concentrate on "three forces": 1) a court injunction—"I think it is just a problem of finding the right judge"; 2) "an order from LBJ inspired by Humphries" (Hughes meant the then Vice-President Hubert Humphrey, who had earlier shown an inclination to oppose testing); 3) direct negotiations—"I personally am positive that the AEC by now is seeking only a graceful exit without getting their clothes torn off any worse. Somebody should start negotiating with the AEC, just like buying a hotel. I want somebody to wheel and deal. . . ." (The AEC went ahead with its test program.)

A more cryptic but illuminating offering from the archive, penned in 1970, expressed resentment of Bill Gay for failure on some delicate assignment involving Mrs. Hughes. In it Hughes achieved the ultimate in delegated authority: he was able to blame *somebody else* for the loss of his own wife. Hughes complained: "Bill's total indifference and laxity to my pleas for help in my domestic area, voiced urgently to him, week by week, throughout the past seven or eight years, have resulted in complete, I am afraid irrevocable loss of my wife. I blame Bill completely for this unnecessary debacle. . . ." (Mrs. Hughes, who lived in California while Hughes was in his Desert Inn penthouse, divorced her husband in June 1970.)

Not all of this graphic material appeared in the press at the time, but intimations of its existence were powerfully broadcast. And when, on December 8, 1970, Davis and Maheu were finally in confrontation in a Las Vegas courtroom, the revelations came thick and fast. Maheu contested Davis's right to take over, on the grounds that he had no word from Hughes confirming his dismissal. He argued from this that the Hughes signature on the proxy document must be a forgery. Expert testimony by Charles Appel, former head of the FBI forgery school, supported this claim.

But Davis had his own expert, who argued otherwise. As the case rolled on, Maheu's old tennis partner, Governor Laxalt, made desperate efforts at conciliation, but to no avail. "I've put my neck on the line for this," said Maheu, "and I'm going to see it through."

As the hometown boy, Maheu was buoyed up by some popular support in the struggle. For a man who had wielded such great and sometimes arbitrary authority in the town, he was curiously well thought of. Vegas liked men who obviously enjoyed their wealth and power, which made it equivocal in its attitude to the great benefactor Howard Hughes, but warmly disposed toward his chief executive. Maheu had style. But there was another current in Vegas which was running against too deep an attachment to Maheu's cause. No town in the world has a more finely developed sense of smell for a loser, and, as the courtroom battle proceeded, its subtle fragrance settled on Maheu.

After two members of Hughes's hitherto anonymous palace guard, Howard Eckersley and Levar Myler, appeared at the court, it was fairly clear that rumors of Hughes's death had been much exaggerated. But how alive he was, was in dispute. It emerged that Hughes had been given a series of blood transfusions several weeks before his trip to the Bahamas and that he had been suffering from pneumonia and anemia. He normally ate well but sometimes went for days without food in a state of near total withdrawal. Hank Greenspun, who sided with Maheu in the struggle, was going around town with his own deduction from the medical grapevine: "Hughes couldn't have signed that goddam proxy because he was in catatonia at the time."

But Davis had the clincher which underwrote the proxy— a two-and-a-half-page letter from Hughes in Nassau, beginning "Dear Chester and Bill." Its contents complained about the "very damaging publicity" and ordered the recipients to "take whatever action is necessary" to "terminate all relationship with Maheu. . . ." The court accepted its authenticity. Maheu was out, with plenty of time to prepare his next offensive—a $50-million damage suit against Hughes claiming that his old boss had broken his employment contract. Not that he had anything against Hughes personally. "It's the old story," Maheu bitterly told his supporters. "He who controls the palace guard controls the king." Chester Davis, with the shadow of the ax removed, ascended to a very high place. Recognition of his services was made soon afterward by his formal appointment as general counsel to Hughes Tool and his elevation to the board of directors.

In mid-December *Newsweek* wrote a story monitoring the progress of the dispute under the headline: THE CASE OF THE INVISIBLE BILLIONAIRE. The second page of the article carried an illustration that constituted the real starting point of the Clifford Irving hoax. It was a photographic reproduction of the final paragraph of the "Dear Chester and Bill" letter:

> As I have said, this matter has caused me the very gravest concern, and is damaging my company and all the loyal men and women associated with me in the very deepest and far-reaching way.
>
> My sincere regards,<br>Howard R. Hughes

These eleven handwritten lines had a distinct effect on Irving, who read the *Newsweek* article during Christmas week. They were not much to go on, but sufficient for a modest hazard in forgery. He got in touch with the fastest writer on the Balearic archipelago, Richard Suskind, and set out the essentials of the idea.

A few days later Suskind flew from Majorca to Ibiza for a more detailed consultation. The outline of Irving's idea was as follows: they should work up the "authentic" biography of Howard Hughes. Irving reasoned that the Vegas conflict had whetted the public appetite for a Hughes book, and there were indications of a large fallout of new Hughes material which could—if they laid hands on it—be incorporated in such a volume. But the thing that would distinguish it from all previous books about Hughes, and make it into a major property, would be that it would have Hughes's own imprimatur. It was obvious to Irving from the circumstances of the Vegas dispute that if Hughes would not manifest himself to stop all this adverse publicity, he must be in very feeble shape. By the time they had assembled the biography, Hughes might be dead or in no condition to denounce it. But to be on the safe side they would fashion a book that would portray him in a sympathetic light, which might help the subject overlook some mendacity in presentation. There was still an obvious risk of denunciation, but it was one worth taking.

If they could manufacture a pseudo-Hughes and set him in opposition to the real Hughes, there was a strong likelihood that people might accept the pseudo version. After all, the real Hughes, eternally locked in his air-conditioned nightmare, was already totally incredible. Reconstituting the old man would be almost a service to reality. It would, at the very least, be a lot of fun trying.

No great initial outlay was involved. They had in *Newsweek* a meager but passable crib of Hughes's most recent handwriting. Irving would test the reaction of his New York publishers, McGraw-Hill, by slipping them a few forged letters from Hughes. If they took the bait, he and Suskind could get an advance on expenses and play it by ear from then on. Suskind came in on the basis of a 25-75 split of all the potential proceeds.

In January 1971, *Life* made the forgery task much easier by reproducing in full color the handwritten text of the "Dear Chester and Bill" letter. By this time the conspiracy was well under way. McGraw-Hill had gobbled up the bait.

# ACT III

## A Property Is
## Acquired

# A Modest Proposal

"There is less in this than meets the eye."

Attributed to Tallulah Bankhead

Clifford Irving had been a McGraw-Hill author for twelve years, so it was only natural that he should have an old friend in the company with whom to share the astonishing news that he had opened a correspondence with Howard Hughes. On January 3, 1971, he wrote to Beverly Jane Loo, McGraw-Hill's executive editor, and announced:

> I sent a copy of *Fake!* some time ago to Howard Hughes, and to my surprise received a note of thanks and praise from him. Some wheels are beginning to turn in my brain. Do you know if there is any biography of Hughes, or anything in the works for the near future? Let me know, but please don't mention it to anyone.

Beverly Loo was understandably excited. She told Irving that as far as she knew there were no books planned on Hughes, but that newspaper interest in him was still high after the mysterious departure from Las Vegas.

Her duties included selling serial rights, and she knew the sort of bidding that a biography actually authorized by Hughes would attract. She didn't keep the secret entirely to herself. But those she told were senior enough to see the implications of the idea and to commit, if necessary, the cash it would command.

On January 30 Irving wrote to Beverly Loo again. He was able to report that since writing to her he had received two letters from Hughes, and that the second of them had even talked in terms of a biography. Hughes had asked how and when Irving could do the book and had given him an address to write to in Miami, care of a man called George Gordon Holmes. Irving explained that the letter put him in an awkward position, since he was halfway through his new novel for McGraw-Hill, *The Man in the Mink Collar.* He asked Beverly Loo for advice: Should he finish the novel and then try to get the Hughes biography, or drop everything? The question was engagingly naïve, suggesting Irving's willingness to defer to the higher wisdom of his publishers. He was not surprised by the reply. Miss Loo ordered him to drop everything and come to New York immediately, bringing the letters with him.

Irving arrived in New York on February 10 and went to McGraw-Hill's tiled skyscraper tower on West 42nd Street (known to intimates as "the great green latrine"), where Miss Loo took him to meet a powerful trio: Harold McGraw, the chairman of McGraw-Hill's vast book division; Albert Leventhal, who runs its general publishing section; and the late Robert W. Lock, then the book company's executive vice-president. Only Miss Loo knew Irving well, though Leventhal had met him the previous summer and had read two hundred pages of the new novel.

Irving showed them the first letter he had received, dated December 10, 1970, and explained its origins. He said that during the previous summer he had sent a copy of *Fake!* to Hughes at the Desert Inn in Las Vegas—his father had suggested he do so just before his death. The acknowledgment he had received from Hughes read:

Dear Mr. Irving:

Thank you for the gift of your book, which I thoroughly enjoyed reading. Your inscription was very thoughtful.

I find myself deeply interested in the fellow you have written about, despite a natural inclination to the contrary. I cannot help wondering what has happened to him.

I would hate to think what other biographers might have done to him but it seems to me that you have portrayed your man with great consideration and sympathy, when it would have been tempting to do otherwise. For reasons you may readily understand, this has impressed me.

I do remember your father and I was sorry to learn of his passing.

Yours truly,
H.R. Hughes

Irving explained that he had replied, suggesting almost lightheartedly that Hughes should unburden himself in the same way that Elmyr de Hory had done and, of course, to the same person. He had added coyly that Hughes would no doubt be "horrified" by the proposal. But Hughes had not broken off the correspondence. Again Irving's letter was acknowledged, with a note dated January 8. It read:

Dear Mr. Irving:

I have had your most recent letter.

I have taken note of its content and will give the matter my very serious consideration.

Yours truly,
H.R. Hughes

But it was the third letter which gave the McGraw-Hill executives intimations of a bestseller. It was the longest of the three, dated January 20. It had come from an address in Florida (near Miami, Irving explained), and it said:

•

Dear Mr. Irving:

I thank you again for the pleasantness of your letter to me.

I am not "horrified" by your suggestion, although in times past it has come to me from other quarters and was rejected by me. You must know that a short time ago a man named Gerber published a book which purported to be the story of my life. I found it in part offensive and in part childish [*Bashful Billionaire*, by Albert Gerber, published by Lyle Stuart in 1967].

I am not entirely insensitive to what journalists have written about me and for that reason I have the deepest respect for your treatment of de Hory, however much I may disapprove of his morals. I do not question your integrity and I would not expect you to question mine.

It would not suit me to die without having certain misconceptions cleared up and without having stated the truth about my life. The immorality you speak of does not interest me, not in this world. I believe in obligations. I regret many things in the past, but I have little feelings of shame about them.

I would be grateful if you would let me know when and how you would wish to undertake the writing of the biography you proposed.

In future when you write to me if you would use the address on the attached sheet your mail will reach me more rapidly.

I wish there to be no publicity about this communication for the time being, and I would view a breach of this request very unfavorably.

Sincerely yours,
H.R. Hughes

After McGraw-Hill executives had read the letters, there was little need for editorial conferences. They thought it was a marvelous idea and told Irving to go ahead. The only suspicions they harbored concerned Hughes. They thought he would duck out of the deal, or simply would not let Irving complete the research. They had no worries about Irving himself, and Harold McGraw told him to talk to the corporation's legal department about an agreement with Hughes. Irving was thought to be quite reliable; he had always delivered manuscripts on time before, and manuscripts were McGraw-Hill's business.

Irving was better known around the corridors of McGraw-Hill than some authors whose homes were in Manhattan. He lived abroad, so he tended to use his publishers' office as his when he was in the city, and he had become familiar enough with the editors to deal directly with them. It was typical of the relationship between publisher and author that Irving had no agent. Irving's $150,000 advance for his next three books seems generous in retrospect, but it was made in inflationary times. If it appears high, this is because Irving's literary reputation was not. *Fake!* had not fulfilled the promise seen in it by both author and publisher, and there were some people in the editorial department who, quite frankly, regarded Irving as a hack. But if he was the hack who produced the first authorized biography of Howard Hughes, then good for him.

As if to demonstrate that they were all friends in the same adventure, Irving deliberately drew Beverly Loo into the plot during his first trip to New York. He explained that Hughes had told him to wait for instructions at the Buckingham Hotel. There he had received a telephone call that told him to go to an American Express office, where a plane ticket would be waiting in his name. He wondered if Beverly Loo would accompany him. She was happy to, and when they showed up, there was indeed a ticket which would take him to Mexico City and Oaxaca, 250 miles farther south. He omitted to tell Beverly Loo that a little later he was going to buy another ticket for a traveling companion.

On February 17, Irving was back in New York with the quartet of McGraw-Hill executives who had been drawn into the plot. He had excerpts from a copious diary he had kept in Mexico, which described in vivid detail how he had met Hughes twice, first on a mountaintop near Oaxaca and again at a seaside resort a plane ride away. He explained that he had traveled via New Orleans and Mexico City, and that each time he stopped over he had expected to be spirited away by a Hughes man who would transfer him to another route and prevent his being followed. But it didn't happen. He arrived in Oaxaca on schedule and, he said, met his new collaborator there.

Irving explained that among the things they had discussed was a contract. The legal arrangements had to satisfy a man who knew the intricacies of the law, and the monetary agreements had to satisfy a man who was immensely rich but not averse to accumulating fresh capital. For its part, McGraw-Hill did not want to commit too much liquid cash to a project that was at the whim of the most notoriously eccentric of American capitalists. Leventhal proposed a deal which gave $100,000 in advance, another $100,000 when research for the Hughes biography was completed, and a bumper $300,000 when the manuscript was delivered. The publishers thought they were being cautious; they had two stages at which they might pull out. McGraw-Hill had not offered a larger advance for a single book since it had bought General Douglas MacArthur's memoirs twenty years earlier, but nevertheless it seemed a fair sum for Hughes—if he ever delivered. There was no quibbling about the price.

When the deal was agreed on, the publishers asked Irving whether he would mind if an officer of the corporation observed the great moment of signature. Irving replied that he wouldn't mind at all, but Hughes would be unlikely to sanction it. After all, he had never met his own lawyer, Chester Davis, let alone one of McGraw-Hill's. The point was taken.

Irving next went to San Juan, Puerto Rico, and returned on March 5 with the agreement between himself and Howard Hughes signed and sealed. Hughes's signature was there for everyone to see. The text of the agreement showed that McGraw-Hill had agreed to some stringent secrecy clauses, and Hughes had apparently agreed to allay McGraw-Hill's lawyers' fears about any prior claims on his authorized biography. There was also a paragraph about payments by Irving to Hughes, which said: "The money will be deposited as designated verbally or in writing by H. R. Hughes for deposit in any bank account of H. R. Hughes . . . and shall be paid [i.e. by Irving] within 15 days after receipt of payment from the Publisher." It seemed innocuous enough, suggesting that Hughes was perfectly happy to have all his money paid via Irving.

On March 23, 1971, Clifford Irving and Harold McGraw signed a contract which elevated Irving into the company of the best-paid writers in America. In it, McGraw agreed to publish "an untitled authorized biography of 'H' (Señor Octavio) with a preface by 'H.' "

The contract was remarkable for two things. One was the secrecy imposed on the participants in the project, which was not just a question of their agreeing not to gossip about the book. They were contractually obliged to keep their mouths shut. Clause 22 was quite specific: "The Publisher agrees that it shall undertake no advertising or promotion or sale of the Work prior to 30 days after acceptance by the Publisher of a complete and satisfactory manuscript for the Work." The next clause joined anyone who bought subsidiary rights to the secrecy pact.

The other notable thing about the contract was the quality of the terms. On hearing them, a New York literary agent whose bargaining skill is spoken of with awe said enviously, "Which agent did that?" No agent was involved, but the percentages Irving extracted for subsidiary rights were consistently 5 to 10 per cent higher than the form contract proposed. "It was supply and demand," explains one of the McGraw-Hill negotiators. "There was only one Hughes book, and there was a considerable demand for it."

There was only one detail that had not gone according to Irving's plan. He had suggested that all the money should be paid to him and that he would pass Hughes's share on. Mc-

Graw-Hill refused to do so after the first payment of $100,-
000. It might have seemed a small point to the publishers,
but it was a setback to Irving because it directed attention
to the subplot of his hoax—paying over checks made out to
H. R. Hughes into a bank account controlled by himself.

No flash of intuition prompted McGraw-Hill to start making the checks out to Hughes himself. Ted Weber, the corporation's spokesman, explained, "It's just prudent business
practice. It means you have proof that the right person has
received the money."

On the day Clifford Irving and Harold McGraw signed the
contract there was no celebration: not enough people at Mc-
Graw-Hill knew about Project Octavio to have a party. Those
few who did know were ecstatic. There was Harold McGraw,
who was in charge of all the book departments in the largest
publishing company in the world, and, incidentally, the
grandson of the corporation's founder. He had always confessed that he preferred a man who could clear the memos off
his desk to a man with ideas, but the idea of this project was
attractive to him; its success would bring prestige as well as
profit to a company that was worrying about a somewhat
gray and blurred public image. It might well help him up
the corporate greasy pole, and he was anxious to get to the
top. The enthusiasm of Albert Leventhal, group vice president in charge of general books, was also unrestrained. He
was to claim later in the year that the Hughes book was the
finest publishing deal McGraw-Hill had pulled off in this
century, and Leventhal had plenty of experience to judge,
too. He had worked in publishing for years, been chief
editor at Simon and Schuster, and run his own company.
The McGraw-Hill job was expected to be his last before retirement, and the Hughes book would be a fitting climax to
his career. He looked benevolently on it.

The chief editor was a complete contrast to Leventhal.
Robert Sussman Stewart was only thirty, brought in to
toughen up the book division and find more bestsellers. His

star was in the ascendant following his work on Germaine Greer's *The Female Eunuch,* which was on the bestseller lists. The Hughes book would be too, and that was sufficient recommendation. Beverly Loo, a second-generation Chinese-American from California, had been a house guest in Ibiza and entertained no discernible doubts about Irving as a friend, a writer, or the biographer of Howard Hughes.

The enthusiasm survived its first test. Early in April, Beverly Loo rang Ralph Graves, managing editor of *Life* magazine, and told him she had a proposition which was so secret that she dared not breathe it over the telephone. If he wished to hear it, he should meet her, unaccompanied. They agreed to rendezvous at Barbetta's, an Italian restaurant on West 46th Street whose most significant characteristic is that the tables are far enough apart to deter eavesdroppers.

Ralph Graves had kept a good many secrets in his time too. Only two months earlier *Life* had published Khrushchev's memoirs to cries of "fake" from a few Kremlinologists. Graves and four or five others on the magazine had kept that secret for eighteen months. Nevertheless, Graves remembers the excitement he felt when Beverly Loo revealed the subject of her property. "Journalists go for the person who won't talk," he says, and Hughes demonstrably fitted that description. When they parted, they still had to get down to a price, but Beverly Loo had a sale.

In May, Graves offered $100,000 for United States and Canadian rights, but Beverly Loo wanted a lot more. She threw in world magazine and newspaper serialization rights for good measure. Graves consulted the man who runs Time-Life's syndication service, Gedeon de Margitay, who said that, although the magazine market in Europe was depressed, he didn't disagree to a new offer of a quarter of a million dollars. That covered half McGraw-Hill's outlay, and it had yet to dangle the bait in front of book clubs and paperback publishers.

It was a big commitment for *Life,* especially for a book on a man so notorious for changing his mind, but the magazine was insured against the threat of his indecision. Clause 4 of the agreement finally signed by Graves and Harold McGraw on July 29 stated, in convoluted contractual jargon: "Anything in this agreement to the contrary notwithstanding, if for any reason 'Octavio' refuses to authorize the Work and allow it to be published as his authorized biography, it is understood and agreed that McGraw-Hill shall refund to *Life* all sums paid to McGraw pursuant to this agreement." In other words, unless Howard Hughes personally sanctioned the manuscript, the deal was off. But Graves also had to agree to virtually complete secrecy. No reporters at Time-Life were to be told, for instance, and *Life* was to make no effort to check Irving's story. In short, *Life* was refused the right to do what it did best—investigate the facts.

Clifford Irving and Ralph Graves first met on April 13. Graves thought Irving amiable enough, though *Life*'s editors were never to grow as fond of him as were his mentors at McGraw-Hill. Graves had seen one of the Hughes letters and conceded it was impressive, but he thought Irving less so. One of *Life*'s assistant managing editors, David Maness, described him brusquely as "an untalented schmuck." But Irving could hardly have cared. On that same day, April 13, he pocketed a check for $97,500—half of which he was to make out to H.R. Hughes (Irving had received $2500 a month earlier). He also met Richard Suskind, who had just flown in from Majorca. Irving had told McGraw-Hill he would need a research assistant on the biography—though only Beverly Loo knew that the man in question was a skilled and experienced writer flown in from Europe. Others were under the impression that Irving was talking about a part-time graduate student in Los Angeles. Suskind was never that.

The two of them then began to carry out a certain amount of background research designed to flesh out the great work. Suskind started off with ten days at the New York Public Library; Irving went to Washington, then on to Nassau.

After New York, Suskind went west to Las Vegas and Houston. Then, early in May, Beverly Loo received from Irving the comforting news that the interviews with Hughes had begun in Nassau. Irving returned to Ibiza shortly after that announcement, but he was back by the end of the month, when both he and Suskind did another stint in the New York Public Library. Then, on June 3, Irving went around to the *Life* offices, and Graves introduced him to David Maness, who gave him the Time-Life file on Howard Hughes. Both left New York shortly afterward to inspect more newspaper files in Houston and Los Angeles. In the middle of June they went to Palm Springs, California, where Irving met an old acquaintance called Stanley Meyer, and had what proved to be a fruitful discussion. It was an exhausting schedule, but at the end of July author and researcher returned to Ibiza and stayed there until the end of August, when they flew to Florida. Irving explained that the final series of interviews with Hughes was about to begin.

Graves met Irving several times during the summer and spoke to him once or twice on the telephone. His faith in the project remained unshaken: indeed, *Life* once actually took advantage of Irving's "expertise." A freelance photographer had come into the office offering what he claimed was the first picture of Howard Hughes to be taken for some fifteen years—an 8-by-10-inch picture of a man on a balcony at the Britannia Beach Hotel in Nassau. If it was a picture of Hughes, it was worth thousands of dollars. The picture editors at *Life* took it to Graves, and Graves suggested they leave it with him because he had an unorthodox but reliable way of checking it. When Graves next saw Irving, he asked if the figure on the balcony *was* Howard Hughes. "Certainly not," said Irving crisply.

Irving's attitude toward both his publishers was deliberately thoughtful throughout the summer. On August 28 he cabled Beverly Loo from Pompano Beach in Florida to tell her that Hughes was being difficult about the money: he wanted more. Beverly Loo was furious, even after Irving had explained that Hughes was under the mistaken impression that the half-million-dollar advance was for American rights to his autobiography. Irving said he had tried to explain to Hughes that the sum covered world book rights, but that Hughes, in a fury, had doubled his price; he wanted a million dollars. Miss Loo told Irving that a contract was a contract and, if he didn't realize that, Hughes ought to. Irving, chastened, said that he would go back to Hughes and find out how serious he was about the price increase. Internally, a debate raged at McGraw-Hill; some believed that Irving had persuaded Hughes to push up the price when he realized how good the book was going to be. "It was pure Irving," said one. But a mere two days later Irving wrote to Beverly Loo announcing that he had persuaded Hughes to drop his new demand by the considerable sum of $150,000. He was admittedly sticking at $850,000, but there was one other thing that justified the increased price. The interviews were going well—so well, in fact, that the book was changing character. It was becoming Hughes's own story, an autobiography.

McGraw-Hill's anger at the demand for twice as much money was diluted by the prospect. It was, the publishers finally concluded, one of the tribulations of dealing with Howard Hughes, not to mention Clifford Irving. Still, there was no question that an autobiography was worth more money, and, unethical though the breach of contract might be, Leventhal eventually agreed to renegotiate the asking price. In the meantime, he wanted to make sure of one thing that would make the corporation's lawyers a lot happier.

They wanted a legal assurance that the rights to the autobiography belonged to Hughes and to no one else. Irving said he didn't think that would be a problem and he would talk to Hughes about it. A letter of addendum was accordingly drafted, dated September 10. It contained a significant new paragraph which would quell McGraw-Hill's lawyers' residual suspicions about so secret a project. It became internally known and admired as "the harmless clause." The paragraph read:

> H.R. HUGHES warrants that he has the sole proprietary rights granted to AUTHOR, and in the event that any suit, proceeding or claim is commenced by Rosemont Enterprises, Inc., its successors or assigns, Hughes Tool Company, its successors or assigns, The Howard Hughes Medical Institute, its successors or assigns, or any other person, company, corporation or legal counsel representing or purporting to represent H.R. HUGHES, Hughes Tool Company, Rosemont Enterprises, Inc., or The Howard Hughes Medical Institute, against AUTHOR and/or THE PUBLISHER, H.R. HUGHES will indemnify, defend and save harmless AUTHOR and/or THE PUBLISHER against any expenses, costs, charges or damages incurred in such an event, including reasonable attorneys' fees.

The names were all familiar, except, perhaps, for Rosemont Enterprises, Inc. But it was the inclusion of Rosemont that mattered most. With that in, authorized by Hughes, the lawyers explained, there was no chance of a damaging legal action against the book.

# The Joe DiMaggio
# Bat Theory

A great deal of money can buy a great deal
of publicity—or a great deal of silence.

Attributed to Raymond Chandler

In the secret negotiations with his publisher, Clifford Irving
had no greater ally than the reputation of Rosemont Enterprises. It was a name that struck fear and trembling into
the heads of literary lawyers, and the relief of McGraw-Hill
after it had finally drafted an "immunity" to its claims was
almost tangible. For Rosemont was the final and most elaborate expression of Howard Hughes's aversion to publicity;
technically, it "owned" Hughes's life story. Now McGraw-Hill
was getting, or thought it was getting, Hughes's own undertaking that this subtle piece of legal machinery would not be
used against it.

Historically this was an astonishing *volte face* and perhaps
should have caused rather more than raised eyebrows at
McGraw-Hill. But relief proved stronger than skepticism.

There was no part of Hughes's empire more spendthrift
than that constructed to preserve his own unique concept of
privacy. It was a money-no-object operation, drawing on the

highest forensic talent. For some time past, the star characters on this dimly lit stage had been two high-powered attorneys, Chester Davis and a flamboyant Los Angeles lawyer called Gregson Bautzer. They were remarkable performers. A full narration of their exploits in suppressing books about Howard Hughes would itself require book-length treatment. Here we must confine ourselves to a few vignettes from the record which are relevant to our tale.

Bautzer's experience in this arena actually predated that of Chester Davis and the formation of Rosemont in 1965. He is a big, heavy-shouldered man with a fiercely open smile and is well known in Hollywood for many reasons. His clients are from the upper reaches of the movie and entertainment business. In his private life he has gained an almost Hughesian notoriety as the escort of filmland's more well-favored starlets. He was married, for a time, to Dana Wynter. But Bautzer's most singular claim to fame is his job as Howard Hughes's personal attorney on the West Coast. He has held it down for twenty-five years, and it is very close to his heart.

"There are only three things I'm really sentimental about," Bautzer tells acquaintances. "First, there's my son. Second, there's money. And third, there's Howard Hughes. In that order of priority. I just love that goddam guy."

Over the years his affection for his wealthiest client has been most profoundly demonstrated by his skill in keeping Hughes's name from between hard covers.

Hughes had always inclined to the view that any publicity for himself and his interests ought to be on his own terms. Even as a young man he would go to extraordinary lengths to make this possible. Back in 1938 he found out that a special magazine was being prepared on the plans for his round-the-world flight. He felt it was premature and had the whole print—some 400,000 copies—bought up straight off the presses. But his war with the book-publishing world came later, roughly coinciding with his disappearing act.

In 1954, a New York literary agent called Alex Jackinson lined up a writer to do a biography of Hughes; he found a publisher and secured an advance. The writer, however, failed to deliver, and Jackinson later found out that he had been bought off by men anxious to preserve Hughes's "privacy." This so upset Jackinson that he filed suits against the writer and the Hughes organization and, for good measure, persuaded another author to do the Hughes biography. Unfortunately, his new man, on reading through the available material, concluded that Hughes was a "half-assed hero" and decided to turn the job down. By this stage, however, Jackinson was deep into the confrontation stage with the Hughes organization, represented by Greg Bautzer.

Bautzer had come to New York to discuss Jackinson's book, though without an author there seemed to be no longer anything to discuss. Nevertheless Bautzer offered a very interesting proposition. Instead of Jackinson's extending his search to find a third man to write the biography, Jackinson should become Bautzer's ally. In Bautzer's suite at the Warwick Hotel they drew up an agreement: if Howard Hughes ever agreed to authorize a biography, Jackinson would be the agent, and if the author had a regular agent, some special provision would be made for Jackinson. The deal was made in 1955; in 1972, Jackinson, still a literary agent in New York, is still waiting.

But Bautzer's finest coup—and as far as Clifford Irving was concerned the most relevant one—was the nailing down of Noah Dietrich, the man with the richest store of Hughes memoirs. After some financial complications in the late 1950s, Dietrich affirmed that he would not:

> . . . directly or indirectly, voluntarily or negligently, either use for his own benefit or cause or permit the disclosure to others of:
> 1. Any information (whether true or false, whether laudatory or defamatory, whether of fact or of opinion, and whether previously disclosed to or otherwise known to others or not)

which either was acquired by Dietrich in or as a result of his employment by or confidential relationship to Hughes Tool Company, Howard Hughes, Trans World Airlines, Inc., Hughes Aircraft Company, or any of their affiliate companies, or which by its nature or manner of disclosure is information reasonably calculated to create the inference that, in whole or in part, it was so acquired or

. . . .

4. Any biographical or historical book, article, or other type of writing with respect to the life and affairs of Howard Hughes, or the history and affairs of Hughes Tool Company, whether or not such book, article, or other writing may be covered by the provisions of the foregoing sub-paragraphs, and Dietrich agrees to surrender to Howard Hughes or his attorneys or agents any manuscripts or other documentation of any or all of the above in his possession or under his control.

Under these elaborate terms Dietrich risked being in breach of contract if he so much as intimated that Howard Hughes might be the son of Howard Hughes, Sr.

In the late 1960s Albert B. Gerber began researching a biography of Hughes and noted at an early stage that there was an astonishing number of rumored biographies about The Man which somehow never made it into print. He began to get the message when he came across a Hollywood writer, Leo Guild, who had worked for Hughes for many years. Gerber was hopeful that Guild would prove a rich source of information. The interview did not turn out as he expected.

Guild was open but, of necessity, unhelpful. Gerber's note on his interviewee's remarks read: "I certainly wish I could help you. Unfortunately, I can't. You see, some time ago I started a biography of Hughes myself. Of course, when I began to interview people, the word got back to the Hughes organization about what I was doing and the next thing you know I was visited by a member of the organization. He made me a very handsome offer. I signed a contract." The contract was not to write a book.

Gerber asked, out of curiosity, whether he might have a look at the contract. Alas, there was another snag. Guild explained, "That's one of the provisions of the contract. I can't tell anybody about its provisions."

Around the mid-1960s the "no book" policy was rationalized. There was a pure logic to the new strategy. The whole Hughes phenomenon had been based not so much on business acumen as on legalistic skill in defending patent rights. Hughes's diligence in repelling all potential infringers of his rights over his father's oil-drilling bit had guaranteed him a continuous gusher of wealth throughout his career. It was this, more than anything, that freed him to pursue his multiple obsessions. In the twilight of his public career, Hughes tried, in effect, to patent himself: hence Rosemont.

Rosemont Enterprises, Inc., was incorporated in Nevada on July 2, 1965, qualified to do business in New York and California. In September 1965, Rosemont made a contract with Howard Hughes and obtained, for an alleged $15 million, the exclusive right to publish material about Hughes. It was an incestuous deal. The officers of Rosemont were (and still are) employees of the Hughes Tool Company. There was one exception. The post of secretary-treasurer was assigned to Chester Davis, who, technically at least, was not an employee of Hughes Tool but an independent contractor of his services. His chief client, of course, was Howard Hughes. Rosemont's offices were at 120 Broadway in New York (Davis's office) and at 1700 Ventura Boulevard, Encino, California, on the premises of one of the Hughes empire's many outposts.

Rosemont Enterprises has done very little to bring along its great "property," apart from running all the public source material on Hughes through a computer. It has not, however, been unenterprising. Since its inception, Rosemont has made one thing powerfully clear. It does not simply claim rights to Hughes's personal material; it is in business to pre-empt anybody else's right to publish books about Hughes.

Within weeks of Rosemont's foundation, Chester Davis was explaining the theory to Bennett Cerf, then president of Random House, which was proposing to publish a Hughes biography by John Keats. Davis wrote:

> Recognizing that the name and achievements of Mr. Hughes now have commercial value, being willing to make use thereof in a manner consistent with his interests, my client, Rosemont Enterprises, Inc., has obtained the *sole and exclusive right to use or publish his name, likeness, personality, life story or incidents therein.* The publication of any story about Mr. Hughes would appear to invade such rights, *even if the matters therein are assumed to be factually accurate.* [our italics]

Chester Davis once explained the concept to a reporter in simpler terms as "the Joe DiMaggio bat theory." "Look at it this way," said Davis. "If you are going to bring out a bat and put Joe DiMaggio's name on it, then you have to pay DiMaggio a royalty." He claimed that Howard Hughes had the same proprietary interest in anything written about him. It is an intriguing concept which, if generally applied, would give men of great wealth virtual immunity from any significant comment.

In the particular situation, Chester Davis won what might be described as a Pyrrhic victory. For a time, he managed to halt the distribution of Random House's 17,500 copies of the book, but simulanteously *True* magazine, with a circulation of 2,500,000, went on and printed the same material. Within the higher echelons of the Hughes organization, the episode became known as "the time Chester successfully guarded the mouse hole while the elephant walked by."

But even the mouse roared. Random House rejected Chester Davis's lavish contention that no publisher could even use Hughes's *name* without injuring Rosemont. Greg Bautzer then moved into the picture with a new tactic. He told Cerf that if Random House promised to give up the biography by John Keats, he would arrange for the publisher an "authorized" biography with the cooperation of Mr. and Mrs. Hughes. Such a book, according to Bautzer, would "raise the hair on your arm." Cerf, however, asked the obvious question: How could they be assured of Hughes's cooperation and delivery of the manuscript on a specific date? Bautzer's reply was: "If we don't perform we would be willing to agree to pay a penalty." Cerf concluded that Bautzer's embrace was to be avoided, and stuck with Keats's biography.

Rosemont was still not beaten. It got hold of a copy of Keats's book in advance of publication and scrutinized it to discover its sources. They found that a substantial one was a series of articles by Stephen White in *Look* magazine in 1954. Rosemont promptly acquired the copyright of those articles from *Look*'s parent company, Cowles Publications; it was given in exchange for first refusal on that chimera, the official Hughes autobiography. Rosemont then took Random House to court, contending that the book was an infringement of its copyright on the *Look* series.

The courts had some interesting things to say about this bizarre struggle. The majority opinion in the appeals court case, *Rosemont* v. *Random House,* stated: "When one enters into the public arena to the extent that [Hughes] has, the right of privacy must be tempered by the countervailing privilege that the public has some information concerning important public figures." In a separate opinion, even stronger language was used: "It would be contrary to the public interest to permit any man to buy up copyright to anything written about himself and to use copyright to restrain others from publishing biographical material concerning him."

The court also rejected a claim which Rosemont had made, both before and since the action: that it was independent of Hughes. The judge then went on to review Rosemont's various maneuvers and concluded: "The implication from the above facts is obvious: Hughes wanted nothing written about himself, the publication of which he could not control. The

Rosemont Corporation was created to this end." John Keats's biography of Hughes, after being withdrawn from circulation, was put back in the bookstores. But Rosemont had its "success" stories, of a sort.

Lyle Stuart is a wealthy New York publisher with a strongly combative nature. He wanted a book about Hughes on his list and was not deterred, as others in the trade were, by the prospect of expensive legal action. He actually likes litigation. Late in 1964 he commissioned a Hollywood movie critic called Ezra Goodman to do a Hughes biography. In the spring of 1965, Stuart received a visit from the ubiquitous Bautzer. Finding Stuart resolute in his decision to publish, Bautzer again promised "partnership": if Stuart would wait until the end of the TWA litigation against Hughes, the man himself would cooperate on the book. Goodman would be guaranteed access to corporate records and other secret materials, though not to Hughes himself. Stuart rejected the offer (which was just as well, as the TWA suit, seven years later, is still dragging on).

But Stuart had not reckoned with Goodman. On November 22, 1965, Goodman entered into a contract with Rosemont which stipulated that he would submit his manuscript on Hughes to Rosemont before he showed it to Stuart. Goodman also accepted a generous commission, of over $40,000, from Rosemont to do an outline for a biography about D.W. Griffith, one of Goodman's pet interests. What with one thing and another, the book on Hughes somehow never managed to appear.

Stuart, however, has an unforgiving nature. He started a merry-go-round of litigation that has involved the whole cast of characters—Goodman, Chester Davis, Bautzer, and Rosemont—right down to 1972. At one stage, just to give events a new impetus, Stuart hopped on a plane to Las Vegas, deliberately lost $30,000 in Hughes's casinos, and refused to pay. To requests for the money, Stuart responded, "Sue me."

He took a more practical form of revenge through his

publishing house. In 1967 Stuart brought out "the book that couldn't be suppressed," a biography by Albert B. Gerber entitled *The Bashful Billionaire,* and followed this up a few years later with *Howard Hughes in Las Vegas* by Omar Garrison. Out of only three book-length studies of Hughes which managed to slip by his security apparatus in sixteen years, Stuart proudly claims responsibility for two.

Both the Lyle Stuart books and Keats's biography for Random House were carefully read in the summer of 1971 by Clifford Irving and Richard Suskind, while they researched their own biography of Howard Hughes. But Irving's advantage gained from this history was not the raw material but the knowledge of Rosemont's image.

Rosemont's obtuse zeal in combating any Hughes book, whether good or bad, factual or fanciful, had earned it the dislike of Manhattan publishers. When Irving came to Mc-Graw-Hill with his proposition, he made one thing very clear at an early stage: Rosemont, on Hughes's instructions, was not involved and was not to be consulted. In the light of the record, McGraw-Hill's eagerness to accept this condition was hardly surprising. Nor was its determination to get a watertight indemnity against legal action by Rosemont into the agreement between Irving and Hughes. The agreement protected the publishers from Davis and Bautzer—assuming, of course, that it was made between Irving and Hughes; and McGraw-Hill had no reason to doubt that.

# A Million to One

There was a crooked man
Who walked a crooked mile.
He found a crooked sixpence.
It wasn't enough.

Murray Sayle, *A Crooked Sixpence*

When Irving flew into New York from Nassau on September 12, there was still a money problem. Hughes, he said, was reluctant to budge from the $850,000 asking price for his autobiography. The project was now on the verge of completion, but it could—if the money was not right—be easily offered to another publisher. Irving was sorry about the situation, but there it was, that was Howard Hughes for you.

Irving checked into the Elysée Hotel and, for the benefit of the publishers, assembled the evidence in hand. He had a bulky draft manuscript and two letters signed by Howard Hughes. The first was dated September 11 and written on the notepaper of the Beach Inn on Paradise Island in Nassau, to which Irving had flown from Miami the previous day. It authorized McGraw-Hill to publish the book as an autobiography under the terms and conditions of the agreements between Hughes and Irving. That meant McGraw-Hill had the Howard Hughes autobiography and an indemnity against legal action by Rosemont and anybody else who thought he, not McGraw-Hill, owned the book. The second letter was less pleasing. It read:

Clifford Irving—

In the event that no agreement (on the money question) is reached between you and McGraw-Hill by 9-21-71 concerning the publication of my autobiography, I authorize you to offer my autobiography for sale to another publisher on the terms to which you and I have agreed in our Letter of Agreement, and also to show them the manuscript in your possession. This authorization expires 9-30-71 at which time both copies of this manuscript are to be returned to me.

Yours truly,
Howard Hughes

To make quite certain that McGraw-Hill did not think that Hughes was making an idle threat, Irving also brought with him a check for $100,000 made out to McGraw-Hill, drawn on the Swiss Credit Bank and signed H. R. Hughes. It was exactly the sum that had been so far paid to Irving, who said Hughes had told him to give it back unless the price was increased to $850,000. It concentrated Albert Leventhal's mind wonderfully. Faced by the threat of losing such a valuable property, he was in a poor bargaining position. Nevertheless, he refused to cave in completely. He offered an improved advance of $750,000 instead of the $850,000 asked by Hughes. Irving said he would pass the offer on. Meanwhile there was a manuscript to be read. McGraw-Hill and *Life* were about to see what they were to get for their hefty expenditure.

They got about a thousand pages of roughly edited tape-recorded conversations. The finished product opened with an account of the boyhood of Howard Hughes, and then broke off to outline his philosophy. But the bulk of the book —at least 75 per cent, as the agreement had promised—was in question-and-answer form, and that was what Irving had brought with him. Early on September 13, Ralph Graves arrived at the Elysée, bringing David Maness; the two of them and the McGraw-Hill trio—the ubiquitous Beverly Loo, Leventhal, and Stewart—grabbed handfuls of the tape transcripts and read them through the silence punctuated by occasional laughs and surprised whistles. It took them two days to go through them all, and most of the time Irving hovered about, wandering from bedroom to sitting room, suffering the insecurity of authorship. He need not have worried. "I thought it was terrific," says Graves. So did the McGraw-Hill people.

The manuscript seemed authentic. The paperback publishers, who trooped in when *Life* had finished reading, thought so too. The style was what convinced them. Hughes sounded just as they had expected him to sound. Ralph Graves wrote about it later in *Life:*

> It was outspoken, full of rich and outrageous anecdotes, as well as detailed accounts of Hughes's youth, his moviemaking, his career in aviation, his business affairs, his private life, his opinions and crotchets. He explained why he phoned people on business matters in the middle of the night (he kept strange hours anyway, and it caught them at their weakest moment). He explained his philosophy of business negotiation (one man plays lion, one man plays donkey, and it is always better to be the lion and eat the donkey). He told business yarns ranging from high finance in TWA to the time a high-ranking corporate friend was caught swiping a box of cookies from the supermarket. Even the boring parts were persuasive: Howard Hughes had always been fascinated by the minutiae of aircraft design and performance, and the transcripts had lots of it.

David Maness thought the manuscript was authentic but was troubled by one episode. This was a romantic story about Hughes's discovery of true love with the wife of a Central American diplomat, called Helga. It described how they met during a plane flight and plighted their troth by holding hands. Hughes had found the meeting an elevating experi-ence. He was, it appears, deeply in love. It might have been important to Hughes, but it sounded pretty phony to Maness. He questioned Irving, who accepted the criticism and said he would check it. Hughes had misled him before, he ex-plained. "He said that he still didn't always trust me, and he wanted to be sure that I was checking everything." Maness forgot about it; he was not interested in the story except for the *Life* excerpts.

If further proof of authenticity was needed, there were some scrawled comments in Hughes's handwriting on the transcripts. They were never very explicit. Sometimes there was just one word—"no"—in the margin. On another page the words "aviator of tricks" had been crossed out and "aviatrix" scrawled in. But the handwritten corrections helped confirm that Hughes was involved—not that any members of the tight-knit group who were in on the secret needed much con-vincing.

There remained the problem of the cash. Leventhal's room for maneuver had been narrowed by the quality of the manu-script, but he stuck at $750,000. Irving, by now complaining that too much money was going to Hughes and not enough to himself, decided on a drastic countermeasure. He sought out Ralph Graves at *Life* shortly after he had finished read-ing the transcribed tapes and wanted to know what would happen if he took the package to another publisher. "I told him he couldn't possibly sell to a reputable firm," Graves remembers. Both McGraw-Hill and *Life* were determined to make their contracts stick. Irving went straight back to McGraw-Hill and, somewhat abashed, admitted that he had thought of selling McGraw-Hill down the river. "I'll try to contact The Man." A day or so later Irving met Beverly Loo again: Hughes had finally come around to $750,000, he an-nounced.

But there was one more thing to be done before a new contract was signed. Since so much money was involved in so controversial a project, the book division decided to seek confirmation from its corporate masters. On September 20, Shelton Fisher, the chief executive officer of McGraw-Hill, and ten of his senior colleagues met and read sections of the manuscript. They were told that not only was a good deal of money involved, but there might be legal problems; moreover, there was some pretty filthy language in the book, which invaded the frontiers of the company's taste. What was their advice? Go ahead, the corporate brass said unanimously. The book company did so enthusiastically.

On September 22, Albert Leventhal gave Irving two checks: one for himself for $25,000 and another for Hughes for $275,000. Irving took them and glanced at both. His check looked fine, but he pointed out a small error in the larger check. It was made out to Howard Hughes, rather than H.R. Hughes. He realized, of course, that Leventhal might find this slightly ridiculous, but Hughes had insisted on the use of his initials. Would Leventhal ask the accounting department to make the check out again? Leventhal agreed, and on the next day Irving was given a second one. Again no one at McGraw-Hill suspected anything unusual. "We just thought Hughes was behaving eccentrically, and there was nothing suspicious about that," Ted Weber explains. Irving reminded Leventhal of just one other thing: his expenses. Rather wearily, McGraw-Hill agreed to cover the first $15,000.

While substantial checks were being made out for Irving, promises of even larger sums were coming into McGraw-Hill. Once the publishers had the manuscript, it became abundantly clear that they were going to make a gratifying profit, much more than either Clifford Irving or H.R. Hughes. Besides the $250,000 already pledged by *Life* magazine, Dell had offered $400,000 for the paperback rights, and the Book-of-the-Month Club had guaranteed $325,000. In the fall the first rough estimates of McGraw-Hill's profit were being made. They were rarely lower than $2 million and went as high as $3 million. The prospect of huge profits somewhat reduced the capacity among McGraw-Hill executives for critical analysis. The mere idea of fraud was a nightmare dismissed to the recesses of the mind.

But mistrust and skepticism are not qualities built into the publishing mind. The industry is still tinged with gentlemanly virtues like trust and friendship and loyalty. Men like Harold McGraw belonged to an Establishment that believed in "standards." If a man had been with the firm for some time you trusted him, and Clifford Irving had been with the firm for twelve years. He might not have been one of the most successful authors on the list, but McGraw-Hill had been loyal to him and they were now being amply rewarded. The transaction was, in its way, a justification of the comfortable old relationship between author and publisher. Of course, not everyone in the editorial department was wholly in favor of the gentlemanly virtues. There were younger and tougher men—they would probably describe themselves as "hard-nosed"—but they were in no doubt that Clifford Irving had provided them with an authentic manuscript, though for different reasons. "He's not a good enough writer to have made it up," one of them said, snickering.

By late October the lawyers were at work on the manuscript. Though they never hacked away at it, they did cut down the number of slighting references to Chester Davis and removed the name of President Lyndon Johnson's last Secretary of Defense, Clark Clifford, from an episode involving President Nixon's brother. But Irving was aware of the alterations. He made no complaints and changed a few things himself later on. For instance, he said that, having checked with Hughes about his girl friend, Helga—as Maness had requested —he wanted to make a change there. She wasn't a figment of Hughes's imagination; he had confirmed that. But Hughes had begun to worry that if her real name remained in the book she would be too easily identified. After all, there couldn't be all that many wives of Central American diplomats called Helga. Instead of calling her Helga, Hughes wanted her called Inge. The only thing Irving clung to stubbornly was the punctuation in the transcribed tapes. Robert Stewart, the editor, wanted to tidy it up. No, said Irving, Hughes wanted it that way, so it had better be left.

The Irving-Hughes agreement drawn up in September contained such proposed titles as "The Confessions of Howard Hughes" and "In My Own Words." But they were soon forgotten. In October, Irving plumped for "My Turn" by Howard Hughes. It was a good idea. "My Turn" evoked images of a man who had been written about, analyzed, and attacked for years, and who was going to answer back at last. It was not until late in December that the more explicit, and final title was chosen. The book was to be announced as "The Autobiography of Howard Hughes," Introduction and Commentary by Clifford Irving.

There was only one small cloud on the horizon: another book purporting to be the authentic autobiography of Howard Hughes. It had first surfaced in August, and it was said to have been edited by a Hollywood novelist and scriptwriter of limited literary repute called Robert Eaton. Early in November McGraw-Hill discovered it was to be published in January. This competing manuscript, entitled "My Life and Opinions" by Howard Hughes, began to act as an irritant. McGraw-Hill and *Life* were naturally convinced that it was bogus, and the Eaton book was to act as a catalyst.

Irving was in Ibiza, tidying up the final manuscript, when the call went out from New York. "Something's got to be done," he was told. "There's a limit to the number of Hughes autobiographies the country can stand." Irving replied that he would contact Hughes and, two or three days later, telephoned to say that Hughes would write to Harold McGraw clearing up the Eaton problem and making certain prepublication conditions. McGraw was looking forward to the Eaton solution but got a bad attack of nerves about the conditions. They hadn't been mentioned before. The handwritten letter, dated November 17, was a testy, bad-tempered, and slightly myopic document, nine pages long and signed Howard R. Hughes. It arrived on November 22, and it read:

Dear Mr. McGraw—

The facts placed before me, I find astonishing. I do not understand, in the first place, why it is not possible for your publishing house in possession of a legitimate contract between myself and Mr. Clifford Irving and between yourselves and Mr. Irving, for the publication of my autobiography, cannot deal firmly and forcefully with other publishers which are asserting fraudulent claims to the rights which I have granted to Mr. Irving and Mr. Irving in turn has granted to you, without my intervention.

I have said before, and I will say again, that this Mr. Post and Mr. Eaton in no way represent me and have no rights granted by me to sell articles or books purporting to be authorized or written by me. I have given no material whatsoever to these people and no documents, and any claim by them to the contrary is fraudulent and criminal. I am sure these people are employed by my enemies.

In the event that they or any publisher should attempt to publish any material supposedly secured by me or authorized by me, and you can do nothing to prevent this through normal channels, I assure you—and I ask that you in turn will now assure *them*—that I will do all in my power, and take whatever legal steps are necessary to halt what I consider an outrage on my privacy and my painfully worked out agreements with you and Mr. Clifford Irving.

I have been made aware, although not fully to my satisfaction of McGraw Hill's apparently embarrassing position relative to these fraudulent representatives and other publishers. By that I mean, as I said, that I do not fully understand why your publishing company in conjunction with Life Magazine cannot without my intervention, an intervention very difficult for me under the circumstances of my health and for other private reasons, cannot handle this matter by yourselves.

Be that as it may, I am aware of the gravity of your problem as well as my own, and considering this as well as my very deep desire that my autobiography in Mr. Irving's possession be published as soon as possible, I will accede to your needs.

That is to say—any provisions in my agreement with Mr. Clifford Irving to the contrary notwithstanding, I, Howard R. Hughes, grant McGraw Hill and Life Magazine the right to publicly announce, at any time following your receipt of this letter, that fact that they and their licensees may and will publish my autobiography as defined in my agreements with Mr. Clifford Irving—*provided that* McGraw Hill's final payment to Mr. Irving under the terms of your contract with him is made simultaneously with this public announcement, and provided that payment to me by Mr. Irving is made immediately thereafter, whether this be McGraw Hill's check or cashiers check being beside the point.

Moreover, to assure you of my good faith in this matter, I hereby authorize McGraw Hill and/or Life Magazine to take whatever legal steps are necessary, in their considered judgement, on my behalf, or to retain legal counsel on my behalf, to seek an injunction against any material published or announced for publication by any publisher which is not one of McGraw Hill's licensees, that purports to be authorized by me or purports to be in any way, shape or form my partial or complete autobiography or memoirs or that in any way, shape or form conflicts with the publication by McGraw Hill and its licensees of my authorized autobiography, and to prosecute to the full extent of the law any perpetrations of such impostures.

I have tried to be as clear as possible in this letter and I regret that I could not be more concise under the circumstances, but I trust I have made my intentions very clear.

I would also ask that you provide to me a copy of your public announcement, either before or after it is made, through Mr. Clifford Irving, as I do not read newspapers, and I respectfully request that your announcement lean more to the side of dignity than sensationalism.

I am very sorry that this matter has become so complicated, and please believe me when I say that I earnestly look forward to the successful publication of my book in the very near future. I have already given my approval in advance to Mr. Irving, and I have the utmost faith that he will be faithful to my wishes in his preparation of the manuscript.

Most sincerely yours,
Howard R. Hughes

The letter clinched the question of authenticity once and for all as far as Harold McGraw was concerned, especially since it contained none of the threatened conditions. He instructed his staff to carry on with the job of preparing an announcement and ordered them to make sure that it leaned more to the side of dignity than sensationalism, just as Mr. Hughes had asked. McGraw-Hill had expected to announce the coup in mid-January, but by then the *Ladies' Home Journal* would have come out with an excerpt from the Eaton book, and an announcement before that would certainly reduce its impact. There was no doubt at McGraw-Hill and *Life* that an early announcement would help them, as well as pacify the author of that November 17 letter.

Then Ralph Graves seemed to suffer a small stab of doubt. He suggested to McGraw-Hill that it would be a good idea to have the most recent letter from Hughes analyzed by a handwriting expert. There was a man in New York, he said, called Alfred Kanfer, who had studied the letter Hughes had written to Bill Gay and Chester Davis a year earlier. Why not show it to him? McGraw-Hill agreed, sent off a copy, and asked if Kanfer thought it was the real thing. On December 2 Kanfer replied in a hastily put-together letter in which Hughes's name was actually spelled wrong and then corrected. Kanfer concluded:

> It can be stated that the two handwriting specimens were written by the same person. These are the reasons for this assumption.
>
> Both handwriting samples show full identity in regard to

the strongest and most outstanding characteristic, the very wide and almost disintegrating spacings between words. There is furthermore full identity in the way the margins to both sides of the writing are handled. The ratios between height and width of the letters are identical, and so are the ratios between down- and upstroke pressures, all letters written with the same force and one could almost say the same vehemence, and what is most characteristic, even the irregularities and fluctuations of size and pressure in both writings are identical. To this can be added the identity of letter forms.

The chances that another person could copy this handwriting even in a similar way are less than 1 in a million.

And just in case Ralph Graves was not satisfied by even that remarkably confident assertion, Harold McGraw supplied what he believed to be the absolute clincher: he told Graves that he had a guarantee from the Chase Manhattan Bank that Howard Hughes had cashed the September check for $275,000. (What the Swiss Credit Bank had in fact told the Chase Manhattan was that *H. R. Hughes* had cashed the check, but Graves was not to know that, or even appreciate the significance of the difference.)

At the end of November Clifford Irving came back to New York and helped write the press release which he was taking down to Florida in order to obtain Hughes's clearance of the contents. He looked at the draft and added one clause which stated that his interviews had taken place "in various motel rooms and parked cars throughout the Western Hemisphere." That sounded a bit sensational and undignified to McGraw-Hill. "But it's true," replied Irving, writing it in.

On December 2, the day of his departure, McGraw-Hill made out two more checks and gave them to Irving. One was the last installment of his own advance, another check for $25,000. The second was made out, properly this time, to H. R. Hughes. It was the biggest of all—$325,000, half the sum promised to Hughes. As soon as he received them, Irving left for Florida. He explained that he was going to be met by Hughes's representative, the man called George Gordon Holmes.

Irving had the full sum of the advance now, though there were still the royalties to come. And McGraw-Hill was so confident of the book that he was given to understand that the author's share of the vast turnover the book was expected to generate—from paperback and movie sales as well—could amount to no less than $2 million.

# Life's Untold Story

I'll take care of my problems and you
take care of your problems.

George Gordon Holmes (subsequently anon.)

Throughout an exhausting year Clifford Irving had, from
his publishers' point of view, been commendably frank.
He had taken them into his confidence at every stage of his
dealings with one of the world's most eccentric men. When
that eccentricity had threatened the project, Irving had
done everything in his power to keep it on the rails. He had
borne the brunt of negotiation as well as that of authorship.
And at the end of the day he had handed in a magnificent
manuscript.

There was no doubt in McGraw-Hill's mind that Irving
deserved far more recognition than that normally accorded to
the ghostwriters of great men. Then *Life* made a suggestion
that was both fitting and great journalism: why not run a
story about how Irving had talked the book out of Hughes?
The proposal was incorporated in McGraw-Hill's official
press release on December 7. In addition to the installments
from the autobiography, the release pledged that *Life* would
"publish shortly after the turn of the year an account by
Mr. Irving detailing his involvement with the project and

his impressions of and adventures with Mr. Hughes, who has not been interviewed or photographed since 1957."

Without question "Clifford Irving—My Secret Meetings with Howard Hughes" would have made a great read, but legal complications were to prevent the talks from being told in *Life*. It was not, however, entirely lost to posterity. When the authenticity of the book was challenged, Irving told the story instead to the Supreme Court of New York. It was sketched out in affidavit, index no. 800/72, sworn before Martin S. Ackerman, Notary Public, State of New York.

Compressed into that legal document is a tale as richly textured as any of the novels Irving ever wrote. It describes, in masterly detail and sub-Hemingway prose, the meetings he had held with Howard Hughes and the interviews which served as a basis for his book. Reading it, one begins to comprehend the scope of Irving's achievement. And for a document signed under oath it has one other remarkable feature: apart from the place names and locations, not a word of it is true.

The account begins with the first "meeting":

> *February 13, 1971, Mexico:* After several telephone calls from Mr. Hughes to me in Ibiza, Mr. Hughes arranged our first meeting in Oaxaca, Mexico. This took place on February 13, 1971. An emissary of Mr. Hughes, known to me only as Pedro, picked me up at the Hotel Victoria in Oaxaca at approximately 7:00 a.m. and drove me to a mountaintop called Monte Alban where Mr. Hughes awaited me in a parked car. Mr. Hughes identified himself to me as Howard Hughes and was clearly recognizable to me as Howard R. Hughes by reason of prior photographs that I had studied and by reason of his statements to me concerning his meeting with my father in the early 1940s which corroborated what my father had told me regarding those meetings. Mr. Hughes and I spoke intermittently for between one and two hours and then arranged a meeting for the following day.
>
> *February 14, 1971:* On that following day, February 14, 1971, the man known to me as Pedro flew me by private plane to

Juchitan airport on the isthmus of Mexico, and we then drove
in a car to Salina Cruz, where I went for a swim. Mr. Hughes
and I finally met in the early afternoon in a room in a hotel
in Tehuantepec. Our discussion lasted intermittently for several hours, during which time Mr. Hughes repeatedly left the
room and went elsewhere for periods of ten to twenty minutes.
Mr. Hughes vanished at about 6:oo p.m. and I returned to
Oaxaca and then the following morning to New York. The
man known to me as Pedro gave me what appears to be a
Polaroid photograph, taken of me by a Hughes aide as I descended from the plane at Mexico City Airport enroute from
New York. This, it was explained to me, was for identificaiton
purpose and to insure that I was not accompanied by newsmen.

*March 4, 1971, Puerto Rico:* Following Mr. Hughes's telephoned instructions, I flew on March 2, 1971, from Ibiza via
Madrid to San Juan, Puerto Rico. I was met at the airport by
an emissary of Mr. Hughes known to me only as Jorge, or
George. This man took from me the draft copy of the Letter
of Agreement dated March 4, 1971, between Mr. Hughes and
myself that I had previously prepared in Ibiza, and told me to
register at the El San Juan Hotel in San Juan, which I did.
At approximately 4:oo a.m. on March 4, 1971, George telephoned me to arrange a meeting between me and Mr. Hughes.
Mr. Hughes and I met in a parked car within brief walking
distance of the hotel and I drove Mr. Hughes, following his
instructions, to an area known as the tropical rain forest, near
San Juan. We talked intermittently for several hours and then
I drove the car back to the same parking place near the hotel
and left Mr. Hughes in the car and went back to the hotel.

*March 5, 1971, Puerto Rico:* A meeting with Mr. Hughes
followed on March 5, 1971, at approximately 3:oo a.m., in a
parked car near the hotel, at which time we signed the Letter
of Agreement dated March 4, 1971. I then flew to New York.
Mr. Hughes did not disclose to me where he was staying in
Puerto Rico.

*April 22–May 3, 1971, Nassau, Bahamas:* Mr. Hughes and
I next met in Nassau, the Bahamas, on April 23, 1971, to begin
the interviews per se. I first stayed at the Pilot House Club in

Nassau, accompanied by my wife, and Mr. Hughes and I met on the night of April 23, 1971, in a parked car. I found this arrangement unsatisfactory for purposes of tape-recording and requested that we meet the next time in my hotel. Mr. Hughes then requested that I move to a different hotel, the Montagu Beach Hotel just outside of Nassau, where he believed entrance and exit were less likely to be observed; and I did so. My wife and I stayed in Room 112 of the Montagu Beach Hotel from April 25, 1971, through May 3, 1971, during which period Mr. Hughes came to my room on about four separate occasions, at night, for the purpose of conducting the interviews. On each occasion Mr. Hughes or a telephone intermediary identifying himself to me with a code word arranged the time of the meeting and requested that my wife not be present. My wife thus saw a great deal of Nassau night life on her own and on one occasion had to sleep in a deck chair on the beach from about 4:00 a.m. to 6:00 a.m. Mr. Hughes indicated to me at this time that he was staying in a private residence in a place on New Providence Island (near Nassau) called Lyford Cay. During this period in Nassau, Mr. Hughes and I saw each other for a total period of approximately fourteen to eighteen hours and clocked approximately eight to ten hours of tape-recorded interviews. After each session, Mr. Hughes left the hotel with the tapes (both spool and cassette) in his possession. It was understood between us that Mr. Hughes would assume the responsibility for having the tapes transcribed and give the typed transcriptions to me at our next meeting.

*June 9–18, 1971, Beverly Hills, California:* Mr. Hughes and I met next in Beverly Hills, California, at the Holiday Inn, 9360 Wilshire Boulevard. During the period from June 9 through June 18, 1971, we met approximately five times in my room (interrupted by a separate meeting in Palm Springs described below) at the hotel for periods varying from approximately one hour to six hours. The time of the meetings was always arranged in advance, either personally or by telephone call from Mr. Hughes or an unidentifiable but bona fide intermediary. Mr. Hughes never disclosed to me his place of residence in California, if indeed he was staying in California. During this period I estimate we clocked between ten to fifteen hours of tape-recorded interviews. Mr. Hughes, during this period, gave me two copies of the typed transcript of the interviews we had recorded previously in Nassau, one of which contained numerous handwritten comments, suggestions and spelling changes, all of which Mr. Hughes indicated to me had been written personally by him.

*June 12, 1971, Palm Springs, California:* At a mid-point during the Beverly Hills interviews, Mr. Hughes requested that I meet him in Palm Springs, California, on the night of June 12, 1971. I was instructed to take a room at the Black Angus–President Motel and await Mr. Hughes' arrival "between 10:00 p.m. and midnight." Mr. Hughes arrived somewhat earlier than expected, which was unusual for him since he was invariably late to our appointments, and found Mr. Richard Suskind, whom I had hired as a researcher, with me in the room. After a brief conversation, during which I introduced Mr. Suskind to Mr. Hughes and in which Mr. Hughes identified himself to Mr. Suskind as Howard Hughes, Mr. Suskind left and Mr. Hughes and I conducted tape-recorded interviews intermittently throughout the night. [Suskind, in his own affidavit, lent substance to this story by claiming that Hughes offered him an organic prune from a paper bag he was carrying.]

*August 28 to September 10, 1971, Pompano Beach, Florida:* The final meeting between Mr. Hughes and myself, during which tape-recorded interviews took place, occurred in Pompano Beach, Florida, in my bungalow at the Beachcomber Motel, where Mr. Hughes had previously instructed me to stay. Mr. Hughes had originally suggested the Beach Inn, Paradise Island, the Bahamas, but for some reason changed his mind at the last minute and advised me by telephone to Ibiza. These meetings took place intermittently between August 28, 1971, and September 9, 1971. We clocked approximately five to eight hours of tape-recorded interviews in this period, during which Mr. Hughes indicated to me that he was staying in a private residence in Palm Beach, Florida. During this same period, since I was dissatisfied with the accuracy and skill of the typist used by Mr. Hughes to transcribe the initial inter-

views made in the Bahamas, Mr. Hughes gave me permission
to transcribe and type the tapes made by us in California and
also the tapes we were making at that time in Pompano
Beach. Mr. Hughes informed me that he would therefore arrange a 24-hour-a-day guard on my bungalow to insure that
neither the tapes nor the transcripts would be stolen and also
to insure that I did not leave the bungalow with the tapes.
Mr. Hughes informed me that the guard would always carry
a cane and be under forty years of age and that if I saw such
a man lurking in the vicinity I was not to molest him. I did,
on two occasions during the daytime, observe such a man from
a distance, standing across the street in front of a shop that sold
seashells. I had no conversation with this man (or men). Since
I was overburdened with work at the time, Mr. Richard Suskind, my researcher, who was living in an adjacent room,
helped me to transcribe approximately four to six hours of
the tape.

*September 11, 1971, Paradise Island, Nassau, Bahamas:* The
next meeting between Mr. Hughes and myself took place on
the night of September 11, 1971, in my room at the Beach Inn,
Paradise Island, Nassau, the Bahamas. Mr. Hughes requested
the meeting place and the time of meeting and did not inform
me where he himself was staying. It was during this meeting
that Mr. Hughes gave me two complete copies of the 950
transcript-pages of our tape-recorded interviews, one of which
was annotated with his handwritten comments and suggestions; the letter of authorization of September 11, 1971, the
letter of September 11, 1971, and a check; and it was also
during this meeting that we signed the Letter of Addendum
dated September 10, 1971. I then flew from Nassau to New
York on September 12, 1971.

*September 23, 1971, Key Biscayne, Florida:* The next meeting between myself and Mr. Hughes took place on the night of
September 23, 1971, in the Sonesta Beach Hotel, Key Biscayne, Florida. The time and place of the meeting was at the
request of Mr. Hughes, who had previously telephoned me at
the Hotel Elysée in New York City, where he knew that I was
staying. At this meeting I interviewed Mr. Hughes (without a
tape-recorder) in order to fill in "gaps" in the story of his life;

gave him McGraw-Hill check for $275,000. and returned to him his own check for $100,000, made payable to McGraw-Hill. Mr. Hughes did not inform me of his place of residence at that time.

*December 3, 1971, Florida:* The final meetings between Mr. Hughes and myself took place on December 3 and December 7, 1971, in what I believe to be a private residence within approximately one-and-one-half hours driving distance from Miami Airport. Mr. Hughes had previously planned to meet me about one week earlier in Los Angeles, California, but illness prevented this meeting. In Los Angeles, following Mr. Hughes' instructions, I personally gave to his emissary, a man known to me as George Holmes, a draft copy of the finished and edited manuscript based on our interviews.

As arranged between Mr. Holmes and myself, I arrived in Miami, Florida, on December 3, 1971, and was met at the airport by Mr. Holmes. After I had rented a car, Mr. Holmes requested that I drive with him in his car to meet Mr. Hughes. Mr. Holmes blindfolded me and instructed me that if for any reason we were stopped by the police or anyone else I was to say that I was tired from a long flight and was trying to sleep and did not wish to be disturbed by the sunlight. We drove for what I judged to be about one-and-one-half hours and then entered what I judged to be a private residence. I was instructed to remove the blindfold and found myself in the presence of Mr. Hughes, who was lying in bed and obviously ill. In my opinion he was suffering from a serious respiratory ailment since he found it extremely difficult to talk and gasped and wheezed between phrases. During this meeting, at which Mr. Holmes was sometimes present but generally silent, I was asked several times to leave the room and wait in the adjoining hallway. During this same meeting, which lasted intermittently for about forty-five minutes, Mr. Hughes acknowledged receipt of McGraw-Hill's check for $325,000—which I had given to Mr. Holmes in the car near Miami Airport—and told me that he had read the manuscript I had given to Mr. Holmes in Los Angeles and approved it for publication by McGraw-Hill. All the changes requested by Mr. Hughes were later made by me. After this meeting, I was driven, blind-

folded, by Mr. Holmes, to pick up my rented car; I then drove
to the Newport Beach Motel in Miami Beach, Florida, where
I stayed through December 10, 1971.

*December 7, 1971, Florida:* I saw Mr. Hughes again, and for
the last time, on December 7, 1971, at the same place described
above. I was picked up at my hotel by Mr. Holmes and subsequently blindfolded as before. Mr. Hughes' physical condition was unchanged. During this meeting, which lasted intermittently for approximately one hour, he signed the Preface
to the book which I had typed from our mutual notes and
recommendations. I expressed the desire to see Mr. Hughes
again, while I was still in Florida, and he said that would be
arranged, although we would have to take extreme security
precautions since he did not wish me to be followed and thus
lead reporters or other persons to his whereabouts, which
might easily occur, he believed, following McGraw-Hill's announcement that same day that they were to publish Mr.
Hughes' autobiography. Mr. Holmes, before he dropped me
near my hotel, promised to call me within a day or two.

*December 8, 1971—Telephone Call:* Mr. Holmes did telephone me late the following evening, December 8, 1971. The announcement of publication of the autobiography had appeared
in the press, together with Hughes Tool Company's and the
Byoir Agency's denial of its authenticity. I was upset and I
asked Mr. Holmes to please ask Mr. Hughes to communicate
with the Hughes Tool Company and the Byoir Agency and
inform them that the autobiography was indeed genuine. Mr.
Holmes promised to relay my message. He called me the following day, December 9th, and was extremely agitated. He
said, to the best of my recollection: "The old man's not well
at all. I can't give you the answers to your questions. I've got
problems. I'll take care of my problems and you take care of
your problems." I said that I wanted to see Mr. Hughes again
and Mr. Holmes said he would call me back. He called me a
few hours later and, still agitated, instructed me to fly to St.
Croix (Virgin Islands) the following day. He telephoned again
to find out what flight I was taking and what hotel I would be
staying at, and then said, to the best of my recollection: "I
can't guarantee you anything. I can't tell you anything at this

point. But go to St. Croix and I'll contact you there and we'll hope for the best."

*December 10, 1971, St. Croix:* I flew to St. Croix on December 10, 1971, and stayed through the late afternoon of December 12, 1971. I was never contacted by Mr. Hughes, Mr. Holmes, or anyone else representing Mr. Hughes. I flew to New York, as I had explained to Mr. Holmes that I would do, on December 12, 1971. Since then I have had no word or message in any form from Mr. Hughes, Mr. Holmes, or anyone else known to me to be a bona fide personal representative or emissary of Mr. Hughes.

# ACT IV

## Wise Men
## Rush In

# An Opportunity Lost

How often have I said to you that when you have eliminated the impossible, whatever remains, *however improbable,* must be the truth.

Sir Arthur Conan Doyle, *The Sign of Four.*

There was one man in America capable of strangling Clifford Irving's hoax at its public birth. The trouble was that nobody knew at the time that he could, least of all himself.

Even so, he came within an ace of exposing the whole affair before the literary Spruce Goose took flight. The reasons why he almost succeeded on Day One but was then thrown off the scent for more than two months are intriguing. They had something to do with Clifford Irving's astuteness in hiding behind the authority of McGraw-Hill; they had even more to do with the devious workings of the Hughes organization. But most of all they had to do with the character of the man himself, a rangy, bearded, fifty-nine-year-old reporter called James Phelan.

Jim Phelan is a journalist's journalist. After thirty years in the business, he has yet to win a Pulitzer Prize, but his skill is recognized in the profession at a more fundamental level:

he is the kind of reporter that other reporters least like to find in opposition on a story.

He started in journalism on a labor newspaper in southern Illinois in the 1930s and in 1938 was fleetingly in the offices of *The New Yorker.* "They were trying out a succession of twenty young hopefuls at the time," Phelan recalls. "I was the twelfth." Thereafter he settled down to daily newspaper work mainly in California, until the tyranny of the deadline began to get him down. He felt that he had to stop inquiring on stories just as they were beginning to get interesting. "I quit," Phelan said, "because I thought daily journalism did not give me the time or money to develop a story. You don't turn out an epic in three hours, with the auditor fretting because you spend sixty-five cents on a hamburger." In 1953 he decided to test himself as a freelance investigative reporter and made a piteous $125 in the first six months. Then suddenly he made the breakthrough and has been in demand as a magazine writer ever since, notching up a continuous series of exposé pieces in the political and business fields. Phelan's nickname is "Old Compulsive," and he was one of the earliest and most expert Hughes-watchers.

In 1969 this area of interest led him into collaboration with Noah Dietrich on a book about his memories of Howard Hughes. The relationship had ended two years later without any book being published, though Phelan did produce a draft manuscript.

On December 7, 1971, the day McGraw-Hill announced the forthcoming publication of Howard Hughes's autobiography, Phelan had no way of knowing that Irving's coup was in fact substantially based on his own unpublished manuscript and the other research material he had gathered as a result of his work with Noah Dietrich. Phelan had all along, as he was to say later, "the Rosetta Stone to the whole Irving-Hughes mystery." Yet two months were to go by before the connection could be made.

Few men had less reason to be pleased by the revelation

of Irving's "coup," yet in the space of twenty-four hours
Phelan moved from a position of suspicion that the book
*might* be genuine to one of near certainty that it *had* to be
the real thing. Paradoxically, the change in his attitude was
wrought by his own investigative skill.

On Day One, Phelan happened to be away from his Long
Beach, California, home and at one of the centers of the
action. He was in the office of Hank Greenspun, the publisher
and editor of the *Las Vegas Sun,* when a reporter raced in
carrying a sheet of UPI wire copy. "What's happened?"
asked Phelan. "Did they bomb Pearl Harbor again?"

"It's Howard Hughes," said the reporter. "He's written his
autobiography."

"You're kidding," said Phelan.

Phelan was astonished by the news, but not incredulous.
Hughes was his specialty, and he had learned the basic lesson
of that discipline: nothing, but nothing, about the man was
predictable. Although it was not his story, Phelan decided
to take time out for his own series of checks. For one thing,
his own professional reputation was at stake.

Over the years Phelan had written five national-magazine
articles about Hughes and his organization. His most recent
one was running in the current issue of *Playboy.* The argument of the piece was that Howard Hughes was seriously ill
and that his empire was being effectively controlled by a small
palace guard—part male nurses, part personal aides—irrev-
erently dubbed "the Mormon Mafia." Hughes's illness, Phelan believed, was of a kind that required massive transfusions
of blood at regular intervals. After these transfusions he could
function efficiently for weeks, but then his energy began to
drain away until he sank into something like a coma. Then
came the next transfusion.

The *Playboy* article drew on Phelan's last major series for
the *Las Vegas Sun,* published in the summer of 1971: an
exposé of a major stock scandal in Montreal, Canada, involving Hughes's senior Mormon aide and personal secretary,

Howard Eckersley. Although it seemed that Eckersley had been duped, his name and that of the Hughes Tool Company had been used freely. Phelan's experience on this story convinced him that Hughes was losing his grip: the cardinal feature of all Hughes's endeavors up to this date had been his reluctance to lend his name to anything he did not control. Hence the title of Phelan's *Playboy* piece: "Can the Real Howard Hughes Stand Up?"

Now it seemed that Hughes was capable not only of standing up, but of racing round the hemisphere and exercising a faculty of total recall for the benefit of a writer completely unknown to regular Hughes-watchers. Phelan had apparently been exploded as a Hughes expert.

Phelan borrowed Greenspun's car and drove over to the Hughes Nevada Hotels headquarters on the Las Vegas Strip. In an office at the Sands Hotel, he found an embattled Arelo Sederburg, Hughes's official mouthpiece in Vegas, "no-commenting" down the phone with great vehemence. This was before the Hughes Tool denial came through. When it did, Phelan, like every other reporter, was immediately suspicious: Wouldn't it be more sensible to use the name of Howard Hughes himself?

His instinct told him that even Hughes's intimates might not be absolutely sure that The Man had not somehow contrived to write his memoirs. Phelan went on checking with other friends in Hughes's Las Vegas operation. One told him the inside story of the denial. It had been based on three calls: one to Chester Davis in New York; the second to Bill Gay; the third, and most crucial, to Howard Eckersley at the Britannia Beach Hotel in Nassau. All three had replied that Hughes could not have collaborated with Irving on his memoirs. Eckersley *knew* the McGraw-Hill announcement was untrue because he knew Hughes had not left his ninth-floor suite at the Britannia Beach since November 1970. Phelan's informant said that the elliptical denial in the name of Hughes Tool was probably due to the fact that Hughes himself was asleep at the time.

Phelan asked whether it might not be a little presumptuous, issuing a denial before Hughes could speak for himself. "Oh, well," said the executive, "we'll have this all wiped out in a few hours as soon as The Man awaketh. We'll lay his own personal denial on top of the Hughes Tool denial."

Hours, days, and weeks went by before this personal denial—the only strategy that could get the desperate Hughes PR men off the hook—came through. When it did, it came in such peculiar fashion that many people were disinclined to believe it.

Meanwhile, Phelan had other calls to make. He rang a New York acquaintance to find out whether he could dig out a home number for any of the McGraw-Hill executives (it was now past 10 p.m. in New York). He got the number for Morrie Helitzer, one of the book company's spokesmen, at his home in Princeton, New Jersey, and telephoned him. The call turned out to be the most significant missed opportunity of the entire drama.

Phelan introduced himself as an old Hughes-watcher and congratulated Helitzer on the publishing coup of the decade. Helitzer modestly admitted that McGraw-Hill did appear to have a product that could outsell the Holy Bible for a couple of years.

"There's just one·thing that baffles me," said Phelan. "While no one can predict what Hughes is going to do, it seems odd that a man who has spent millions trying to suppress books and magazine articles about himself is suddenly going to tell all in an autobiography. You are sure this book is kosher?" Phelan went on to explain that if there was the least doubt, he might be of some assistance. He had, he said, just spent the better part of two years working on the (still unpublished) memoirs of Noah Dietrich, and Dietrich had been Hughes's accountant, right arm, and self-confessed "hatchet man" for more than thirty years. Moreover, he was still alive and well and living in Los Angeles. If there was any doubt in the publisher's mind, he and/or Dietrich could fly to New York and check the manuscript.

Helitzer patiently heard Phelan out but did not think that such an extreme measure would be necessary. There was no doubt. He then explained something that was not in the original press release: McGraw-Hill had a great deal of handwritten material from Hughes himself confirming Clifford Irving's story. Still, he would pass on Phelan's offer and call him back after consulting his superiors. He did so shortly afterward. The answer was: "No, thank you very much."

Phelan was not entirely surprised. The offer had been diffidently made, and he reckoned that McGraw-Hill was probably inundated with calls from self-styled Hughes experts. (He was right.) But, with the precious 20-20 vision afforded by hindsight, it is clear that, had the offer been taken up, the hoax's public life would have been abruptly curtailed.

Next morning Phelan noted that most of his professional colleagues had effectively accepted the McGraw-Hill story and downgraded the Hughes Tool denial. He thought the emphasis was about right.

Still, like any professional, he felt the need to compare notes with someone whose opinion he most respected. He called Frank McCulloch, the New York bureau chief of *Time* magazine. They had known each other for fifteen years, and McCulloch, another Hughes-watcher, had the distinction of being the last journalist to have seen Hughes himself, back in 1958.

Phelan was startled by the first piece of information imparted by his old friend. McCulloch had had no advance information of the Irving-Hughes project, although *Time* and *Life* are sister publications occupying the same Manhattan skyscraper. The decision not to use McCulloch for positive vetting on the Irving project could have only one or two explanations: total confidence, or total foolishness. Phelan concluded it was the former.

As they ran over the evidence, they found themselves in basic agreement. The Hughes Tool denial must be suspect. Even the fact that Eckersley seemed to be behind it was no evidence. He could have been acting on instructions; there was even a possibility that Hughes had related his memoirs without Eckersley's knowledge. Hughes's career was littered with examples of his taking secret initiatives without letting top executives know what he was up to. He was quite possibly playing the same old game with his palace guard.

And on the other side there was the massive confidence of McGraw-Hill, plus the handwriting evidence. Phelan and McCulloch ruefully agreed that this upstart Irving appeared to have done what both of them had been angling for for fifteen years; the professionals had been licked by a rank amateur.

Not that they accepted Irving's *whole* story. Indeed, in one respect they felt it had to be untrue.

PHELAN: "This Clifford Irving story about how he got the book has to be a phony, right?"

McCULLOCH: "Very probably. What we don't know is whether the story about the meetings in motels and parked cars was faked by Irving or by Hughes as a condition for giving him the story. . . . The Man is plenty devious."

In this assumption they were ahead of their professional colleagues. Weeks later, when Irving's story about his secret meetings around the continent began to fragment, this simply confirmed their original McCulloch-Phelan hypothesis. It did not touch on the question whether the memoirs were genuine; if the transcripts had been dictated at all, both assumed from the outset that they had probably been recorded at Hughes's bedside in the Britannia Beach Hotel. Phelan and McCulloch became the victims of their own expertise.

The evidence, as Phelan saw it, was all stacking up in the

McGraw-Hill corner. But there was another, deeper reason for his attitude. Right from the start he had conceived a private theory about why Howard Hughes might be eager to have his memoirs published. He did not go into this even with McCulloch, because, for one thing, it touched on a period when his own ego had been badly bruised; and, for another, explaining it meant explaining the incredible.

The theory went to the roots of Phelan's difficult partnership with Noah Dietrich. Dietrich, a frisky octogenarian, was an impatient man; Phelan was a slow writer. When they started on the project of compiling Dietrich's memoirs, Phelan had stopped all other work and got down to tape-recording the old man's recollections. They had almost a hundred taping sessions (curiously enough, the same number as Irving was said to have had with Howard Hughes), and transcribing the tapes took a stenographer three months. Then came the laborious business of cross-checking Dietrich's raw material. Finally, in the summer of 1970, he started to write the first draft of the book.

There were problems all the way. At one point Dietrich became worried about whether the work would be sufficiently long. Phelan's estimate was 85,000 words. Dietrich was still worried. "How big is a book, Jim?" Phelan tried to explain that this was rather like the question posed to Abe Lincoln about how long a man's legs should be. (They should be long enough to reach the ground—a book should be long enough to tell the story.) Dietrich, still not happy, went the rounds of bemused librarians and bookstore owners with the same question: "How big is a book?" Fortunately, one told him that a work of nonfiction normally ranged from 75,000 to 120,000 words. Dietrich rang Phelan with reassurance. "It's OK, Jim, we've got a book."

But, as it happened, they hadn't. Phelan slogged through his draft and finished it in April 1971, whereupon Dietrich dismissed him from the project on the grounds that he had professional advice that the manuscript was "unpublishable." There are no more hurtful grounds to a writer, especially one like Phelan, who had earned his living at a typewriter for most of his life. He just locked his manuscript away and tried to forget the whole costly and unhappy episode. Some time after, Phelan heard that Dietrich had engaged a new writer, but he, too, was having difficulty finding a publisher.

The odd thing was that both Phelan and his successor thought the memoirs were highly marketable (Dietrich himself immodestly envisaged an advance figure with six zeroes after it). At the same time Phelan knew that Howard Hughes considered the prospect of Dietrich publishing his memoirs as appetizing as a glass of hemlock. Dietrich's "no book" contract, drawn up in 1959 by Greg Bautzer, was still in existence. But before re-embarking on his memoirs, Dietrich had ascertained that the legal attitude to such contracts had become more hostile. His most recent legal opinion was that his contract might be deemed "unconstitutional"—a cruel and unusual infringement of his right to free speech and expression of opinion. But Hughes's lawyers could not be expected to see it that way. Nor did they.

On December 7, Phelan's mind went back to a ferocious letter sent by Chester Davis more than a year before, in November 1970, to a friend who was a literary agent in New York; it had warned the friend off having anything to do with Dietrich's memoirs. When Phelan remembered this, everything suddenly slipped into place. He thought he had the explanation for Irving's Hughes autobiography.

The incredible theory in Phelan's mind was this: The difficulties experienced in finding a publisher for Dietrich's memoirs may have been due, in large part, to the efforts of Hughes's legal arsenal. The prospect of expensive litigation with the Hughes machine would be, to say the least, an inhibiting factor in selling Dietrich's material. Now, suppose Hughes was simply trying to stall Dietrich to gain time while getting his own memoirs in shape? This would effectively cut the ground out from under Dietrich's feet; nobody would give a dime for Dietrich's revelations after The Man himself was in print. On the morning of December 8, Phelan could just imagine Hughes shaking with mirth at the discomfiture of his old friend, hatchet man, and, latterly, enemy.

Phelan's incredible theory was not incredible enough. Though he was right in his assumption that the Hughes secrecy machine had been balefully monitoring progress on the Dietrich memoirs, he had guessed less than half of the real story. What he did *not* know was that the Hughes machine had been alerted by a man who was supposed to be helping to sell the Phelan-Dietrich book. And that this same man had supplied Clifford Irving with Phelan's work, which had provided a cornucopia of raw material for the hoaxer. The man was called Stanley Meyer, a would-be Hollywood tycoon who was down on his luck. But Meyer's name was not to surface in the public drama till February 1972, and then only in the most innocent of contexts.

Ignorance of Meyer's role was the factor that threw Phelan and all the other experts off. Phelan's own inquiries on Day One had convinced him that his initial response to news of the autobiography was right. He did not feel inclined to call off the bet he had made with Hank Greenspun when the original UPI wire message had come in.

Greenspun, a man of fine instincts, had immediately adopted the skeptic's position and wagered on it. "Jim, I'll kiss your ass 130 times in the middle of the Vegas Strip if that book isn't a fake."

"OK, Hank," replied Phelan. "But if I'm right and it does turn out genuine, I only hope I don't have to collect."

# The Authenticity Game

Where ignorance is bliss, 'tis folly to be wise.

Thomas Gray, "On a Distant Prospect
of Eton College"

Four days after the public announcement of the autobiography, a McGraw-Hill executive, meeting a colleague in a corridor, clutched his sleeve and said in an excited whisper, "Listen, if Hughes hasn't denied it by now, then he's not going to deny it at all." The Hughes Tool Company had issued its condemnation of the book, but the man whose book it was had not fulfilled expectations by adding his denial. "We figured that even Hughes couldn't sleep that long," remembers a McGraw-Hill editor.

Even some of the Hughes PR men were beginning to experience doubts. By Day Four, one conceded, everybody's palms were getting sweaty. Perry Lieber admitted to a reporter on December 12 that the McGraw-Hill release had shaken him. He had read and reread a passage quoted from the preface to the memoirs.

"There's a line in it," he said, "that really bugs me. It's Hughes saying, 'I'll not apologize, but I'll try to explain.' That's pure Hughes. I've heard him say that fifteen or twenty times."

In the offices of *Life* magazine anyone who questioned the authenticity of Irving's book was treated with mild contempt. When editors of other publications, approached by *Life*'s syndication salesmen, asked for proof of it, they were told that they had the word of the editors of *Life*. That was not enough for everyone's taste, but by the end of the month *Life* had called in other experts, and they were still convinced.

The first expert to be consulted was Time-Life's own, Frank McCulloch. McCulloch is fifty-two and has spent all but three of his last twenty years in journalism at *Time*. He is an arresting presence—physically because of his shaven head, and professionally because he has done just about everything a reporter can do at *Time*. Recently he was made New York bureau chief, which became a prestigious post with his appointment. It was not exactly *Life* which brought him into the plot; it was Howard Hughes himself.

McCulloch, who last interviewed Hughes in 1958, still knows as much about him as any journalist, and significantly more than anyone else at *Time* or *Life*. Even so, he was astonished in mid-afternoon of December 16 to receive a call from Richard Hannah and Perry Lieber in Los Angeles. They offered McCulloch the first interview with Howard Hughes for fourteen years—exclusive, too. Hannah explained that Hughes wanted to talk to someone he trusted about the book controversy. McCulloch's delight was diminished only by his ignorance of the project. Hughes might want to talk to him about the book, but so far no one else had. "I was not in a position to ask intelligent questions," McCulloch says. He told Hannah that he would of course take the call, but could they do it tomorrow? He explained that he needed to brief himself; and, he added, he had a date with Governor Rockefeller that evening, which he wanted to keep. Hannah was sorry: McCulloch knew the old man, and the old man had not given them any room to bargain. It had to be that evening.

The events of the next two hours closely resembled a

Feydeau farce, taking place on the thirty-third and thirty-fourth floors of the Time-Life Building instead of the Hotel Paradiso, with a cast of characters as diverse, if not quite as ludicrous. McCulloch first asked Graves for as complete a rundown as time permitted on the project. So Graves and David Maness called Beverly Loo and Albert Leventhal, who hurried over from McGraw-Hill. Then Clifford Irving himself, sneering at the very suggestion that Howard Hughes would actually speak to anyone outside his world, arrived with Richard Suskind in tow. They all gathered in Donald Wilson's office to brief McCulloch. The briefing was necessarily short but was cut even shorter by the unexpected arrival on the thirty-fourth floor of Chester Davis. "Hold him!" Wilson cried, and Graves, Loo, and Leventhal scuttled off down one corridor as Davis, armed with two Washington lawyers, strode in along another.

The next to exit was McCulloch, who had concluded that the chances of making his date with Rockefeller were minimal and that he had better cancel it. He arrived at his office on the floor below to be met by a stricken-looking secretary holding out the phone, gingerly, as though it might melt in her fingers.

"What shall I do with this?" she asked.

McCulloch was not sure.

"It's Howard Hughes," she explained. It was the first time in seven years that Howard Hughes had been on the phone to any journalist. "Hang up," McCulloch commanded. He simply had to have witnesses. The girl did so gratefully. McCulloch rushed back upstairs, praying that Hughes would call again. The farce would turn into black comedy if he didn't.

McCulloch took his place behind Wilson's desk, notepad and tape recorder ready for the call. It did come through. The first questions he addressed to Hughes were technical: Could he tape the call, and was the conversation on the record? The reply was in a nasal, raspy voice, and it was "No" to both. McCulloch knew that it could only be Hughes. At the other end of the phone, Howard Hughes launched into a tirade which lasted half an hour. The book was a phony, he said, and he had never met Clifford Irving, who was also a phony. Sure, some people on his staff were preparing biographical material about him, but there was no way that Clifford Irving could have got hold of it, and it all belonged to Rosemont anyway. Did McCulloch get that? Yes, Mr. Hughes, he did.

The only person who seemed agitated in the audience of four lawyers (one *Time,* three Hughes) and a PR man (Wilson) listening to McCulloch's side of the conversation was Chester Davis. He started to wave at the phone and whisper hoarsely, "Tell him to put it on the record." Finally, he said urgently, "Tell him I authorize him to put it on the record." McCulloch would have liked nothing better, but he felt he had made his bid and could not make another. When he finished, however, he passed the receiver over to Davis, who grasped it and spoke firmly into the mouthpiece.

"Now look here, Howard, it's Chester here—"

There was a silence. Then Davis spoke again. "Yes," he said, rather more subdued, "yes, Mr. Hughes. . . . Yes, I will, Mr. Hughes."

Chester Davis put down the phone, reached for Donald Wilson's bottle of bourbon, and poured himself a whole glass.

But it wasn't so much the humiliation that was preying on Davis's mind at that moment. His scheme had gone wrong. He had intended Hughes to speak for publication so that the autobiography of Howard Hughes might be exploded in *Time,* the stablemate of the magazine that was planning to serialize it. It was a smart idea, but it didn't work, and the failure had implications not only for the privacy of his boss but for his gambling interests as well, since the announcement of the book had thrown Davis's delicate relationship with the Nevada Gaming Control Board into turmoil again.

When Chester Davis left—still followed by the two Washington lawyers—Graves, Loo, and Leventhal rushed back in. But they were not followed, as expected, by Clifford Irving and Richard Suskind. Irving had left earlier, muttering that the whole affair was ridiculous and certainly not worth his passing up a dinner engagement with his lawyer, Martin Ackerman; he said he would call later. He was spared McCulloch's description of the Hughes call. But McCulloch informed everyone else that Hughes had confidently dismissed the book as a fraud and Clifford Irving as a fake. The reaction was a mixture of shock and outrage. Beverly Loo was particularly angry, and she thought she had reason to be. Only the day before, Irving had told her that he had personally delivered the check for $325,000 to George Gordon Holmes, Howard Hughes's representative, in Florida.

The argument became fierce and subsided only when Clifford Irving telephoned. The call was passed to Frank McCulloch.

"What happened?" Irving asked.

"Hughes says you are a phony," McCulloch told him.

"But that's not possible," Irving blurted after a silence.

"Well, I just talked to him. I'm just telling you what he said."

"How do you know it was Hughes you were talking to?"

"I know him. I've talked to him often enough before."

"How do you know you weren't talking to a faker?" Irving asked.

"Well, I can't be absolutely sure, I suppose, except I know it was Hughes," McCulloch said firmly, and the call ended there. McCulloch had no way of knowing what impact the exchange had had on Irving, but Martin Ackerman, his dinner companion, said later that for the first time Irving lost his composure and began railing obscurely against the unfairness of it all. The call must indeed have been a stunning blow, since it removed one of the foundations of his carefully structured plot. He had always assumed that

Howard Hughes would remain completely silent. But now he had spoken and might well do so again.

The world outside, however, was not to know this, since neither *Life* nor McGraw-Hill intended to release such a juicy bit of news to rivals. McCulloch had been drawn into the plot now, and, pledging him to secrecy, Ralph Graves decided that he must see the reason for *Life's* continuing confidence. Next day David Maness carried over to McCulloch's office the first half of the manuscript.

McCulloch read it that evening and found it a revelation. The style, the pace, the earthiness of the language all sounded so true to Hughes's form that when he went into the office next day he was able to inform Graves that he was a convert. Graves suggested that he next meet Irving, and McCulloch did so, that afternoon at McGraw-Hill's offices. While he was talking to Irving, he noticed the manuscript open at a page that had not been part of the section he had read. It described a conversation between a *Time* reporter and Howard Hughes. There were, McCulloch believed, only two people who knew about that particular exchange, since it had been an off-the-record interview between Howard Hughes and himself—he was the *Time* reporter. It was the final authenticating detail for McCulloch. His conviction delighted the editors at McGraw-Hill as well as those at *Life*. But it was not clear to anyone at the time which sections of the manuscript McCulloch had read.

He had seen enough to persuade him that the tone was right and the facts, so far as he could see, were accurate; and he had glimpsed his own interview with Hughes. But he had read only those parts of the manuscript that covered Hughes's earlier life. When, in the weeks that followed, other experts—such as William Lambert, another Time-Life reporter—came to read bits and pieces of later sections, they were by no means so impressed. Lambert remembers saying of a section about Hughes's departure from Las Vegas that he could have done better himself. The material was so thin that it occupied barely a couple of paragraphs.

Nevertheless, the book had survived its first exposure to an expert outside the magic circle privy to its secrets. But if the book was genuine, how was Hughes's phone call to be explained? It did not, in fact, cause the *Life* editors much difficulty. They were rationalizing from a position of strength. Don Wilson explains that they had two theories at the time. "One theory was that his advisers had come to him and said, 'You're crazy to have done it—it'll just add to your legal problems,' and had persuaded Hughes to change his mind. The second possibility was that Hughes knew exactly what he was doing; that he still wanted the book to come out but, for some reason, he wanted it under a cloud of suspicion."

Meanwhile, Chester Davis had decided to put a brave face on the incident at Time-Life. On December 17 he wrote a peremptory letter to Harold McGraw saying: "There is no doubt that you have been deceived into thinking you have acquired material which you could publish and that someone is responsible for most serious misrepresentations to you and through you to the public. The only question remaining is what must be done to remedy the widespread misstatements which have appeared in the press."

But Chester Davis's faith in his case was misplaced. The two theories on which the confidence of *Life* and McGraw-Hill was based have not survived the passage of time, but they seemed credible enough then for Harold McGraw to ignore Davis's letter for six days, until December 22, and for *Life* to reject an offer from Davis of another Hughes-McCulloch conversation (in return for which Davis insisted on inspection of the manuscript and its supporting documents). The publishers were in no mood to bargain.

Nevertheless, *Life* decided that one more precaution should be taken. At a meeting with McGraw-Hill on December 17, Graves said that he would feel happier if the letters were subjected to another handwriting examination. McGraw-Hill's lawyers did not seem overjoyed at the prospect. One of them held the countersigned checks close up to his chest, as though they were four aces, and insisted that they were evidence enough. Another claimed confidently that there were quite simply no legal problems about the book, authentic or not. Graves argued that credibility was just as important as legality and pressed McGraw-Hill again to agree to another handwriting test. McCulloch, who was now consulted freely, said that he believed they could get access to some recent specimens of Hughes's handwriting. Finally they all agreed that there was nothing to lose. But McGraw-Hill had no experience of handwriting experts. Did *Life* know whom to go to? It did: a New York firm called Osborn, Osborn and Osborn.

Osborn, Osborn and Osborn is a family business, founded in 1905 by the present senior partner's father. Both of the grandsons also work in the cramped office suite in the Woolworth Building in Manhattan. The grandsons, Paul and Russell, are obviously and naturally proud of the tradition and the fact that their father was one of the founders of American holography—the art of analyzing handwriting. Technology has caught up with the art but has by no means passed it by. There are now mechanical aids such as infrared viewers, which can show that two apparently similar pieces of handwriting were done at different times, and ultraviolet lights help the analyst spot cunning chemical erasures; but the best tools for the job are good eyesight and experience. Whether an ambitious handwriting analyst ends up in the FBI, the Post Office or a state police force, as most do, or in a family firm, like the Osborns, he has first to serve an old-fashioned apprenticeship. It is not a flamboyant trade, and, there are some skeptical lawyers who hold that there is sometimes a tendency to find in favor of the person paying the fee. "We are not infallible," Paul Osborn says.

The normal procedure for deciding whether or not a document is forged is a simple one. Paul Osborn explains it deliberately, rather as though he were giving evidence. First, the analyst obtains copies of the questionable documents. Then, for comparison, there must be as generous a sample as possible of the subject's genuine handwriting. It is important that the samples, or exemplars, as they are known, should have been written at roughly the same time as the questioned documents, because the style and character of writing changes.

It is also important that the samples should not have been done deliberately for a specimen. "Writing is a semi-conscious act and it's as difficult to do naturally if you have been asked for a specimen as it is to walk into a room naturally if you are being filmed," says Osborn. He adds pointedly that the analyst should always work from originals. In copies the focus is not exact, and the subtleties of handwriting style will either be eliminated or overemphasized.

When the documents, real and questioned, have been brought together, they should all be placed on a table. The genuine ones are examined first. Everyone's handwriting varies—it is different when the writer is tired or elated, for example—and the variations have to be discovered. It is not just a matter of dots over the i's and crosses on the t's. Only after these exhaustive preliminaries does the handwriting analyst turn to the dubious examples. He looks for the variations to see if the basic characteristics remain the same, and he examines the microscopic details of the ink lines. "The trouble with forgers," says Osborn, "is that they are their worst critics. Nine out of ten draw the writing slowly and tediously, and that produces an unnatural tremor." The most suitable instrument for forgery is a soft pencil. Next best, Osborn claims, is a felt-tip pen, because it tends to hide some of the minute habits of a writer. Only slightly less good for forgery is a ball-point pen. Best for the handwriting analyst, worst for the forger, are pen and ink. The twentieth century has not been kind to the handwriting analyst.

There is, therefore, a right way of undertaking handwriting analysis and a wrong way, and when the Osborns were called in by McGraw-Hill and *Life* on December 17, it seems they went about the job the wrong way. "There was a tremendous amount of pressure on us: they wanted the report by yesterday," Paul Osborn complains. Within twenty-four hours of receiving the commission, Paul's brother, Russell, was on his way to Nevada to examine genuine examples of Howard Hughes's handwriting and signature. Bill Hannifin, the chairman of the Gaming Control Board, had been called by Frank McCulloch, and had agreed to allow Russell Osborn access to the letters which Hughes had allegedly written earlier in the year.

"It was in our interests as well as in his," Hannifin explains. "We were just as concerned as McGraw and *Life* to discover whether all the examples we had were written by Hughes." That helped Russell Osborn; but he was severely hindered by McGraw-Hill's adamant refusal to let him take the letters Irving claimed to have had from Hughes, and the contract signatures, with him when he traveled to Carson City and Reno, Nevada. He had to photograph the examples of Hughes's writing in Nevada and bring them back to New York for comparison. Another drawback was that the Nevada authorities were not 100 per cent certain that the writing was actually Hughes's. They had not witnessed him doing it.

Russell Osborn returned from Nevada and went straight to McGraw-Hill's offices, where Irving's Hughes letters (many written with a felt-tip pen) and signatures were unlocked and revealed to the expert. Again he was not allowed to take the documents away, so for a second time they had to be photographed. When the analysis began at the Osborn offices, the experts were comparing two sets of photographs. "It was," as Paul Osborn was to confess later, "a very unusual procedure in the Hughes case."

But none of those uncertainties was reflected in the oral report which Russell Osborn delivered to *Life* and McGraw-Hill on December 23. Everything in the letters and signatures which Irving had produced to authenticate the autobiography, Osborn, Osborn and Osborn reported, was utterly consistent with those examples of Hughes handwriting with which they had been compared. It must have been the best Christmas present Harold McGraw and Ralph Graves had that year. "We were jubilant at the totality of the report," Graves concedes.

The written report, delivered on January 10, confirmed Osborn's verbal judgment. "Both the specimen and questioned documents reveal great speed and fluency of writing. Yet the questioned documents accurately reflect in every detail the genuine forms and habit variations thereof which make up the basic handwriting identity of the author of the specimen documents. Moreover, in spite of the prodigious quantity of writing contained in the questioned documents, careful study has failed to reveal any features which raise the slightest question as to the common identity of all the specimen and questioned signatures and continuous writing."

But the best was yet to come. Osborn's conclusion was not quite so confident that it would confirm Alfred Kanfer's odds of a million to one against the letters being forgeries (quoted for McGraw on December 2), but it was good enough. "These basic factors, we believe, make it impossible as a practical matter, based on our years of experience in the field of questioned handwriting and signatures, that anyone other than the writer of the specimens could have written the questioned signatures and continuous writing."

Just before Christmas, Chester Davis must have concluded that he was not being treated with the respect due him. Howard Hughes was on the telephone daily with requests for progress, and there was none to report. In New York, not only were his denunciations of the autobiography ignored, but on December 22 Harold McGraw actually questioned Davis's credentials. "If you represent Mr. Hughes as legal counsel, we must insist upon the receipt by us of a copy of your specific written authorization from Mr. Hughes relating to the autobiography," he wrote. If Davis did not explode when he read that, he was overinfluenced by seasonal good will. He would have been even more upset if he had heard

Clifford Irving's jocular proposal that he and Davis should both submit to lie-detector tests to see who was telling the truth.

But Irving was nearly hoist with his own petard, for if the application of the idea to Davis was the subject of some mild hilarity, the suggestion that Irving should take the test was greeted with considerable enthusiasm. It would provide another piece of expert evidence with which to plague Davis. Irving, who did not have much option, submitted, but he warned Harold McGraw and Ralph Graves that he was leaving to catch a flight to Ibiza at 5 p.m. that same evening to spend Christmas with Edith and the children. He would take the test, but under no circumstances would he miss the plane.

A lie-detector test, or polygraph, as the experts know it, is not a wholly reliable guide to a man's honesty, but if it is undertaken by a skilled operator, it helps. The machinery consists of three recording units attached to the body, which relay information electronically to a recording device. This has a moving roll of graph paper on which three pens draw the jagged lines from which an expert polygraph operator judges the truth or otherwise of answers to specific questions.

To begin the test, operator and subject retire to a quiet room. The subject sits in a comfortable chair and tries to relax, which is not always easy. One band, a pneumonographic unit which measures the speed at which a man breathes, is strapped around his chest. The second unit, which consists of two electrodes, is wrapped around separate fingers to measure galvanic skin response, or the amount of sweat the questions produce. A third unit, like the band a doctor wraps around the arm to measure blood pressure, records what is called plythesmatic resistance, or the manner in which arteries beat against the skin. The test is uncomfortable, experts agree, but it is not thought to be especially taxing. If the tests show that the patient is breathing fast and sweating profusely, and his arteries are banging wildly against the wall of his arm, there is a fair chance that he is not telling the truth.

An operator called Rudy Caputo Jr., from Burns International Security Services of New York, arrived at the McGraw-Hill offices on the afternoon of December 23, and Frank Mc-Culloch began to brief him on the case and the subject. This is an unavoidable preliminary to the test. For a test to be significant, a polygraph operator should spend at least a day familiarizing himself with the case. He can then refine the problem down to a few key questions, most of which can be answered yes or no. But the man from Burns did not have time on this occasion to complete the preliminaries. McCul-loch had barely half an hour in which to rush through the background facts before Caputo set up equipment in a con-ference room. He also knew that Irving wanted to catch the Ibiza plane.

They went into the room alone, because a third party can disturb the concentration of both operator and subject. But the two were closeted together for only forty minutes before Irving jumped up and insisted that he had to catch his plane. The attachment to and then the disengagement from the gadgetry had taken up so much time that there was not much left for the actual questions, but the few that were put to Irving narrowed the affair down to money. During the operator's brief rehearsal of the facts with McCulloch, this had seemed to be the single most significant item.

The polygraph machine immediately showed that Irving was desperately nervous. He was asked if he had kept any of the $650,000 that McGraw-Hill had given to H.R. Hughes and he fudged the answer. Irving replied that he was not sure whether the money had actually gone to Hughes or to some-one who worked for him. That was more than he had ever told McGraw-Hill or *Life,* to whom he had never admitted any doubt. The operator concluded that there were incon-sistencies in Irving's story, but they were not yet conclusive evidence of dishonesty. Had he formally told the people waiting for the lie-detector test of these results, he might have dashed the confidence inspired by the oral report just received from the handwriting experts.

Caputo told McCulloch privately that he did not think much of Irving's story, but he refused to write a report because the test was incomplete, and he happened to believe that a partial report on an incomplete test of a man's honesty is a serious curtailment of his civil liberties. "Before you call a man a liar, you have to be damn sure," Caputo says. Unlike Osborn, Osborn and Osborn, Burns International Security Services refused to be rushed. Anyway, there did not seem to be much urgency at that stage. Caputo understood that Irving would complete the test when he got back from Ibiza. He was confident that another thirty minutes on the polygraph would completely destroy his story.

Irving must have thought so too, because he never gave the operator another chance. For his part, McCulloch mentioned to the others that Irving had not sounded especially convincing. But they replied that it meant nothing, really, because, as Caputo himself said, the test was incomplete.

Clifford Irving arrived back in Ibiza on December 24, briefly celebrated Christmas, and was back at work two days later. If the basic idea had been baroque in style, Irving now began to add the meticulous detail, which made it positively rococo. On December 26 he wrote a letter to Hughes and sent a copy to Shelton Fisher. It is the only letter extant from Clifford Irving to Howard Hughes, and it suggests an intimate, conspiratorial relationship.

26 Dec. 1971

Dear Howard,

I hope I haven't screwed up by using this address but I consider it something of an emergency. I was distressed, naturally, that no contact was made on St. Croix—not just distressed that it left me totally out of touch but also worried on your account, having last seen you flat on your back. A word as to your good health would be reassuring.

It's also occurred to me that you may not be reading the newspapers and therefore unaware of the current situation. Briefly, Davis and the Tool Company and Richard Hannah of the Byoir Agency have been loudly and publicly denying the authenticity of the autobiography. Davis has gone so far as to arrange a telephone call at Time-Life's offices between Frank McCulloch and someone pretending to be you. I say "pretending" because the man on the other end of the wire, claiming to be you, told McCulloch that he'd "never met Irving, never met his father" and the book was "a hoax." I have to assume, therefore, that Davis is in the dark, and frantic, and has a lot of balls to pull a stunt like that.

What happens next I don't know, but if Davis keeps up his campaign to discredit the book it may cast serious doubts on its authenticity, which I'm sure is not what you want and certainly not what McGraw-Hill wants. All the publishers, by the way, are not just delighted and thrilled by the quality of the finished manuscript, but believe that its publication will be a major event and that the book will become a major document in American contemporary history.

What I'm asking you, in essence, is to make some effort— whatever's possible under the circumstances—to call off the dogs. You really should give some clue to Davis and Holliday [vice-president of Hughes Tool Co.] which would either make them recant or shut up, preferably the former. Also, it might be apropos to get in touch, either by letter or telephone, with Shelton Fisher, who is President of McGraw-Hill, Inc. He has a book he'd like to send you, anyway, a McGraw-Hill tome on the history of Rolls-Royce, which you would like. You would like Shelton also; he's a very straightforward guy and it would be worth communicating with him.

I'm not asking you to come out of the woodwork altogether, but do let me know at least how you are and if possible how I can get some leatherbound copies of the book to you. Let's not lose touch after all we've been through! That would sadden me.

You have my warmest wishes and thoughts for this new year.

All best,
Clifford

Shelton Fisher at McGraw-Hill, overjoyed at the handwriting analysis and unaware of the incomplete lie-detector results, must have looked at the bit about leatherbound copies and wondered only how much they were going to cost.

There was a lull in the week after Christmas. McGraw-Hill and *Life* were resting on their laurels, and Chester Davis was wondering what on earth he could do next. Then, on January 3, a Hughes Tool spokesman again called *Life* from Los Angeles and offered new bait: The Hughes Tool Company would make members of Howard Hughes's immediate entourage available for interviews, and also provide documents demonstrating conclusively that the autobiography of Howard Hughes was a fake. *Time* and Hughes Tool could combine complementary talents to investigate the fraud.

Donald Wilson remembers that the management and senior editors were skeptical about the offer. They believed it was just a ruse to obtain sight of the manuscript (which was still more difficult to get than a Shakespeare first folio) and the letters supporting its authenticity. There were a few reporters who thought it might be worth trying, but they were overruled. Two days later Wilson returned Hannah's call and made a counterproposal: Why not arrange a meeting between Howard Hughes and Clifford Irving, attended by Frank McCulloch? "The key to the offer was the confrontation with Irving," says Wilson. But it did not unlock the door because Hannah never returned the call.

Instead, *Life* decided to test the documents just one more time. There was only one kind of expert who had not studied them by now—the fingerprint men. On January 7 the letters and signatures were taken out again and dusted. They showed innumerable prints, though none of them belonged to Howard Hughes. "They were such a mélange of other people's prints that the evidence was dismissed as unimportant," Don Wilson remembers.

So of three expert analysts brought in by *Life* and McGraw-Hill, one had found no proof of authenticity, and another had intimations of fraud, but had not felt able to make formal charges. The third was the Osborn firm of handwriting analysts, and on their unsteady foundation the publishers based a remarkable display of confidence in themselves and their book.

Meanwhile, the Hughes people, worn down by McGraw-Hill's intransigence, concluded that a really dramatic move was called for. On January 7, Chester Davis wrote an uncharacteristically subdued letter to Harold McGraw, in which he concluded that he was forced to question McGraw's good faith. "I simply cannot understand the basis or justification for your position," he said sadly. It was the tone of a man who is having a hard time from his boss, and it was written on the same day that Davis's boss emerged to confirm his dissatisfaction with the counsel. For the Hughes people had decided to unveil their own expert witness: The Man himself. On January 7, Howard Hughes broke silence for the first time in fourteen years and, among many other things, informed seven journalists in Los Angeles just how critical he was of Chester Davis.

# Hi, Howard!

I'm not seriously in a deficient condition.

Howard Hughes, January 7, 1972

The return of Howard Hughes to public contact with the outside world revealed more about himself and the kind of man he had become during the long years of his seclusion than all the articles and books he had inspired during his lifetime. The form it took was bizarre—a telephone interview with seven West Coast journalists sitting in a Los Angeles hotel room—but the occasion itself was a tour-de-force. The interview turned into a two-and-a-half-hour marathon in which Hughes failed, in spectacular fashion, more than half the test questions designed to prove his identity but supplied instead a morass of technical detail on the subject of his airplanes, his legal battles, even the shoes he used to wear, which convinced everyone present that the voice on the end of the line could belong only to Howard Hughes.

The interview, which was set up in two days, was booked for 3 p.m. on January 7, when Studio III, a conference room on the ground floor of the Sheraton-Universal Hotel, was hooked up through one of the Hughes Tool Company's switchboards in Miami with the ninth floor of the Britannia Beach Hotel in Nassau. It involved, at the Los Angeles end,

seven microphones, two loudspeakers, one television net-
work, and a small army of technicians. When it was all over,
one calculation was that the bill would run to about $5000.
Even by Hughes's own standards it was an extraordinary
event. It was also absurd: seven grown men, clustered around
an electronic box, frantically posing questions to a disembodied voice, while television cameras solemnly recorded the
whole charade. It was McLuhanism gone mad.

The journalists had been selected by Hughes's public-
relations team on the West Coast. With one exception they
were men who had known him well in "the old days," when
they had followed his career, reported on his exploits, charted
his eccentricities. Four of them were old aviation hands who
shared his enthusiasm for planes and could be expected to
engage him in intimate talk about them (a somewhat one-
sided discussion, as it transpired). The others had written
about his Hollywood days, the ups and downs at RKO, the
TWA deal, and his flight around the world. All of them, again
with one exception, had been on terms of some intimacy with
him and remembered the times when it was still possible to
hold a man-to-man discussion with Hughes over a late-night
scotch about the vagaries of government agencies or the problems of designing an airplane cockpit. Most of them remembered him with affection. Their average age was fifty-seven.

They met, the day before the interview, to discuss the way
it should be handled. The agency had supplied a few suggested questions as guidelines, but these were sternly rejected
and each reporter instead prepared two test questions designed to establish whether Howard Hughes was genuinely
on the other end of the line. It was agreed that everybody
would keep off the subject of the women in Hughes's life
and, in particular, Jean Peters. Knowing his irascibility (a
characteristic which did occasionally surface during the course
of the interview), they decided that it was not worth provoking his anger and risking an abrupt end to the interview.
Even the most hardened confessed to some excitement.

In the event, the carefully arranged scenario was scrapped almost from the word go. Only six of the test questions were put, and Hughes fell down hopelessly on four of these. But the failure rate was irrelevant. As the reedy voice, with its barely discernible Texan twang, came through with growing confidence on the loudspeakers, those listening began to realize that this was more than just a convenient means for denying the authenticity of a book. It was the return of the hermit, the resurrection of a myth: Howard Hughes was actually talking again to real people, and finding, to his surprise, that he enjoyed it. "I'd be happy," he said at a late stage in the interview, "to talk to you all just as long as you want."

His weak point, it emerged, was people; his strong point, hardware. Asked to supply the name of a pilot with whom he had once worked, he had to confess no recollection of the man, though the admission obviously bothered him. On the subject of the plane involved, however, he would gladly supply details about the windshield he had designed, down to the last quarter-inch of its thickness. Asked to recall the name of a friend who had helped on the construction of a plane engine, he made another game attempt, searched through his memories of the period, and failed again. But the cockpit of that same plane—now, that was of particular interest and he would gladly explain the scope of the elevator controls, their arc of movement, and the space into which they fitted.

This attention to detail, the almost obsessive concern with accuracy, became apparent right from the start, when Roy Neal of the National Broadcasting Company asked the first question: "Where are you speaking from right now, sir?"

"Paradise Island," replied Hughes. "Nassau seems to be a more widely known name. I notice from the accouterments here at the hotel that it is called Paradise Island, Nassau. That must be because Nassau is a more widely known name than New Providence. But in truth, New Providence is the main island here in this group, and Paradise Island, which used to be called Hog Island, is a part of that group, and that is where I am."

The preoccupation with detail was shown in more spectacular fashion when Gene Handsaker of the Associated Press, the only one of the seven who did not claim intimate acquaintance with Hughes, asked about the H-1 airplane, which Hughes had designed and built. It was like feeding a data-card into an enthusiastic computer:

> We first called it the Racer, and it was designed by me in conjunction with Dick Palmer, and we built it in a small building of what later became Lockheed Air Terminal. I think at that time it was called Union Airport, or United Airport. It had several names before it became Lockheed. And this airplane was designed and built in a very small building at the corner of the main road, north and south, that bordered the east boundary of the field at the corner of that road, and the road which entered the Lockheed . . . what is now the Lockheed property. And right at that corner was this small building. I'm sure Lockheed later took it over. Jack Real is certainly familiar with the building I'm talking about, and it was there that this airplane, which had a wooden wing and a metal fuselage and single engine, a single two-row Pratt & Whitney, well, it was one of the first two-row engines they built before the one that—the 1830 that powered the early DC-4s. It was before that building—that's right, before the building of that engine. This was the first two-row engine that Pratt & Whitney built and it had a very small diameter in relation to what we had before that. And this airplane had a metal fuselage with butt joints, of which we were very proud, flush rivets, which were later standard in the industry, as you know, and it had a wooden wing which, of course, did not become standard, but was the only material at the time that would give us the smooth surface we were looking for. And this was, as I say, a single-seat, single-engine airplane, a beautiful little thing. And I still have it actually. It's out—the last time I saw it, it was out at the factory at Culver City. What was the question originally?

Handsaker, somewhat stunned, conceded that his simple test question had been more than adequately answered, but Hughes was now too far launched on the subject of the H-1 to stop. The waiting journalists put down their pencils, leaned back, and mopped their brows under the arc lights as, for the next eight minutes, he reconstructed in loving detail that plane and the time he had flown it at 352 miles an hour, capturing the world speed record from the French on a dramatic day at Santa Ana, California, which ended with a wheels-up landing on the metal-riveted, flush-butt jointed fuselage.

As he reached the end and abandoned, reluctantly, a further digression on the subject of its successor, the D-2, there was a pause, broken by Hughes.

"Don't you fellows have the D-2 in your historical material there at all?" he asked testily.

"Yes, sir," came the resigned reply. "Our files are very rich in your aircraft background."

At this point it might have occurred to anyone studying the interview that a man so obsessed with the finer points of airplane construction and so reluctant to abandon the topic would hardly endorse as authentic a book about him which did not contain a heavy proportion of meticulous detail on the subject. The authorized biography of Howard Hughes would thus be about as racy as a flight manual.

Hughes's next statement, however, dealt in no uncertain fashion with the present book and with Clifford Irving himself. "I don't know him," he said. "I have never even heard of him until a matter of a few days ago when this thing first came to my attention." He went on to confirm that he had never left the Bahamas and had certainly not traveled to the places Irving claimed to have visited in his company. As Hughes began to discuss the motives of a man who could work up a plot as far-fetched and devious as this one appeared to be, another part of him emerged. This was the Howard

Hughes who had been driven into seclusion by the scheming of evil men and the envy of lesser beings. It was clear that, like his lawyers, he believed in a plot of some magnitude, and one that probably came back to the man he had fired a year before—the grudge-bearing Robert Maheu. While still restricting himself to the kind of statement that could not be faulted for bias or inaccuracy, he conceded, "To assume that it's all an accident certainly takes a lot of assuming."

He went on to repeat the complaints that Chester Davis had been muttering for the past four weeks about the unfriendliness of McGraw-Hill and *Life* in refusing to help trace the checks and find the money; and in a phrase which reveals much about the relationship between the man and his lawyer he commented, "Chester Davis will tell you that I have been very, very critical of him for not being able to uncover the path of these funds. . . ." The overtones to that "very, very critical" sounded chilling indeed, especially for Chester Davis.

The questioners came back to Nevada, to the court actions he would face if he returned to Las Vegas, to the Maheu "controversy," as Hughes preferred to call it. "If some of these people would get off my back I could come closer to [returning]," he snapped at one point.

It was here that Hughes came closest to articulating the philosophy that lay behind his continuing absence from the public eye and the United States mainland. "I don't deny one thing," he said. "I don't want to spend the rest of my life sitting in some courtroom being harassed and interrogated by some disgruntled discharged employee. That I will frankly admit and so if the serving of the process would mean endless hours of exposure to harassment, interruption of what work I want to do before I die, I can certainly say, I don't want it and I don't relish it and I would certainly not welcome it or encourage it or make it easy."

There was some warmth in his voice as he said it, and the

questioners were drawn back in fascination to his relations with Maheu. Why, he was asked, had he left Nevada in the first place, and had he done it willingly?

It was a key question, and Hughes hesitated. "You've asked me a very difficult question," he said slowly. "In light of the Maheu litigation and this struggle and harassment that he has embarked upon, it's very, very difficult for me to tell you precisely all the motives that led to this trip without, as I said, having some effect on the devastating, horrifying program of harassment that Maheu and his associates have launched against me." The voice rose in anger.

Why had he fired Maheu?

Hughes's answer snapped back. "Because he's a no-good dishonest son-of-a-bitch who stole me blind."

"That's the old Howard," whispered someone admiringly.

The remark was undoubtedly the high point of the interview—perhaps the only uncensored sentence Hughes had allowed himself. But there was some good clean fun to be derived from the rumors about his personal appearance, rumors which had built up steadily over the years. The interviewers began to ask about the six-inch fingernails, the hair down to the waist, the emaciated body. Could he confirm that these rumors were without foundation?

He could indeed. Why, a man with six-inch fingernails, for example, would find it extremely difficult to sign his name. Nobody thought to suggest that a small incision at the top of the six-inch fingernail would convert it into a perfectly serviceable six-inch quill pen. Hughes went on to reveal, with no small detail, that he personally cut his own fingernails. The reporters leaned forward and listened intently. This was pure gold.

"I do it myself. I never had a manicure. I don't know, maybe it is an outgrowth of my childhood when they used to teach people about males and about having manicures. Anyway, I never have had them. But, I have always kept my fingernails a reasonable length. I cut them with clippers, not with scissors and a nail-file the way some people do. I use clippers because they don't leave a rough edge afterwards. Anyway, I take care of them the same way I always have—the same way I did when I went around the world and times when you have seen me, and at the time of the flight of the flying boat, and every other occasion I have come in contact with the press. I care for my fingernails in the same precise manner I always have in my life."

His physical condition, it emerged, was "tolerable" ("but I certainly don't feel like running around a track at UCLA and trying to break a record"). Somewhat tortuously he managed to describe how he felt after fifteen years in the air-conditioned nightmare.

"I keep in fair shape," he said. "Not great; not as good as I should, I can tell you that. I certainly am not happy about my condition. I mean I'm not in any seriously disparaging—or, that's not the word. What the hell is the word I'm looking for? I'm not in any seriously derogatory—or that's not the word either. I'm not in any serious deficient—now there's the word. I'm not seriously in a deficient condition."

The mental pressures, however, were obviously a greater problem. He confessed reluctantly that he was not a happy man, that the constant flight from litigation brought its own kind of suffering. But someday, very soon, he intended to break out, to break free of it all. There was more than a hint of forced optimism in his announced intention to end his long exile: Soon he would return to Las Vegas; soon he would give his first face-to-face interview; soon he would have his photograph taken and distribute it to the press. And he would fly again. "Yes. Positively. . . . it would be the best possible thing in the world for me. I have not only contemplated it but planned it definitely. And it will, I think, be the best conceivable therapy for me, because—well, it's just something that I like doing rather than something I don't like doing."

One of the journalists present, asked to say how he thought Howard Hughes had changed since he last met him, picked out his emphasis on all the things he was determined to achieve before he died. "In the old days," he said, "Howard never talked about dying. That would have been unthinkable. Now he seems to have got around to thinking he's mortal."

For Hughes's lawyers, the interview gave much cause for rejoicing. But for observers of Hughes as a person, it had been a sobering revelation. This was a disappointed man, a man who had held all the cards, chosen his own game, played by his own rules, and still, in the end, lost out. Faced with the massive problems of the present, he took refuge in the halcyon days of the past, dwelling on those times when the biggest problem around was the design of a flush-butt jointed fuselage; or else he wove plans for an undetermined future when everything would be as simple again as he believed it once had been.

The fact that a mere six weeks later Howard Hughes was on the run again, forced to flee the doubtful pleasures of Nassau for the even less predictable ambiance of Nicaragua and then Vancouver, was proof, if proof were needed, that those same plans were still as fragile as ever.

The interview ended, finally, when the exhausted interviewers persuaded Hughes that enough was enough. The arc lights by this time had reduced most of them to rivers of sweat, and the air-conditioning had been switched off because it made too much noise. A swift—and unnecessary—poll determined that they all agreed without reservation that the man they had spoken to was Howard Hughes; most of them felt that he sounded in good shape, in his right mind, and in essence at least the same unpredictable old son-of-a-gun he always was. It had been, without doubt, the interview of a lifetime.

The incident that most of them delighted in recalling afterward was the account of the tennis shoes. Hughes had been asked by Jim Bacon, Hollywood correspondent of Hearst newspapers and the most ebullient of the interviewers (his questions had invariably begun: "Hi, Howard! Jim Bacon here."), to clear up one of the Hughes legends, the story that he used to be seen around during World War II days wearing tennis shoes with his tuxedo. His answer is as good a demonstration as any of the way in which the Hughes mind works:

> They were shoes made of nonstrategic materials, some kind of canvas or imitation leather and I had a pair of these that I liked and wore and these were termed by some newsmen, tennis shoes. They weren't really tennis shoes at all, they were simply a shoe that was sold in normal shoe stores and which did not require a ration coupon to procure them. In other words, they were not strategic material and that is where that one came from, because I haven't played tennis in quite a while. I am certain they didn't come from any exposure on the tennis court or any appearance in what were truly tennis shoes. But the tennis shoes story definitely derived from those gray-green-colored—I think that is what you would call them—mostly gray—gray-green—yes, nonstrategic semi— no, they weren't canvas, they were an imitation shoe leather, I am certain. They were not ranked as canvas in the normal sense.

# A Damn Good Imitation

Hain't we got all the fools in town on our
side? And ain't that a big enough majority
in any town?

Mark Twain, *The Adventures of Huckleberry Finn*

Howard Hughes is the only man in the world whose outright
public denial of the authenticity of his autobiography could
actually convince a skeptic that it must be genuine. There
was a remarkable unanimity among the countless armchair
commentators who judged the quality of the unseen autobiography of Howard Hughes. A powerful consensus concluded that Hughes had, of course, dictated his autobiography
to Clifford Irving and had then been persuaded to retract on
the advice of his lawyers. It seemed a good guess that they
had frightened him off with stories of ever more expensive,
time-consuming, privacy-invading law cases.

It seemed for a time that Hughes's re-entry into public
controversy had only succeeded in adding to this already
monumental legal burden. After the press conference, Bob
Maheu, the badly bruised loser in the Las Vegas power
struggle, lost no time in issuing another suit against "the
man who, by telephone, identified himself as Howard R.
Hughes" and who had labelled him "a no good dishonest,

A man and his property: Clifford Irving in New York with the "autobiography" of Howard Hughes *(Camera 5/John Robaton)*.

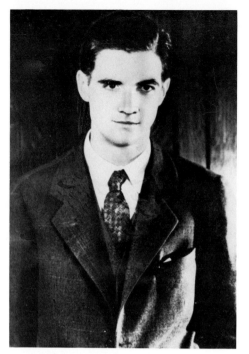

Howard Hughes: at 21 *(left),* owner of the $10-million Hughes Tool Company *(UPI);* at 41 *(right),* he defends his wartime defense contracts before a 1947 Senate investigating committee. *(Wide World Photos).*

A man in his element: Hughes, as test pilot, at the controls of his own plane, the XF-11, in 1946. Shortly after this picture was taken, the plane crashed and Hughes was seriously injured *(UPI).*

The last published picture, taken in 1957, of Howard Hughes, aged 51 (*Wide World Photos*).

Hughes's two wives: Ella Rice *(left)*, the Texas belle, was married to him for four years until their divorce in 1929 *(UPI)*. Hughes remarried, in 1957, Jean Peters, the Hollywood actress *(right)*. They were divorced in 1970 *(Culver Pictures Inc.)*.

The love of his life: the world's biggest airplane, nicknamed the "Spruce Goose," was constructed by Hughes and flown by him for the first and only time in 1947. It was aloft for one mile. "My reputation is bound up in this plane," Hughes once said *(Los Angeles Times)*.

Hughes and the ladies: with Ginger Rogers in 1933 *(top left) (UPI)*; Ida Lupino in 1935 *(top right) (UPI)*; Ava Gardner in 1946 *(bottom left) (UPI)*. Jane Russell *(bottom right),* a Hughes discovery, starred in his film *The Outlaw (Culver Pictures Inc.).*

"Dear Chester and Bill": Chester Davis *(right)* with Frank (Bill) Gay, victors in the Las Vegas power struggle within the Hughes empire which turned out to be the seedbed of the hoax *(UPI)*.

Robert Maheu, the ex-FBI man who ran the Hughes gambling interests in Las Vegas. *(Above)* at the height of his power *(Camera 5/Curt Gunther)*; *(below)* following his controversial defeat by Chester Davis, he leaves a Las Vegas court with his son Peter *(Wide World Photos)*.

The Ibizan milieu: Clifford and Edith Irving in their home on the island with *(left to right)* Elmyr de Hory and Gerald Albertini *(Pierre Boulat—Life)*.

Long afternoons in the sun with little to do except gossip—about art, literature, and each other. The Café Montesol in the center of Ibiza town *(The New York Times/Richard Eder)*.

On the veranda, *en famille,* Clifford and Edith with sons Nedsky, 4 *(left)* and Barnaby, 2 *(UPI).*

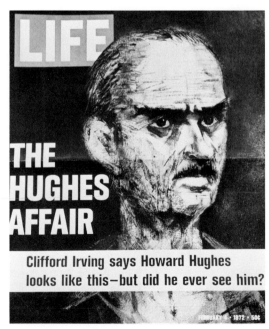

Two works of imagination: *(left)* the fake autobiography as it would have appeared; *(right)* the *Life* cover with its picture of an imaginary Hughes.

Edith Irving, artist, mother of two, co-conspirator, at the Chelsea Hotel, New York (*Harry Benson—Life*).

The artists: Elmyr de Hory *(left)*, whose career as an art-forger gave Clifford Irving much of his inspiration for the hoax, with David Walsh, who drew pictures of Hughes from descriptions invented by Irving *(Pierre Boulat—Life)*.

De Hory with the portrait of Clifford Irving he painted for the cover of *Time* *(Roger Beardwood—Time)*. Gerald Albertini, in whose safe the manuscript was kept *(Wide World Photos)*.

The publishers: Beverly Loo *(top left)*, first at McGraw-Hill to hear about the Irving project *(McGraw-Hill News)*; Albert Leventhal *(top right)*, who runs the general books division *(Hans Namuth)*; Robert Sussman Stewart *(bottom left)*, editor on the autobiography. *(Bottom right)* Ralph Graves, managing editor of *Life*, which bought the serial rights *(UPI)*.

The researcher: Richard Suskind, Irving's co-conspirator and wordsmith (*Camera 5 / John Robaton*).

26 Dec. 1971.

Dear Howard,

I hope I haven't screwed up
by using this address but I consider
it something of an emergency. I was
distressed, naturally, that no contract
was made on St. Croix — not just
distressed that it left me totally
out of touch but also worried on
your account, having last seen
you flat on your back. A word
as to your good health would be
reassuring.

After the balloon had gone up, Irving wrote a solicitous letter *(above)* to an unreal Howard Hughes. The real Hughes replied *(below)* in unreal fashion via an electronic box. Dick Hannah, his PR man in Los Angeles, dialed the call as the television cameras rolled on seven expectant newsmen *(UPI)*.

In the spotlight: Irving in New York plays the injured innocent to the world's press *(UPI; Wide World Photos)*.

Dear Chester and Bill —

I do not understand why the problem of Maheu is not yet fully settled and why this bad publicity seems to continue. It could hurt our company's valuable properties in Nevada, and also the entire state.

You told me that, if I called Governor Laxalt and District Attorney George Franklin, it would put an end to this problem.

I made these calls, and I do not understand why this very damaging publicity should continue merely because the properly constituted board of directors of Hughes Tool Company decided, for reasons they considered just, to terminate all relationship with Maheu and Hooper.

Model: Howard Hughes's letter to Chester Davis and Bill Gay as it was published in the January 1971 issue of *Life*.

11-17-71

NOV 22 1971
McGRAW-HILL BOOK CO.

Mr. Harold McGraw
McGraw Hill
New York., N.Y.

Dear Mr. McGraw —

The facts placed
before me, I find
astonishing. I do not
understand, in the
first place, why it is
not possible for your
publishing house in
possession of a legiti-
-mate contract between
myself and Mr. Clifford
Irving and between your-
selves and Mr. Irving,
for the publication of
my autobiography, cannot
deal firmly and force-
fully with other
publishers who which
are asserting fraudulent
claims to the rights
which I have granted
to Mr. Irving and Mr.

Forgery: the "Howard Hughes" letter to Harold McGraw, dated November 17, 1971, composed and forged by Clifford Irving.

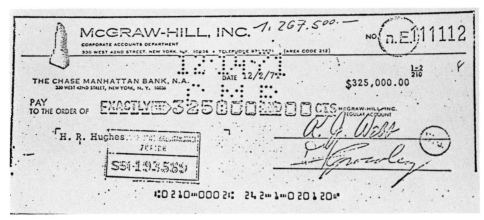

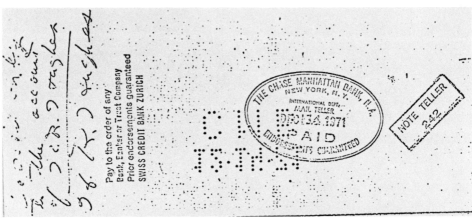

Solid proof? *(Above)* the $325,000 check paid out by McGraw-Hill on December 2, 1971, with its endorsement by "H.R. Hughes"; *(bottom left)* signatures on the contract for the book; *(right)* the imposing façade of the Swiss Credit Bank in Zurich, where the money went *(Wide World Photos)*.

this Agreement, signing each in the other's presence, on this Fourth day of March, Nineteen Hundred Seventy One.

ACCEPTED AND AGREED TO:

*Howard R. Hughes*

HOWARD R. HUGHES  (L.S.)

*Clifford Irving*

CLIFFORD IRVING  (L.S.)

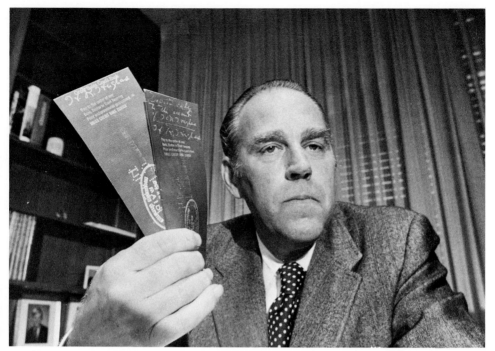

Before and after: At his press conference on January 10, a confident Harold McGraw brandishes two of the countersigned checks as evidence of his firm's belief in the authenticity of the Irving book *(New York Daily News/Dan Farrell); (below)* five weeks later Mr. McGraw admits, "We've been taken" *(The New York Times).*

The women in his life: *(top right)* Irving's first wife, Nina Wilcox *(Graphic House Inc.),* and his third, Fay Brooke *(Michael Ward). (Top left)* Anne Baxter, the scuba-diving instructress who gave Irving lessons in the Virgin Islands, relaxes in her Miami apartment *(UPI). (Bottom)* the singing Baroness, Nina Van Pallandt, with her manager, John Marshall, and attendant reporters, parades down Fifth Avenue *(Wide World Photos).*

Nina Van Pallandt, a bad alibi witness for Clifford Irving, but a boon for the photographers. "This is ridiculous," she told them, but she went on posing (*New York Daily News/Ken Korotkin*).

A tale of two lawyers: *(above)* Irving with Martin Ackerman, his civil lawyer, explaining a case of laryngitis at Kennedy airport on his arrival from Spain *(New York Daily News/Paul de Maria)*. *(Below)* with his criminal lawyer, Maurice Nessen, outside the DA's office. "The grand jury investigation is being conducted in a goldfish bowl," complained Nessen *(New York Daily News/Gordon Rynders)*.

Together again and still smiling: The Irvings and Richard Suskind outside the Chelsea Hotel *(Wide World Photos)*; *(below)* a question of supplies at the local delicatessen *(Camera 5 / John Robaton)*.

**8.** When is the last time you personally endorsed a check for any reason?

*More than 10 years ago*
*Howard R. Hughes*

EXHIBIT "1"

*'one should be available*

**12.** Did you ever start to write your autobiography or did you ever tell any of your assistants that you were writing an autobiography and ask any of them to deny it if questioned?

*Absolutely not*

*Howard R. Hughes*

Evidence for the existence of Howard Hughes: thumbprints at the bottom of the Hughes affidavit and two of his written answers on Chester Davis's questionnaire. *(Bottom left and center)* voiceprints taken from the January 7 press conference and a Hughes speech in 1938 *(UPI)*; *(right)* how the cartoonists saw it *(Wright—Miami Daily News)*.

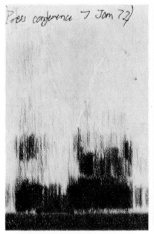

Press conference 7 Jan 72

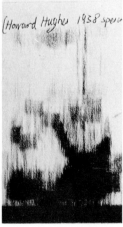

(Howard Hughes 1938 speech

Wright—Miami Daily News
'Frankly, Mr. Hughes, this is getting pretty silly'

The investigators: John Tigue *(left)* and Robert Morvillo, leaders of the federal investigation, talk to reporters before leaving for Switzerland

Whitney North Seymour, the U.S. attorney, offered cooperation to District Attorney Frank Hogan *(right) (all UPI)*.

Reporters on the trail: Jim Phelan and Frank McCulloch compare notes shortly after Phelan's confrontation with McGraw-Hill executives *(David A. Loggie)*.

Other journalists who cracked Irving's story were: *(left to right)* Bill Lambert of *Time (Time-Life)*, Wallace Turner of *The New York Times*, and John Goldman of the *Los Angeles Times (Los Angeles Times)*.

"Old compulsive": Jim Phelan in combat gear outside McGraw-Hill's offices on West 42nd Street *(David A. Loggie)*.

Noah Dietrich on his hospital bed the day after Irving's book had been denounced as a hoax based largely on Dietrich's own memoirs. "I haven't felt so good since I was 75," he said *(Los Angeles Times)*.

The middlemen and a man in the middle: *(top left)* Gregson Bautzer, Hollywood lawyer *(Wide World Photos)*; *(top right)* Paul Gitlin, New York agent *(Alfred Statler—Time)*; *(bottom left)* Stanley Meyer, who gave the Dietrich memoirs to Clifford Irving *(Time)*; and *(bottom right)* John Meier, who became a suspect because of an unfortunate phonetic similarity *(Wide World Photos)*.

Howard Hughes's hideaway on Paradise Island, the Britannia Beach Hotel, with its impressive array of Hughes communications equipment *(Camera 5/Ken Regan)*.

The flight to Managua: airport workers load a curious assortment of Hughes's possessions onto a plane at Nassau airport *(Wide World Photos)*; *(right)* the Intercontinental Hotel, Managua *(UPI)*.

Members of the palace guard: Howard Eckersley *(left)* and Levar Myler, the two men closest—physically, at any rate—to Howard Hughes *(Hank de Lespinasse)*.

Bob Peloquin *(left)*, President of Intertel, which runs Hughes's security *(Hank de Lespinasse)*, and Hank Greenspun, editor and publisher of the *Las Vegas Sun,* which is dedicated to piercing it *(Donald Donero—Time)*.

Indictment day *(New York Daily News/John Pedin)*.

son of a bitch." And Maheu's new claim for $17.5 million libel and slander damages looked, if anything, more ominous than his original $55 million suit for wrongful dismissal. The post-Maheu regime in the Hughes empire had already spent over a year trying to dig out evidence of Maheu's larceny with dismally poor results. It appeared that Maheu had some deficiencies as a businessman but that deliberately dishonest use of his employer's funds was not one of them. Word to this effect had evidently not got back to Howard Hughes himself.

From early on Sunday, January 9, the day on which the Hughes telephone press conference was finally shown on television, Ted Weber had been receiving inquiries about McGraw-Hill's reaction to it. The recording was not scheduled to appear until the 6:30 news that evening, but Weber had heard enough, privately, by midday to propose that Harold McGraw and James Shepley, president of *Life*'s parent company, Time, Inc., should be available to make counter-denunciations. But their immediate and confident assertion that they would go ahead with the "authentic autobiography" was not strong enough news to invade the time and space which newspapers and television devoted to Howard Hughes's curious performance. "The thing we were most upset about was not Hughes's denial of his autobiography, but that the networks cut McGraw and Shepley down to two sentences," says Weber.

The next day, Monday, Harold McGraw easily took the second round in the battle of the press conferences. But it was not so much his words that carried weight as the facsimiles of two checks made out by McGraw-Hill to H. R. Hughes and countersigned by H. R. Hughes. A picture of Harold McGraw, a stern-faced man of integrity, brandishing the checks, appeared in newspapers throughout the nation. Unfortunately, the impact of his message was somewhat blunted by his author. Clifford Irving had also given a press conference and he had announced—unlike his publishers, the voice-print experts, and the interviewers—that the disembodied voice on the telephone to Los Angeles was not that of Howard Hughes.

"In my opinion it was a damn good imitation of his voice as it may have been three or four years ago," Irving told a chosen audience of three reporters—his cousin, James Norman of AP, John Goldman of the *Los Angeles Times,* and Douglas Robinson of *The New York Times.* But if his intention was to divert reporters from the authenticity of the book to the authenticity of the voice, it failed. Irving also revealed publicly for the first time the contents of the letter from H. R. Hughes thanking him for the gift of *Fake!* But he refused to take the story any further. "My obligation, of course, is to Howard Hughes and not the voice on the telephone," Irving said.

The hectic charge and countercharge of those two days acted as a catalyst. The affair was now referred to as the Battle of the Book, and after loitering for a month on the inside pages of newspapers, it had become a front-page story. The subdued treatment which the press was giving to the controversy had been the fault not of reporters, who sensed that something was happening behind the scenes that they should know about, but of *Life* magazine, which had worked with some ruthlessness to keep the story to itself. Irving was told not to give interviews; and although Time-Life's own reporters were becoming more intimately involved, they were told that they were "working for the thirty-fourth floor," where the management office suites are situated. Both Mc-Culloch and William Lambert, *Time*'s specialist investigative reporter, were bluntly informed that they were to report to *Time* executives, not *Time* editors. Hughes's press conference made it more difficult for *Life* to retain the story exclusively, but this did not prevent it from trying.

One of the first to sense the quality of the intrigue was John Goldman of the *Los Angeles Times,* who had gone hopefully to Kennedy Airport on January 8 to meet Irving's return flight from Ibiza. The two men had not previously met, so

Goldman, feeling a bit foolish, had held a sign asking Irving to identify himself. Irving had obliged and rewarded Goldman's reportorial endurance by joining him for a drink and showing him a draft of the article he was preparing for *Life* about the extraordinary business of getting the Hughes story. It revealed, among other things, that Irving first met Hughes when he was nine, on the set of *The Outlaw*. Irving interrupted the conversation to call his lawyer, Martin Ackerman, and when he returned, Goldman noticed a single word written on the back of a piece of paper Irving was carrying. "Leak," it said. "Leak" is journalists' jargon for the process of making confidential information available without disclosing its source. Irving proceeded to Ackerman's house, where he was staying, and, from that point on, started to leak like an old bucket.

Martin S. Ackerman was familiar to American writers and journalists. He was one of the most successful of that happy breed of businessmen in the 1960s who understood enough about the principle of the corporate merger to become barons of industry almost overnight. A graduate of the University of Syracuse, he left the Wall Street firm for which he had specialized in corporation law during 1962 to take over a small company of photofinishing shops called Perfect Photo, Inc. By 1968 he was president of one of the largest printing and publishing companies in the world, the Curtis Publishing Company, owners of an institution, the *Saturday Evening Post*. On May 2, 1968, Ackerman first met the magazine's staff and made an indelible impression when he announced, "I am Marty Ackerman, I am thirty-six years old, and I am very rich. I hope to make the Curtis Publishing Company rich again." Marty failed. A little over eight months later the *Saturday Evening Post* died and Marty became known as "Marty the Mortician." Within months he had been overthrown at Curtis. But all was not totally lost. Marty still had an ornate town house on Park Avenue, a nice place in the country, and a small law practice. His problem was, in Harry S. Truman's immortal phrase, that he was a twelve-ulcer man in a three-ulcer job.

By the end of 1970 he had begun to pick up the pieces, and one of those was Clifford Irving, who became a client in October. Ackerman, despite his personal delivery of the mortal blow to the *Post,* always liked writers and journalists, and he talked to them at length, at some two hundred words per minute. In January 1972 he enthusiastically talked to anyone who could get through to him about the qualities of his client's manuscript.

*Life* was, naturally, less enthusiastic about this verbosity than were Marty and Cliff. The magazine already had the three 10,000-word excerpts chosen, and these were checking out nicely. Each incident described in them could be traced to something that had actually happened. *Life* decided that, because of the quality of the material and the danger of its leaking out, it would bring publication forward. Instead of beginning in March, the first installment was now scheduled for the issue of February 11.

David Maness, who was editing the excerpts for *Life,* arrived at Marty Ackerman's town house early on January 10, together with Faustin Jehle, the McGraw-Hill lawyer, in order to check the final draft of the excerpts with Irving. They immediately became aware that they had been right to be worried about security. Not only were they kept waiting for two and a half hours, but they discovered that the reason for the irritating delay was a conversation taking place between Irving and the producer of CBS's Sunday-evening news feature program *Sixty Minutes.* In another room the program's reporter, Mike Wallace, was reading the precious manuscript. Maness eventually blew up, and told Irving what he had always thought: that he had a small talent and a huge ego, and Maness wanted him to turn the talent, rather than the ego, to the *Life* articles. Irving, chastened, did so; but before applying himself he asked Wallace to sneak off with the manuscript, so that he could read it in peace. "Irving seemed manic that day," Maness remembers. "He just seemed to have been carried away by the storm."

Meanwhile, Mike Wallace's colleagues had negotiated a deal with Irving. If they were to broadcast an interview the following Sunday, they did not want to show spoiled goods, so Irving had agreed that he would make it an "exclusive" for *Sixty Minutes*. McGraw-Hill was pleased enough at the prospect of such generous television coverage for an unpublished book. But Maness saw *Life*'s story beginning to slip away.

The Wallace interview was to be taped on January 13, and for the next two days Irving's friends at McGraw-Hill—Leventhal, Loo, and Weber—played devil's advocates, testing Irving's story as Wallace would do. At no point did he waver, though he was excitable, especially when asked, "Will you take a lie-detector test?"

"Never," he answered brusquely, "I wouldn't want to go through it again. It's horrible being all taped up like that."

He exaggerated the horrors of the test, but the McGraw "interrogators" had apparently never seen one, so they were in no position to analyze his reluctance. "We didn't press the point," Ted Weber says, "because we were aware that lie-detector tests are questionable evidence, and anyway we thought he was in too emotional a condition to prove anything one way or another."

Irving was certainly emotional. At one stage he turned on Weber and complained that McGraw-Hill was not associating him closely enough with its corporate conviction that the book was genuine. "It's my integrity at stake," Irving charged. It was, perhaps, the truest thing he ever said to his publishers.

Marty Ackerman was certainly unworried by imputations against Irving's honesty. He had personally tested it, and had not found it wanting. A friend who knew of his interest in the Irving book had sent him copies of two long articles from the *St. Louis Post Dispatch,* printed on the two days after

Christmas. They were written by a *Houston Chronicle* reporter called Charlie Evans, and both were based on extensive interviews with Noah Dietrich. The tone of both was curiously similar to the conversations between Irving and Hughes that Ackerman had been reading avidly in his copy of Hughes's autobiography while Irving was in Ibiza for Christmas.

Ackerman confronted Irving with Charlie Evans' interview. "Look here," he said, "what about this Dietrich stuff?" Irving was interested and they both went through it. "Of course they're similar," Irving argued, "they're by the same man, aren't they? Both Dietrich and I were talking to the same man." That was good enough for Ackerman; after all Irving was his client.

Mike Wallace's interview was filmed in Ackerman's house. During the first half of the interview itself, Wallace revealed more of the Irving-Hughes letters than had been seen before; he talked about the checks and waved the manuscript in front of the cameras, and he and Irving went over the incident in which Suskind had seen Hughes.

Irving described Hughes as wearing a $9.95 wig bought from a chain store; claimed that Hughes did not, as the voice from the Bahamas had said he did, wear a beard; but confirmed that his fingernails were normal length. He concluded with a description of his attempts to reach Hughes.

> IRVING: I don't know why he hasn't surfaced. It puzzles me. It upsets me. It distresses me. And I don't mean on my own account because I can handle this. And we have the proof and that's no problem. It just distresses me that he seems unable to respond.
>
> WALLACE: There's no doubt that he's alive, is there?
>
> IRVING: No, I assume that he's alive.

Wallace privately concluded that the autobiography seemed genuine, although he just did not know whether Clifford Irving had actually met Hughes or had obtained the transcripts of conversations with Hughes from another source.

There was only one exchange which he remembers as being less than convincing:

> WALLACE: If he's such a sick man, what in the world is he flying around the Western Hemisphere meeting you in all these assorted places for?
>
> IRVING: Who said he was such a sick man?
>
> WALLACE: Well, you say that he's so sick that he couldn't stay through any more than twenty minutes in a taping session.
>
> IRVING: I said it was physically impossible for him to talk for two and a half hours without long breaks. That doesn't mean that the man can't travel. When you travel, you don't talk.
>
> WALLACE: Well, what was the necessity of traveling if he's in that kind of shape? Why couldn't you simply come to Nassau, to the Britannia Hotel, go upstairs, and that's it?
>
> IRVING: Well, he likes to travel. And also, at the very beginning the specific arrangement between Mr. Hughes and myself was, he said to me, "None of my people, in my organization, know about this and none of them are going to know."

"I confess that was the one spot at which I said, 'Well, come on, that was a foolish answer,'" Wallace remembers. But he reports that not all his colleagues shared his confidence in Irving. There were cries of "phony" and "liar" from the truck outside on Park Avenue, where technicians and producers watched a monitor. Wallace had an unanswerable response. Wait till you read the manuscript, he told them: then you'll see why I think it's genuine. It was exactly what senior editors at *Life* were saying to their friends that week. They conceded that they might not think much of Irving, and, like Wallace, they were not altogether sure whether the tape-recorded interviews had happened quite as Irving described them, but they were utterly certain that the book was genuine Hughes.

It was a paradoxical situation. Usually hoaxes convince people who do not have intimate access to the dubious material; once it is scrutinized, their veracity crumbles. But in the case of the autobiography of Howard Hughes it was the editors and publishers—the people who had read it—who believed passionately in it and who managed to communicate some of their enthusiasm to a less credulous public.

Chester Davis was able to derive a single crumb of comfort from the failure of Hughes's personal denunciation of the autobiography; he finally discovered the identity of the bank into which the H.R. Hughes checks had been paid. When Harold McGraw had shown off the countersigned checks to the photographers, he had accidentally revealed the name of the Swiss Credit Bank too. So on January 11 Chester Davis appeared at the Nassau branch of Swiss Credit, asked for the manager, and told him that since Howard Hughes, his client, was not the H.R. Hughes to whom $650,000 had been paid, he would like to know just who H.R. Hughes was. Davis was offered a short lecture on the secrecy of Swiss bank accounts and left with a flea in his ear. There was only one place left for him to go—the courts of law.

On January 12 Chester Davis swore an affidavit in the Supreme Court of the State of New York, County of New York. It was a legal document, but a very angry one. It demanded that McGraw-Hill and *Life* be prevented from publishing the autobiography of Howard Hughes. It claimed that the book infringed Rosemont Enterprises, Inc.'s rights to Hughes's memoirs. And Davis went further: He wanted to see the publishers' proof of authenticity too. He complained that they had refused to participate in efforts to determine whether the so-called autobiography was authentic or a fraud upon the public. And the affidavit concluded:

> If, as there is reason to believe, an elaborate fraud is being perpetrated and somebody with the ability to forge the handwriting of Hughes and to create a fake autobiography is at large, then only through prompt disclosure may the identity of all those who are threatening to destroy Rosemont's right be disclosed.

The docket was titled *Rosemont Enterprises, Inc., Plaintiff, against McGraw-Hill Book Company, McGraw-Hill, Inc., Time, Incorporated, Dell Publishing Company, Inc., Clifford Irving, John Does 1 through 111, Defendants,* and it was numbered 800/72. (The "John Does" were in case other unidentified people were involved in the attempt to undermine Rosemont's rights to the memory of Howard Hughes.)

Then there was a brief legal diversion. Rosemont was also engaged in an action against the *Ladies' Home Journal,* which was printing excerpts from Robert Eaton's version of a Hughes autobiography. On the evening of January 14 a judge ordered distribution of the magazine to be stopped. This looked like a promising precedent for the more important case against McGraw-Hill and *Life.* But whatever rejoicing the judgment may have caused in Chester Davis's offices was short-lived. In a special appeal hearing the following morning, a Saturday, the judgment was overturned. John Mack Carter, publisher of the *Journal,* explained that the magazine would be ruined if the injunction was not lifted. The judge ruled against prior restraint and said the case ought to be heard later. As a precedent, the case had become decidedly unhelpful to Davis.

On January 16 the floodgates began to leak seriously. Mike Wallace's interview with Irving was broadcast, and *The New York Times* carried a long article resurrecting from the autobiography's manuscript an incident involving Howard Hughes and President Richard Nixon. In 1956 Donald Nixon, the President's brother, had borrowed $205,000 from Hughes on somewhat flimsy security, and a few months later, in one of those coincidences with which politics abounds, the Howard Hughes Medical Institute in Miami had been awarded tax-exempt status after a long struggle. Since the Medical Institute owned the Hughes Aircraft interests, it was clearly an important decision. The memory of it was potentially embarrassing to the administration and to the Howard Hughes industrial network.

The leak was also embarrassing to *Life* magazine. Ralph Graves was to complain in his affidavit to the court: "News, and the Hughes autobiography is news, is a perishable commodity. The intense effort by competing news media to learn the autobiography's content will continue and increase. If the United States government cannot safeguard the security of its own confidential papers, surely McGraw-Hill, *Life,* and Dell cannot long do so.

Meanwhile, the principals in the affair at McGraw-Hill and *Life* were preparing their case against Rosemont's demand for an injunction to stop publication, and the defense led naturally to the production of the records Chester Davis had so anxiously sought. To prove their right to publish and to prove that Rosemont's claim was invalid, McGraw-Hill and *Life* had to demonstrate the authenticity of their product.

As a result, the affidavits of the defendants contained some remarkable hostages to fortune.

*Harold McGraw:* "McGraw-Hill's reputation is of primary importance to me, and, as the papers submitted by the plaintiff are full of claims of hoax and fraud, I make this affidavit in order to set the record straight. . . . I believe the book Clifford Irving has produced is precisely what it is represented to be: the story of Howard Hughes in the words of Howard Hughes himself.

"Both as a novelist and as a writer of nonfiction, he had produced works which had received substantial praise by serious critics. We have known him as a writer of integrity and as a serious and hard-working practitioner of his craft. . . .

"All of us [working with him] are completely convinced of Irving's integrity. As we read the manuscript we were convinced it was an authentic work. . . . It is very hard for me to believe, based on some years' experience in publishing, that if a work were not genuine, it could deceive so many publishing staffs."

The affidavits from *Life* concentrated less on the author

and more on the book. This was an accurate reflection of the magazine's preference for the material over its producer.

*Frank McCulloch:* "I am convinced beyond reasonable doubt as to the authenticity of the Howard Hughes autobiography. This conviction is based upon my long-standing personal familiarity with Howard Hughes, my readings of the manuscript, and my interviews with Clifford Irving. My belief in that authenticity is not shaken by denials of that story, nor is my belief in the authenticity of the autobiography shaken by the denials which I have heard from a man I believe to be Howard Hughes. Such actions are perfectly consistent with the Hughes I know."

*Ralph Graves:* "I respectfully submit that the unanimous opinion of highly respected journalists, the handwriting analysis by three of the foremost examiners of questioned documents, and the unhesitating conclusion reached by Mr. McCulloch (a conceded expert on Hughes) can leave no reasonable doubt that the Howard Hughes autobiography is authentic and was authorized by him."

All these affidavits in defense of the publishers were submitted on January 18. On the same day, Clifford Irving and Richard Suskind submitted their affidavits, and they were manna to the investigators, for they contained a wealth of unrevealed detail. The Hughes-Irving correspondence was finally made public, as were the extraordinary itinerary Irving had followed in quest of Hughes and the documentary basis for *Life*'s confidence in its experts. The affidavits were a considerable boon to the historian too. But to the principals they were a ghastly embarrassment, for the date on the assertive affidavits coincided with the day on which McGraw-Hill and *Life* finally learned that "H.R. Hughes" was not quite the man he seemed.

# ACT V

## The Ladies
## Are Revealed

# A Mention of the Unmentionable

There are two ways of revealing information.
You can either reveal it positively, or
you can reveal it negatively.

Dr. Joseph Morger, Manager,
Swiss Credit Bank, Nassau

Chester Davis's angry visit to the Nassau branch of Swiss
Credit on January 11 had not been entirely without effect.
Even as Davis stormed out into the sunshine, Dr. Joseph
Morger, the manager, placed a discreet call to his headquarters in Zurich, a suitably imposing building in heavy
baroque on the Paradeplatz. He discussed Davis's request for
information with his superiors, and suggested that it might
be worth inquiring just a little more closely into the dealings
of Mr. H.R. Hughes.

It was the first indication the bank had received that there
might be anything wrong with the account. But the bank
officers were not unduly concerned. After all, who could tell
whether Herr Davis was really speaking for this Howard
Hughes? There had been no direct communication from
him, nothing in writing. The whole affair was *unordentlich*,
typically American. On the other hand everything relating
to the H. R. Hughes account within the bank's premises had
been conducted with exemplary regard to protocol, so far as

they could see. There had been no hint of trouble at all. Still, perhaps a few quick checks might be in order. Internal, of course. There could be no question of releasing any details. That would be highly unethical, not to say against Swiss law. . . .

A message was dispatched to Nassau, requesting more information about the checks involved, and details were instantly sought about the account itself. It seemed that Frau Sonhild Schaffner had dealt with the customer's withdrawals, while Felix Holz, cashier at No. 1 window in the ground-floor banking hall, had handled the paid-in checks. Both were questioned closely. No, they said, there had been no irregularities. The sums involved had been large, but not out of the ordinary. The customer, who held a Swiss passport, had spoken a curious kind of Hochdeutsch, rather than the Schweizerdeutsch one might have expected, but these days business people often like to adopt a more sophisticated accent, do they not? Quite so, agreed the official, but perhaps they could give a description of Mr. Hughes.

"Mr. Hughes?" came the puzzled reply. "But there was no *Mr.* Hughes. The customer was a lady, not a gentleman."

Swiss bank officials are not noted for the betrayal, in public, of their emotions. But it is safe to assume at this point that they responded to the news with a thoroughly un-Swiss double take. Something, somewhere, was definitely not in order.

What had happened could have occurred only in Switzerland. Arguably, only in Zurich, the banking capital, where the main Bahnhofstrasse is punctuated during working hours by groups of earnest raincoated men clustered around windows which display an invigorating range of stock prices and exchange rates.

The main banks vie with each other in the opulence of their halls and reception rooms, and at Swiss Credit, for instance, you can sit for hour after bemused hour slumped in a soft armchair, watching a rotating cylinder spell out with electronic precision the changing minutiae of the world's trade. In this atmosphere business dealings can become routine to a point that would be inconceivable, given the circumstances, in any other city in the world.

On May 13, 1971, a woman who called herself Helga R. Hughes had walked into Swiss Credit's main office and, by paying over a small deposit of 1000 Swiss francs ($229), had opened a current account. Her Swiss passport and a specimen signature were all she needed, and she had only one special request—she would be grateful if the bank would hold on to any documents or letters relating to the account which it might from time to time receive. It was a significant request in the light of later developments, but perfectly normal practice. Later that day she returned to the bank, picked up her checkbook, and, almost as an afterthought, improved the account's standing with a check made out to her for $50,000, drawn on the Bankers Trust Company.

Over the next seven months the fortunes of Helga Hughes's account fluctuated dramatically. A withdrawal of 15,000 francs ($3900) two weeks later was followed by a transaction which in retrospect seems remarkable but which attracted no attention at the time. Walking into the bank with an airline bag slung across her shoulder, Helga Hughes withdrew 184,-000 francs ($45,000) and tucked them, in folded 1000-franc notes, into the bag before·walking out. Then on October 14 she deposited $275,000, a process which went so smoothly that no one to this day remembers it; five days later she removed 1,092,000 francs ($266,000), again in cash, leaving the account with a mere $470.

On December 6 a letter arrived containing a check made out by McGraw-Hill to H.R. Hughes for the largest sum yet—$325,000. It was accompanied by a handwritten letter which asked the bank to confirm the check's arrival, and gave an address in the Rue du Bac, Paris. A letter was duly sent off but returned a week later with *"inconnu"* (unknown) scrawled across it. Suspicious? Not really, thought the cashier.

The customer had, after all, specifically requested that all correspondence be retained by the bank, and the check seemed to be in order. These business people, they move around so fast these days you never know where they are. Just in case, however, a Telex was sent to the Chase Manhattan Bank in New York, on which the check was drawn, asking for clearance. On December 16 clearance came, and the check went through to make Helga Hughes's account once again one of the healthiest personal accounts on Swiss Credit's books.

It was not to remain so for long. Three days after Christmas, Helga Hughes arrived with an ominously large brown traveling bag and withdrew everything the account contained except for a token 600 Swiss francs ($156). And there they remained, forlorn remembrance of a fertile period in which the turnover of Account No. 320496 came close to a million dollars and then ran down to nothing.

"We do not ask our clients many questions if we get the impression that they are engaged in business," commented a laconic Swiss Credit official some weeks later, summing up in a phrase the philosophy of his country's banking system.

On that day of surprises in early January, however, as those same officials tried to work out how a trim five-foot-three, respectably dressed brunette, carrying out business as a company director, could conceivably be holding an account in the name of a six-foot-three eccentric millionaire named Howard Hughes, there was nothing laconic about their attitude. Swiss Credit appeared to be heading toward some very distressing publicity.

The bank's legal adviser, a shrewd financial lawyer called Rudolf Hegetschweiler, decided to adopt a course of action familiar to many a Swiss banker—he did nothing. In Swiss Credit's own words, "We sat tight and waited."

They did not have to do so for long. The first tentative approach from outside came the very next day, January 12. Dr. Hans Mast, a director of the bank, received a call from

*Time* magazine's economic expert in Brussels, Roger Beard-wood. Diffidently Beardwood explained that he was making a few inquiries, not as a journalist, and certainly not for the purposes of a story, but as a representative of Time, Incorporated, the parent company. He would be grateful if Dr. Mast could spare him some time. Surprisingly, Dr. Mast found that he could, and an appointment for lunch at Zurich airport was fixed for the following Friday.

Thus, eight months after making the down payment on their $650,000 bid for glory, McGraw-Hill and *Life* magazine were sending their first corporate scout into the Swiss banking jungle to find out who had swallowed it up. The reasons for this not inconsiderable delay are simple. Everyone had said the jungle was impenetrable, so what was the use of even trying to get into it? In other words, faced with the awesome tradition of Swiss banking secrecy, no one had thought there was the slightest chance of getting any information about the Hughes account.

Beardwood, however, seemed at least to have opened up a footpath, and at Friday's lunch Dr. Mast dropped the first hint that his bank might not be quite as inflexible as tradition demanded. He gave Beardwood a stern lecture about the laws relating to secrecy and the Swiss banking system, but promised to ring him the following Tuesday.

There followed a weekend of suspended animation, a tense three days during which a number of anxious men in New York City waited for the word from Zurich.

It came, as promised, on Tuesday, when Dr. Mast telephoned Beardwood and explained, with delicate understatement, that there was good reason for believing that the account held in the name of H.R. Hughes was not the account of Mr. Howard Robard Hughes. What that "good reason" was, Dr. Mast felt unable to reveal, unless called upon to do so by the forces of the law.

It has been pointed out, in the aftermath of the event, that the privacy of a Swiss bank account is watertight only

up to a certain level and that, where there is strong evidence
that it is being used to conceal crime, the police can insist on
a bank's cooperation, which must then be given. By this token
Dr. Mast's revelation was not all that surprising. But set
against this is a stern tradition of banking secrecy which
stretches back to the nineteenth century and which has become ingrained in the system. It was given concrete form by
the formidable Bank Secrecy Act of 1934, framed originally
to protect accounts opened by German Jews in face of Nazi
persecution, which is still the basic law governing the country's banking ethics. It makes Switzerland one of the few
countries in the world where a bank manager who violates
the secrecy of a customer's financial affairs can be found
guilty of a criminal offense and liable to a maximum 20,000-
franc ($5200) fine, a six-month sentence, or both.

Its effect, somewhat naturally, has been to encourage most
Swiss bankers to err heavily on the side of caution. Two years
ago Pierre Leval, a former Assistant United States Attorney in
the Southern District of New York, giving evidence to a Con-
gressional committee on banking practices, pinpointed the
basic dilemma faced by any investigator whose suspect re-
treats behind the screen of a Swiss bank account. "Bank secrecy in Switzerland," he explained, "technically can be lifted
by the government of Switzerland when a bank is being used
to harbor stolen funds. But that is easier to say than to do;
if a prosecutor needs the proof that the stolen funds are in the
account there in order to get the bank secrecy lifted, and if
he can get that proof only by seeing the account records, then
he has succeeded only in chasing his tail; the secrecy will not
be lifted and he will not have proof of the crime." And of
course while both the United States and Switzerland agree on
the definition of what constitutes a crime when it comes to,
say, drug-running or diamond theft, the area of fraud or tax
evasion is heavily blurred.

Only in recent years and in the very rarest of instances has
a Swiss bank agreed to reveal details of private accounts

when either of these is alleged. There is, for instance, only one case on record in which the Swiss courts have accepted the defrauding of American tax authorities as sufficient grounds for causing a bank to divulge its secrets. The case, against a United States citizen, which was anonymous and which attracted virtually no publicity when it was finally decided in December 1970, may well have far-reaching implications, but it is, so far, unique.

Swiss Credit was thus going out on a limb when it revealed that the Hughes money might not, in fact, have gone in the right direction. By doing so it undoubtedly saved itself from much of the adverse publicity it saw looming, but the action contrasts strangely with that of the larger Swiss Banking Corporation across the road, which turned out later to have received much of the money withdrawn at intervals from Swiss Credit. Even after a criminal inquiry had been undertaken, Swiss Banking played it by the rules and kept quiet.

Dr. Mast's information was flashed to New York the same day—January 18—together with the warning that his bank could say nothing more until a prosecution was launched, in which case it would be happy to cooperate with the police to the best of its ability. This attitude was confirmed next day when a weary delegation of Time-Life and McGraw-Hill executives, bleary-eyed after an overnight flight, called at the headquarters of Swiss Credit. There they were given the same scant information which Beardwood had already heard. Nothing more.

"When you know the identity of the person concerned," explained Rudolf Hegetschweiler patiently, "you will know it could not have been Howard Hughes." More than that he could not say.

The agonized Americans felt as if they were taking part in some nightmare guessing game, with the mocking Swiss holding out a clue whose nature was somehow too simple to guess. They retired to another room, feeling tired, clumsy, and baffled. From here on the battle would have to be a legal one, fought on foreign ground. Turning to their lawyer, Dr. Paul Gmür, who represented the *Time* interests in Switzerland, they gave him the go-ahead to approach the Zurich police and the District Attorney's office and launch a criminal prosecution. The grounds would be suspected fraud, and forgery.

Dr. Gmür, however, was beaten to it. The Zurich police had already been engaged in a most fascinating discussion about the Hughes case with an American gentleman from Washington, who knew rather more than McGraw-Hill, *Time,* or *Life* about the H.R. Hughes account. He knew, for instance, that the account had been opened by a woman. He had written proof that Howard Hughes had nothing to do with it. And he too was most anxious that a prosecution should be launched.

Robert D. Peloquin, President of Intertel International Intelligence, Inc., would not relish the idea of being called a gumshoe. His detective agency is described in a glossy Intertel brochure as "an international management consulting organization" which advises large firms on security with an impressive program called "Cost Reduction through Total Asset Protection." It operates from a luxurious office in downtown Washington, where shades of Sam Spade are well hidden beneath close-fitting carpets and the teak walls with their brass fittings.

Nevertheless, Bob Peloquin is a detective and lawyer, not a management consultant. Brought up in the tough school of the Justice Department's Organized Crime and Racketeering Section, he had left in 1967 and formed his own agency in 1970, after making his name as a man who knew how to tackle the Mafia on previously undisputed territory: the gambling resorts of America and the Bahamas. This asset was, of course, particularly attractive to Howard Hughes, and it was not long before the Hughes account became Intertel's biggest. Intertel was adept at solving all manner of problems which the Hughes life style threw up—such as removing him secretly from Vegas to Nassau. When news of the Irving autobiography reached him, Peloquin had no hesitation in clearing his desk and concentrating all his energy on nailing the hoaxer.

Like Chester Davis, he had been a frustrated man for the past month, a detective with no clues to work on. But the appearance of the Swiss Credit checks waved importantly by Harold McGraw during his press conference on January 10 gave him a vital break. Now he knew the name of the bank, and Intertel was not the sort of agency to be put off by minor considerations like Swiss banking conventions.

Chester Davis had already written a letter to Hughes, requesting information that would be extremely useful as soon as the bank was identified. It asked, among other things, for confirmation that he, Davis, was indeed the true and only representative of the Hughes interests, and to help establish the authenticity of the reply he had enclosed twelve key questions, for which he required twelve key answers. They included one which, he hoped, would encourage any bank involved to yield some information: "When is the last time you personally endorsed a check for any reason?"

A week later he received the answers, complete with fingerprints to back them. Hughes denied any knowledge of Irving, the book, a projected autobiography, or any kind of agreement to write one, and he had not endorsed a check personally for more than ten years. He also confirmed the role of Chester Davis as his legal representative and authorized him to approach the bank involved to obtain details of any transaction. He added, with an eye for the obvious, "Also, please concentrate on who received the money."

Chester Davis was doing just that. Hastily putting together an affidavit with the questionnaire as a basis, he found a fingerprint expert to pass the Hughes prints as genuine, and Levar Myler of the Nassau palace guard, who had witnessed the signature, to swear to the document's authenticity.

Peloquin meanwhile had approached his alma mater, the Department of Justice, on Davis's behalf, to lodge an official complaint. He pointed out that all the available evidence pointed to a fraud, and he suggested that the department should launch an investigation into the affair. The suggestion was heard with respect but not enthusiasm. The department likes to have its complaints of impropriety from directly injured parties, and it did not appear that Mr. Peloquin represented the victims in this case. Peloquin proceeded to put forward an eloquent and somewhat complex argument which claimed that Howard Hughes *was* a directly injured party, but the department's lawyers were not convinced. "It was," conceded Peloquin, "a fast-talking area to get into."

As a fall-back, he dispatched a letter the same day to the Internal Revenue Service, raising the pointed question of who owed tax on the $650,000 which McGraw-Hill had paid over to someone. Any allegation, he said, that Mr. Hughes himself had had sight or sound of it would be vigorously and immediately denied. Whatever happened, Mr. Hughes would not be paying tax on it, and the letter should be regarded as formal notification of that refusal. He also added that, *as a citizen*, Mr. Hughes would like the IRS to investigate who precisely *should* be paying the taxes. It was public money, after all. The IRS, which had for years been fighting an unequal battle with Howard Hughes over the vexed question of his own taxes, undoubtedly found his concern for the state touching in the extreme.

Both approaches were made on January 17, and that same evening Peloquin managed to catch a plane for Zurich and the most important part of his investigation. He took with him the Hughes questionnaire with its unambiguous responses (the affidavit followed next day), a pile of newspaper clippings, and the address of a useful Swiss attorney. He was exactly twenty-four hours ahead of the McGraw-Hill party.

On the plane he read through the clippings and made a mental note of one in particular, a chatty article which contained a fairly detailed physical description of Edith Irving. Detectives like physical descriptions; they make a habit of remembering them; and Peloquin's mental note on this occasion was not just useful, it was decisive. For he had already discovered, before leaving the United States, something that certain parties in New York would have given much to hear. He knew that H.R. Hughes was a woman. How he knew, Mr. Peloquin, being a good detective, is not prepared to say. An explanation would, after all, embarrass some people in Zurich. But his information was sound, and when he called on the Swiss police on the morning of Tuesday, January 18, he was able to pass it on.

The Swiss were impressed, and they were doubly impressed by the questionnaire. But there was a problem. Like the Department of Justice in Washington, the Prosecuting Attorney in Zurich required a complaint before he could start investigation. And the complaint should logically come from an injured party—McGraw-Hill or *Life*. Although Herr Peloquin was undoubtedly well informed, he would have to wait a few more days. This was disappointing, but at least the machinery of justice had been primed. Peloquin filled in the time by hiring a Swiss attorney and enjoying the sights of the town with his wife, who had come over for the trip.

By January 20 McGraw-Hill's complaint, filed by Dr. Gmür, had overcome the formalities, and Detective Corporal Lack of the Zurich police was able to call at the offices of Swiss Credit and demand the closest cooperation. It was willingly given. Cashiers stood by to be questioned, records were thrown open, figures added up. That evening word crept up the hill to the Dolder Grand Hotel, where a tense party of McGraw-Hill and *Life* executives was waiting. The appalling news was absorbed and funneled back to New York: H.R. Hughes was female, the account she had opened was current, and the money was long gone.

Resistance to shock is undoubtedly helped by a rationalization of the event after it has taken place. Whether the diagnosis applied in this case or not, McGraw-Hill rode the latest body blow with almost unnatural cool. Clearly, it pointed out in a statement of the obvious from New York, these latest revelations would have to be "cleared up," and in the meantime publication of the book would be suspended. But, the company said, the very questions raised had been generated by its own "thorough and continuing investigation," a statement which somehow managed to imply that it had been expecting complications all along. But it did not affect the main issue. "We continue to believe," McGraw-Hill added doggedly, "that the material contains the authentic language and views of Howard Hughes."

McGraw-Hill executives might have been less disposed to optimism if they had been privy to the revelation which had just flared in the mind of Bob Peloquin. He was reading a description of Helga R. Hughes given to the Swiss police by Frau Schaffner, the Swiss Credit cashier, and he felt that he had seen it somewhere before. Then he remembered: Those very same words had been used in the newspaper clipping he had read and noted on the plane, and they had been used to describe Edith Irving. He telephoned New York, and a batch of pictures of Edith Irving was immediately dispatched, air freight, to Zurich. As soon as they arrived, Peloquin, with a police officer, paid another visit to the bank.

Frau Schaffner looked at the pictures for a long time. She was unhappy about the hair, which seemed, somehow, different, but it was the face which seemed to transfix her. "I cannot be one hundred per cent certain," she said at last. "But it is very, very close."

That was close enough for Peloquin. And it was just as convincing to the Swiss police, who dispatched a man by the next plane to Ibiza, Spain.

# Womanhunt

"There is only one thing in the world worse
than being talked about, and that is not
being talked about."

Oscar Wilde, *The Picture of Dorian Gray*

Now the world's press was off on the kind of exhilarating
quest which brings out the best—and the worst—of its investigative skills: *Cherchez la femme*. Since none of the reporters at this stage possessed the inside information which Bob
Peloquin was in the process of acquiring, their task was
apparently awesome. It involved locating a beautiful blonde
(the hair color had got mixed up somewhere along the line,
but nobody minded much, since "blonde" sounded better),
with fluent German (or broken German, according to which
reports you read), a forged Swiss passport (or stolen Swiss
passport), who was wearing a dark wig and lipstick (or not,
as the case might be). Her name was Helga Hughes, but the
chances of her answering to it were slim.

It was a brief but riotous chase, with Clifford Irving cast
in the role of Pied Piper, one which he clearly relished since
it guaranteed him continuous attention. Always just ahead
of the ratpack, he dropped tiny but misleading clues with

confident abandon and during the next few days talked sol-
idly to anyone who would listen. Everybody listened.

It began on the day on which word got back to New York
that H. R. Hughes was a woman—Thursday, January 20. An
immediate conference was called by McGraw-Hill, and it was
attended by *Life* executives, by Clifford Irving, and by Martin Ackerman. The atmosphere was heavy with suspense, but
Clifford Irving took the lead immediately by explaining how
he personally interpreted the latest revelations. There were,
he suggested, three possible theories to be extracted from the
evidence: 1) He had been dealing all along with an impostor.
2) Howard Hughes had, for his own inscrutable purposes,
used a "loyal servant" to cash the checks for him. 3) He,
Irving, was a hoaxer.

He looked carefully around at his audience. "The last of
these possibilities I intend to discard," he announced. "And
I hope that you do too." Everyone nodded, some a trifle less
quickly than others. The first theory, Irving went on, was
very difficult to accept, and so, given all the circumstances
he personally favored the second—the concept of the loyal
servant. It sounded quite good if you didn't examine it too
closely.

A long and tortuous discussion followed on the relative
merits of available clues; but nobody was prepared to question seriously Irving's motives. Then, just as everyone was
preparing to leave, Irving announced casually that he would
have to return to Ibiza next day. There was immediate and
loud-voiced consternation. How could he go, now of all
times? Even Ackerman suggested that he might have chosen
a better time, and Ralph Graves was adamant that he must
stay. Irving listened to their arguments but appeared uncon-
vinced. Edith wanted him back. She was worried about what
was happening to him in New York, and he wanted to reas-
sure her. He would try to speak to her on the telephone, but
he could not promise anything.

The reasons for Irving's desperate need to return to Ibiza

were not, as it turned out, quite so straightforward as they seemed; Edith was worried, true, but for very different reasons. The Swiss police had approached her and indicated that there was compelling evidence to link her with Helga Hughes. They had also discovered that the passport used by Helga was one which she herself had reported lost and which appeared to have been forged; two figures on the serial number looked suspiciously as if they had been altered. They would appreciate it if she and her husband could come to Zurich to help them clear the matter up. It was essential, Edith said, for Clifford to return.

Next day in New York, Irving said that he was sorry, but he would have to fly to Ibiza. He had talked to Edith, and there was no reversing the situation. Making the best of a bad business, *Life* arranged a final grilling—the toughest Irving had yet faced—for that morning. Frank McCulloch and Bill Lambert went through with him the whole story once more from beginning to end.

They concentrated on the evidence contained in Irving's affidavit and pressed him to expand on his description of the various incidents it covered. It is a useful interviewing gambit, since the details can always be checked later, and besides, the subject, if he is concealing something, will tend to overdo the elaboration in an attempt to convince his listeners that he is telling the truth.

Irving played it brilliantly. He was happy to supply a whole range of detail, but there were moments when he confessed he simply couldn't remember. Then from time to time he would amplify a tiny incident, quite unprompted, in a way which had both Lambert and McCulloch shaking their heads in admiration. One exchange particularly impressed them. They had been talking about Irving's blindfold journey by car from Miami airport in the company of the mysterious George Gordon Holmes, the man who, according to Irving, had acted as go-between, driver, and prime contact during his meetings with Howard Hughes.

"What was this blindfold, Cliff?" asked Lambert. "Was it a handkerchief, a scarf, or what?"

"Well, Bill"—Irving grinned—"it was black; it was like a black Kotex, to be honest."

"Was it pinned, tied?"

"Jesus, I can't remember that, I'm afraid."

"About this stop on the way, how long was it after you left?"

"No . . . I just can't remember how long it was."

"What happened?"

"Well, the man said, 'Do you want to fasten your seat belt?' and I said, 'No, I'm constrained enough already with this thing on!' Then I heard the click as the guy fastened his belt, and we went on."

So confident was Irving that he even confessed to having met a very senior figure in the Nixon administration during one occasion in California when he had been to see Hughes. At 3 a.m. one morning he had been driven out into the country for a nocturnal rendezvous, and there, in a parked Cadillac with a government flag on the front, he had been introduced by Hughes to Spiro Agnew, Vice-President of the United States.

It was no wonder that at the end of the interview both journalists emerged convinced of one thing: If Clifford Irving was a con man, he was the best they had ever met. But of course that didn't mean that Clifford Irving was not a con man.

"We were very sore," said Ralph Graves later, describing Irving's decision to leave. "Very sore, and very, very suspicious. We were so suspicious that we sent somebody to the airport to see he got on the plane he said he was going on."

And so, under escort, the chief suspect left New York. He had, however, no intention of confirming suspicions by running away. He was wondering how best to allay them. His mind was still on the problems raised in the final interview with McCulloch and Lambert. The "loyal servant" theory about the H.R. Hughes bank account was all very

well, but the trouble was that none of Hughes's known intimates were women. Moreover, his own account of his
secret meetings with Howard Hughes did not at any stage
mention a woman. As he pondered this grave omission on
the first leg of his flight, Irving decided that a suitably mysterious hint of a female presence would greatly buttress his
credibility. He decided to pass it on as a "helpful" tip to
Frank McCulloch. He did so in a letter, a work of great
imaginative power, which read:

en route N.Y.–Madrid
21 Jan 1972

Dear Frank,

I've been sitting on the plane thinking and thinking about
our discussion this afternoon, and playing detective, and a
lightbulb has exploded in my brain—triggered by some of
your questions, particularly about the room and the house in
Florida on the last trip. I'm not sure of the significance; and
memory can play tricks especially when you're forcing it as
hard as I am now.

But, for whatever it's worth—

I remember some more details of the bedroom in which I
last saw Hughes. I think I told you there were blinds on the
windows. There were also, I believe, flowered curtains—or at
least patterned chintz-type curtains. The bedspread, I believe,
matched them, or was similar. The furniture was relatively
light in both color and appearance, and in good taste but
not showy. The easy chair in which I sat was not a big chair,
or so I remember it. In other words, what I'm trying to say
is: in retrospect it does not strike me as being a *man's* bedroom.

Also: and maybe even more important—on both the Dec.
3rd and Dec. 7th meetings, I'm sure that Holmes left the room
for several minutes prior to my final departure. On both occasions he came back to get me, lead me into the hallway,
blindfold me and guide me out of the house. On the second
occasion (Dec. 7th), I'm almost positive the car was not in
front of the steps where Holmes had originally parked it. I

remember his having to guide me some distance along gravel or concrete. I got in first; then he got in behind the wheel. He muttered something I didn't catch and then *shòved the seat back*. The sound is unmistakable. As I've told you, Holmes is about six feet tall. Also, he turned the air-conditioning on full blast (as he always had it), and as it must have been when we originally arrived at the house.

The conclusions, unless I'm really losing my memory or fishing blindly, are obvious. I don't know what significance they have, but I'm zeroing in on this curious hint that the person opening the account in Zurich may have been a woman.

My conclusions are that the house in which Hughes was staying in what I assume to be the Palm Beach vicinity (a) most probably belonged to a woman or (b) he was staying in a woman's bedroom. Secondly: after Holmes parked the car in front of the house, a woman (or short man) moved it into a garage or out of sight, then returned it to the front of the house when Holmes was ready to drive me away.

(I wish I could go further and say that I smelled perfume, but I didn't.)

I don't really know if this will aid our manhunt (or woman-hunt), but that's it, for what it's worth. You can give this information on a need-to-know basis to anyone at Time Inc. or McGraw-Hill's; and I do request that you Xerox this letter and give a copy to Marty Ackerman.

Hope I haven't gone off the deep end with this theorizing. This is possibly the first moments of relative tranquillity I've had for a while and I have to say I'm getting more and more tranquilly pissed off at Mr. Hughes and Sherlock Holmes. Or maybe I'm wrong and I should feel sorry for them. I just don't know. But there's more to this tale than I've told and my loyalty, whatever the hell that is, is damn near strained to the snapping point.

If you have any hot news, shoot it to me. Otherwise, I'm sure I'll see you soon, either New York or Ibiza. Let me know how things work out with Mike H.

Best,
Cliff

When his plane landed in Madrid, Irving posted this beautifully proportioned red herring and hurried on to make his connection with the Ibiza flight. There was one final hurdle before he could make it to the dubious peace of his own hearthside. On landing in Ibiza he was told that *Life* had issued a statement strongly condemning his abrupt departure from New York.

"Don't pay any attention to that," said Irving confidingly to the journalists. "They weren't against my going. Why, they even sent somebody to take me over to the airport."

Momentarily the stage was left free for Marty Ackerman, acting as Irving's spokesman in New York, to indulge in an improbable piece of slapstick. Clutching his client's theories in one hand, he began to deal them out at lightning speed with the other, confusing everybody in the process. First he announced that he was personally "leaning" to the theory that Irving had been hoaxed by a sinister gang of at least six people, two of them master forgers, the other a six-foot-three giant, the spittin' image of Howard Hughes, dangling a withered left hand. As reporters digested this information, Marty changed his mind and "leaned" to another theory, the "loyal servant" concept. This would have Howard Hughes, prudently avoiding responsibility for the punitive damages his book might attract, entrusting the money side of things to a loyal and discreet employee in one of his companies. She would, of course, have been a German-speaking blonde. Observers of Mr. Ackerman's performance voiced the fear that if he did any more leaning the chances were he might fall flat on his face.

In spite of this diversion, most attention was fixed on Helga, whoever she was. There was much discussion about a romantic proposition from the CBS reporter Mike Wallace, who had read the transcript of the book before his interview with Irving. He revealed that in the original version there had been a reference to a lady named Helga, the wife of a diplomat in Mexico, with whom Howard Hughes had been deeply in love. In the final version her name had been discreetly changed to Inge, but no matter, she was obviously Teutonic or whatever, why should she not be the missing broad?

Why not indeed? The London *Daily Express,* dubbing Helga "the most wanted woman in the world," suggested that she was in reality Hughes's new wife, the woman he divorced Jean Peters for. Even Henry Kissinger, President Nixon's foreign affairs adviser, got into the act by expressing to some delighted members of the Washington Press Club his keen desire to meet Helga. "If any blonde shows up in my bank claiming to be Helga Kissinger, she's welcome," he said. It brought the house down.

But most of the action was now in Ibiza, where the Irvings, once again amongst their own people beneath the blue skies and the budding almond blossom, entertained the press to a running dialogue on the whole affair. The *Beggar's Opera* cast list of friends and hangers-on began to achieve a global notoriety as they warmed to the spotlight. Those who knew something but wouldn't tell wove parabolas of teasing innuendo; those who knew nothing but wouldn't dream of admitting it waxed confidential and important and hinted at a wealth of information to come, "when things clear up for Cliff." The bets were hedged, because the stakes were high, and if Clifford Irving somehow came out on top there would be rich pickings to soften the hardships of life on the island.

At the cafés and in the bars along the harbor the talk was of promises made and debts to be honored, of Cliff's generosity and Cliff's meanness, of whether he was a man to be trusted or a con man. Opinion favored the former, but if he turned out to be the latter, then, the consensus was, he was a good one who deserved to succeed. After all, if he had fooled one of the world's biggest publishers into parting with three-quarters of a million bucks, then he had hit the quintessence of Ibizan expatriate philosophy; he had thumbed his nose at the materialists and beaten them on their own ground.

Amongst the Irving set a more subtle game was being played. People began to observe the striking similarity between Edith Irving and the published description of Helga Hughes. Edith was about five feet, three inches tall, Swiss-born. Her hair was streaked both blond and brunette. As the wine flowed in the Irving farmhouse, more than one quizzical reporter fumbled with the question: "Hell, Cliff, I know it's ridiculous, but, well, Edith . . . er, Helga . . . you know . . . is there a possibility?" Irving's brow would darken and his smile fade. "Do you really think I'd involve my family in an enterprise like this?" he would say. "My wife, my children, whom I love?" And later, when the questions grew more insistent, he threatened publicly to sue anybody who repeated the suggestion.

In those brief five days, life in the Irving household became one of hectic activity. Almost daily Edith Irving would serve wine to parties of half a dozen journalists as they swapped yarns with Clifford and got nowhere. Sometimes she would open the door with a cheerful "Hello, I'm Helga Hughes," but the joke wore off fairly soon. Irving delighted in pointing out the inconsistencies in the stories coming out of Zurich, such as conflicting descriptions of Helga passed on by newspapers. "I guess it must have been Howard Hughes in drag," he joked. Watchers caught the odd moment of tension between the two, however, and when Edith joked at one point, "Listen, if I'd taken that $650,000, do you think I'd be sitting here with this man?" there was just a hint that maybe she wouldn't.

Occasionally the party was joined by friends, like Gerry Albertini, the neighboring millionaire, whose air of well-bred indifference to the fuss did not conceal the fact that the manuscript of Irving's book had lain for protection in the wall safe of his superb mansion down the road. He too was in the mood for an occasional jest. Talking on the phone to a reporter in New York, he quipped, "You can tell the line's being tapped because it makes such a racket. I've tried to get them to put a quieter machine on, but they won't pay any attention."

Then there was Elmyr de Hory, drawn to the limelight once again like a brilliantly colored moth, waving aside suggestions that he would make an ideal forger and pouring scorn on Irving's own abilities. "He would have to be a genius, and Cliff, dear boy, is no genius at anything."

David Walsh, another painter, whom Irving had selected to effect a portrait of Hughes for the forthcoming issue of *Life,* hinted mysteriously that he could vouch for the meetings with Hughes; in what way, he was unable to reveal, but suffice it to say that he knew more than he could possibly say at this point—later, perhaps, when things became clearer . . . but meanwhile he was keeping his front door firmly locked. There were enemies on every side. Walsh had not in fact as many secrets as he pretended, but the proposition of enemies on every side was an attractive one, and it appealed to the Irvings as well.

"The people who are trying to discredit me are ruthless, and they will stop at nothing in order to stop publication," announced Irving. "There are two billion reasons behind attempts to stop it, and all of them are green and have rectangular shape."

"Someone is trying to get us into a mess," said Edith. "The Swiss police think it's a frame-up."

This was, in fact, a slight misrepresentation of the Swiss position. Peter Veleff, the Zurich prosecutor, had already repeated his request that both Irvings present themselves at Zurich police headquarters in order to answer a few questions, which were becoming daily more pointed, and he was not suggesting that either Clifford or Edith might be an innocent or injured party.

Everyone noted Irving's description of a chilling incident in which two men had apparently confronted Edith on the island and threatened her with dire things to come. Approaching her on the street, they had muttered, "We're here on a job that involves murder. You can call me James Bond." It rang chillingly true to the assembled party. Those Hughes people, they stop at nothing.

But again, this was wide of the mark. There were no Hughes agents on Ibiza. Peloquin had decided that the forces of the law had the situation reasonably well under control by this time, and there seemed to be so many journalists around that it was hard to beat a path to the Irving door, let alone pick up some useful trail in peace and quiet.

Besides, another and more formidable team of investigators had entered the crowded field.

The United States Postal Inspection Service is a federal agency which predates the FBI by 133 years, and has a remarkable 98-per-cent success rate in tracking down its man. Its area of inquiry is mail fraud, and since there are relatively few fiscal crimes which do not at some stage involve sending material illegally through the post, the inspectors find themselves turning down more work than they can take on.

Their entry into the case on Monday, January 24, was a devastating blow to the interests of Clifford Irving, and it was instrumental in exploding his case. So it is a startling irony that the man who brought them in by filing a complaint was, not one of the Hughes team, not McGraw-Hill, not *Life*, but Martin Ackerman, Irving's own lawyer.

On January 21, the day after his fruitless interrogation of Irving, Bill Lambert of *Life* had discussed with Charles Miller, head of the service's criminal investigation department, the possibility of the service helping out on the inquiry. Lambert explained that he had persuaded Irving, before his departure for Ibiza, to take part in an interesting experiment which would, he hoped, prove whether or not he was telling the truth. The experiment involved sending a letter, written and signed by Irving, to George Gordon Holmes, his direct contact with Hughes, at the address in Miami referred to in his affidavit. Irving had agreed and had written the letter. Now, suggested Lambert, all the postal inspectors needed to do was to get a man down to the mail drop and wait to see who picked it up. Miller was impressed, but had to insist on a written complaint before he could come in on the case. He suggested that Irving himself might be interested in making the complaint; but by now Irving was out of touch, in distant Ibiza.

Time was getting short. It was a Friday, and Lambert wanted to go down to Miami on Monday, the twenty-fourth, when the letter was due to be mailed. Already people were leaving their offices for the weekend. Then fate, in the improbable shape of Martin Ackerman, came to his help. Marty was in the middle of his "leaning" act and was at this precise moment "leaning" to the theory that his client had been hoaxed. Lambert, who had phoned him to hear the latest developments, explained his problems with the postal inspectors.

"Hey, listen," said Ackerman. "Why don't I write to them? I'm his lawyer, after all."

Gratefully Lambert dictated Miller's full name, title, and address, even adding the zip code for Ackerman's benefit. Provided it was mailed in time, the letter should be in Miller's hands first thing on Monday morning. Lambert decided to go on down to Miami.

In fact, the letter did not arrive until late on Monday afternoon—an indication that not even the Post Office can speed up its own mail—but as soon as it did, Miller was able to tell Lambert that one of his best agents, Lex Callaghan, would be calling him that evening in Miami. The name was straight out of a detective story, and the chase which followed had some of the better ingredients of a high-class thriller.

If Lambert was lucky to get the postal inspectors working on his side, the inspectors were just as lucky to get him. For he had a wealth of detail, obtained first-hand from Clifford

Irving, with which to check every stage of Irving's trip to Miami and his subsequent meetings with Hughes.

The most important part of it referred to Irving's movements after he had arrived at Miami airport. The timing was fairly precise. He had arrived, he said, at half past two in the afternoon and had hired a car. Then he had driven to a side street, where he had met George Gordon Holmes, who was sitting in his own car. They had driven for about one and a half hours, interrupted by a brief halt when Holmes put on his seat-belt, until they reached the rendezvous and met Hughes. The talk with Hughes had lasted about forty-five minutes, and they had then driven back to Miami, the journey lasting again one and a half hours. He had picked up his hired car in the side street where he had left it and driven out to his hotel, the Newport Hotel, a trip of about forty minutes. Lambert calculated that the whole operation, including delays at the airport, must have taken at least four hours, and probably nearer five. He and Lex Callaghan decided that they would repeat the movements step by step.

But first they had some checking to do. The postal inspectors had already put an alarm on the mailbox where George Gordon Holmes was due to collect his letter, but they did not hold out high hopes of his arriving; they had already discovered that Clifford Irving's original letter to Hughes, written at Christmastime, was still lying there, unclaimed. Lambert reckoned that in the meantime he and Lex could drive out to the hotel at Pompano Beach, thirty miles north of Miami, where Irving had supposedly stayed during his August and September meetings with Hughes. There they had a setback. The hotel records had been removed, apparently at the insistence of the local District Attorney, who was doing his own investigating. However, they were able to inspect the bungalow which Irving and Suskind claimed to have rented, and they immediately noticed a curious discrepancy.

It concerned "the man with the cane"—the agent allegedly

posted near Irving's bungalow on Hughes's orders, to guard the manuscript. Irving had testified that he had seen the man on several occasions walking up and down across the road, in front of a shop which sold seashells. But Lambert and Callaghan discovered that the view from the bungalow was so restricted that it would have been impossible to see him. And they picked up another clue when they strolled over to talk to the man who ran the shop. No, he said, he had noticed no one, with or without a cane. What is more, he would have been the first to stop a suspicious stranger.

"I happen to be an insomniac," he explained. "If there had been anybody hanging around here, I'd have noticed right away. But I didn't."

It was an interesting piece of evidence but, of course, far from conclusive. Lambert and Callaghan turned to the main task—checking Irving's route. They went to Miami airport on Wednesday afternoon and checked the car-rental counters. They started with Avis, and, inevitably, it was the wrong one. The dockets revealed nothing. Turning next to the National desk, they repeated the process. Forty dockets later, they hit the right one. Irving had indeed hired a car on the day in question—December 3—and had taken it out at 2:37 p.m. That was about right, so, given the time-scale calculated on the basis of his evidence, he could not have checked into the Newport Hotel before 6:30. It would probably have been nearer to 7:30.

Lambert and Callaghan set out for the hotel and met with their second setback. The manager had left for the night, and no one else would give them permission to inspect the records. Even Lex Callaghan's impressive credentials failed to convince the hotel staff. "OK," said Callaghan grimly. "If they want to play games, we'll get the United States Attorney to subpoena the records."

Which explains why next day Bill Lambert, reporter, found himself sitting in the back of a government car driving out from the hotel, and leafing excitedly through a pile of hotel records. He turned back to December 3, found Irving's name, looked at the date-time stamp against his name. It was 4:51 p.m.—more than two hours too early.

"Goddammit, Lex!" he shouted. "We've caught the guy in a lie."

For the next two hours Lambert tried to reach Frank McCulloch in New York by telephone. The only information he could get was that McCulloch was out with another reporter, John Goldman of the *Los Angeles Times*. They were apparently on to some important story and were moving about, but finally Lambert managed to track them both down at Goldman's New York home.

When Frank McCulloch heard Lambert's news, he knew that the first thing he had to do was to stop the *Life* magazine presses, which were even at that stage beginning to churn out a new issue carrying a lead story written by Ralph Graves about Clifford Irving. It was, of course, cautiously worded, but now it would have to be changed. Nobody at *Life* will reveal how much the change cost, but the run had almost certainly begun by this time, and to stop a run in mid-flow, break the plates, and begin again is a step which is only taken in the most drastic circumstances. On this occasion the decision was amply justified, for in the meantime the cause of all the excitement had returned to face the music.

It is arguable that Clifford Irving need never have come back from Ibiza. He could have taken the $100,000 which he probably had at this stage and headed with his wife and family for the sanctuary of South America, or simply have stayed on the island, where his chances of being extradited were perhaps no greater than those of his friend Elmyr de Hory, who, after all, had spent only two months in Ibiza jail.

But for Irving that course would have been unthinkable. Just as the game was beginning to reach its climax—that was the moment when he needed to be back in the middle of the action. His confidence was unimpaired. He could call the shots again. And even if, to the rest of the world, it seemed impossible that he could ever pull his tattered story together again, he was certainly not going to run away from it. There was still a lot of talking to be done.

His arrival at Kennedy Airport on Wednesday, January 26 (the pleas from Zurich had been ignored), was more reminiscent of the early days of a Beatles tour than the return of a minor novelist. More than a hundred reporters and photographers milled around him as he came through the doors of the customs shed with his Sancho Panza, Marty Ackerman, beside him. The questions hit him with a roar, and the names Helga and Hughes bubbled to the surface with angry insistence. For once Clifford Irving was stunned into silence. Clutching at his throat, he pleaded laryngitis. "Gentlemen, this is a horrible experience," he whispered. "It's not my cup of tea." He pushed his way through the crowd, half-answering a few questions in spite of himself, then slumped into the seat of a waiting car where his wife and two bewildered children were already sitting. Edith's face was taut and suffering. A reporter watching her remembered one of Irving's quips: "D'you really think I'd involve my family in an enterprise like this?" But he didn't put it in his story.

Next day there were about a thousand people who wanted to ask Clifford Irving questions, but there were only two whose needs were insistent enough for them to wait through until 11:30 at night. John Goldman and Frank McCulloch now believed they held a vital clue. They believed they knew the identity of George Gordon Holmes. Irving's description of him fitted, to an astonishing degree, that of John Meier, a thirty-eight-year-old ecologist who had worked for Hughes in the late 1960s and was now seeking the Democratic nomination for the United States Senate in New Mexico. Goldman and McCulloch reckoned that if they could put a photograph of Meier in front of Irving they could tell, from his reaction, whether they were on the right track.

The theory, good as it seemed, was a red herring. But the

approach, late at night, after Irving had spent a grueling evening with the District Attorney, achieved a result far more spectacular than anything the two reporters had counted on.

They arrived at the Ackermans' town house on Park Avenue at 6:30 and were ushered upstairs by Mrs. Ackerman, She said she was sorry, but Irving was simply not available.

"Just tell Cliff we know all about Meier," said McCulloch.

The Clifford Irving saga has its fair share of ironies, but this was perhaps the richest. Nobody realized that there were two Meiers—phonetically speaking. John Meier, who appeared to be significant but was not, was blessed with a name which sounded exactly the same as that of Stanley Meyer, who was at this stage unheard of. But Stanley, nevertheless, was the one who mattered.

So when Mrs. Ackerman went downstairs to where Irving and Marty were hiding out in the basement kitchen, and told them what McCulloch had said, the shock was pulverizing. If McCulloch knew about Meyer, reasoned Irving, then the game really did seem to be up. Knowing about Meyer meant knowing about the main source for the book, knowing about . . . well, everything. There was only one thing to do now and that was to go back to the District Attorney's office and make a clean breast before anything got into the papers. Well, a relatively clean breast, anyway.

Mrs. Ackerman went back upstairs, apologized again to the waiting reporters, and suggested that they might be able to see Irving later. Perhaps they could wait at the end of a telephone.

The call came, finally, just before midnight. Clutching a sheaf of pictures (they had collected together half a dozen headshots, including Meier's, in order to make it more difficult for Irving to compose a reaction), McCulloch and Goldman went into the living room, where Irving was waiting. He was tired and gray, but, more than that, he was desperately nervous; his voice was no more than a whisper. The pictures were laid on a table and Irving began to leaf through them, scarcely daring to look as he picked them up one by one in trembling fingers. None of them seemed to register. When he came to the photograph of Meier he picked it up and dropped it immediately, shaking his head. "No, I don't know him," he said slowly. He looked up at McCulloch, and there was a long, puzzled silence.

What had happened was unbelievable. Clifford Irving, the con man, had himself been conned. By the simplest, most idiotic accident in the world, he had been fooled into believing that the game was up. As a result he had gone and spilled to the District Attorney details that he could have kept to himself. And nobody in that room knew it except him.

Finally he looked up. "There's something I have to tell you guys," he whispered. "But it's got to be off the record, OK?" He glanced at Ackerman, who nodded. Finally Goldman and McCulloch agreed as well.

"Well," said Irving, "you may have guessed or you may not. Helga Hughes is Edith. Edith is Helga."

There was a long silence in the room. John Goldman, at a loss for words, looked at his shoes and noticed they were covered with fluff from the new carpet he and his wife had bought the other day. "Oh, God," he thought. "Now I've gone and messed up Marty's nice rug."

Within twelve hours of Clifford Irving's admission that Helga R. Hughes was his wife, Ackerman telephoned a terse statement to the Associated Press in New York. It read: "I am not a criminal lawyer, and I think Clifford Irving needs a criminal lawyer in a case like this."

It was an abrupt end to Ackerman's and Irving's sixteen-month relationship. But Marty had known the good times. He had helped Irving draft his Letter of Agreement with Hughes back in March, and he had notarized Irving's fantastic affidavit describing his working relationship with Hughes. It was not the sort of relationship that could be cut cleanly, and although Marty was to complain that Cliff left without paying phone and laundry bills, let alone his fees, he did lend the Irvings his country house in the less excitable atmosphere of Lakeville, Connecticut, so that they could acquaint their newly appointed criminal lawyer with the details of the case.

The lawyer was called Maurice Nessen, a man who stood no higher than Edith—a good head smaller than his client—and who bore an astonishing resemblance to the young Eamon de Valera (though the comparison ends there). He had first appeared at Irving's side on January 28, when Edith's role was first admitted publicly, and thereafter he was the couple's faithful—and much-needed—companion.

# The Mexican Connection

Gentlemen always seem to prefer blondes.

Anita Loos, *Gentlemen Prefer Blondes*

Early in the morning of Wednesday, February 2, the Baroness Nina Van Pallandt left her cottage in the grounds of the Treasure Cay Hotel on a small out-island in the Bahamas and went to the beach. It was the third day of her escape from a damp, chilly, and ill-lit London, and she was beginning to relax.

Nina was a singer, Danish born, thirty-nine years old. She had been married to a Dutch folksinger called Baron Frederik Van Pallandt, and together they had established a modest but steady reputation in Europe during the 1960s. When they separated in 1969, Nina kept the title and the act. She worked alone and appeared regularly on British television. She is a striking blonde, who looks her best on television when the camera highlights her fine high cheekbones. She is slim and dresses elegantly and expensively—the sort of woman who is noticed when she walks into a restaurant—and she was about to become one of the more unforgettable figures in the Irving affair. Two days after she was first heard of in the United States she was referred to fondly and universally as "Nina."

That Wednesday morning four groups of people were looking for Nina. The first was the postal inspectors, who had acted on information from Clifford Irving's old friend Beverly Loo. Miss Loo had once heard from Irving that he had been accompanied on his trip to Mexico by a woman. Her name, she thought, was something like Nina Marshall, and she was, possibly, an English folksinger. This morsel had been followed up by investigations in Ibiza, which had revealed a warm friendship between Irving and a singer called Nina Van Pallandt ("investigation" is, perhaps, too strong a word to describe the process of ingesting Ibiza's café gossip), and the inspectors had then traced Nina's immediate whereabouts through her American agent.

The second group was Clifford Irving and his new lawyer, Maurice Nessen, who were understandably keen to talk to her, preferably before anyone else. A third party consisted of John Goldman and Frank McCulloch, still working together, who had a vague tip about Nina from a friend in the Postal Inspection Service but nothing else. They had no real idea of where she might be and made nearly seventy calls to places in Europe, the United States, and the Caribbean, before somebody had the bright idea of calling Nina's mother in Copenhagen. "Mothers always know where their daughters are; it's a pity we didn't think of it earlier," says Goldman.

The fourth group was Intertel, working for Howard Hughes, and its investigators claim victory. They reached Nina by telephone at breakfast time on February 2—forty-five minutes ahead of the postal inspector—and confirmed that one year earlier she had accompanied Clifford Irving on his trip to Mexico to see Howard Hughes. But it was the inspector who made the significant break in the case. He must have been an incongruous spectacle on Treasure Cay, dressed in a business suit and carrying a briefcase. He explained that he was called Brady, that he had come from Atlanta, and he just wanted to ask the Baroness a few questions. He did not stop asking questions for three hours, and by the time he had finished it was evident that Irving could not conceivably have met Hughes in Mexico. And if he had not seen him there, the chances of his ever having met him were slim indeed.

Nina gave her devastating information on the advice and at the instigation of John Marshall. Marshall is an all-purpose figure in Nina's life: her manager, press officer, and alter ego. Most simply—and most usually—he speaks for her. He is small, stocky, and assertive, and as soon as he heard of the postal inspector's impending arrival he took charge. Of course Nina would see him, he said, and on the way up to the hotel he informed her that she would cooperate completely with the investigation. "If he asks you whether you slept with Cliff, there's to be no beating about the bush, you say 'yes,'" he told her.

The three of them retired to the coffee shop, and the postal inspector began on the long list of questions he carried with him. He was "an absolutely charming chap," according to Marshall, and he started by asking Nina whether she had traveled under the name of Baroness Nina Van Pallandt on a flight from New York to Mexico City on February 11, 1971. She had. Had she then flown from Mexico City to Oaxaca in southern Mexico? She had. Had she then stayed at the Hotel Victoria, Oaxaca? She had. Had she registered as Mrs. Clifford Irving? A pause. She had.

It was abundantly clear from the first few questions that there was nothing on the record about that trip that the postal authorities did not know. They had inspected the airline records. They had been to the Hotel Victoria and had showed pictures of Nina to the bellhops, the barmen, and the pool attendants.

The inspector slowly brought his interrogation to its climax. He wanted to know what the two of them had done during the day. He wanted to know whether they had rented a car, what time they had gone to the beach, when and where they had been shopping. Had they spent any time apart? he asked. "It was a holiday," Nina replied, "so obviously we were together most of the time." How long were they apart? "Oh, for a couple of hours during the afternoon when Cliff scooted off to get the plane tickets," she remembered. So they were together for the two days, February 13 and February 14, except for a few hours? Yes, said Nina, all the time.

The inspector did not mention Clifford Irving's affidavit, but he knew that Nina had just exploded the story of his meeting with Hughes in a parked car at the top of Monte Alban. Nor was there the slightest possibility that Irving had, as he claimed, spent the second day of the trip in a hotel room in Tehuantepec. He was, in fact, a liar of spectacular proportions.

The other Nina-seekers were not far behind the postal inspector from Atlanta. During the afternoon Clifford Irving called the hotel, but Nina and Marshall were out. Marshall took a second call in the late afternoon, from Maurice Nessen. He remembers the call vividly.

"What the hell is going on?" Nessen barked down the phone.

"That's what we want to know," Marshall barked back.

"We've been trying to get you for days; we've had private detectives out looking for you," said Nessen.

"So were the postal inspectors, but they beat you to it."

"What did you tell them?" asked Nessen urgently.

"We told them what happened in Oaxaca," Marshall replied. It must have been a bad moment for Nessen, because it informed him that his client's old friends were not going to rally round. It was *sauve qui peut* from that moment on.

"Why did you have to talk to them?" Nessen asked.

"We have been put in an embarrassing position," Marshall replied, using the royal plural, "and we had to protect our reputation."

But if one reputation—Irving's—was about to suffer badly, another was about to be made. Shortly after Nessen's call,

John Goldman got through from New York. He read Nina the relevant part of Irving's affidavit; it was the first time she had heard his imaginative version of those two days' holiday in Mexico.

"I'm flabbergasted. I can't understand the whole thing," she told Goldman. She said she remembered that Irving mentioned Hughes once, and had even said that he planned to interview him, but he did not do so in Mexico.

Marshall then came on the line to sugar-coat the poison pill. "We obviously don't want to say he's lying. But his story and our story are very different."

Goldman put down the phone and, with his colleague Robert Jackson, wrote his exclusive story about the collapse of the Irving affidavit.

Frank McCulloch rushed back to his office. Shortly afterward, *Life* changed the subject of its cover. The plan had been to put Edith Irving on in full color. But the art department found a picture of Nina—head and naked shoulders. The mistress was not only a better story than the deceived wife; she was better-looking too. Within hours, newspaper headline-writers had christened her "the Danish pastry."

During her interview with the postal inspector, Nina had been asked whether she would be willing to appear before a federal grand jury. Marshall said she would, thus saving the federal authorities a subpoena. Soon New Yorkers would be able to watch the Nina Van Pallandt show as well as read about it.

By the time she arrived in New York there was another blonde on stage—a tall, striking lady who had accompanied Clifford Irving on one of his later adventures. She was called Anne Baxter, and she had traveled with Irving to St. Croix in the Virgin Islands early in December.

Later on, Anne Baxter was equipped with an agent to whom she referred all inquiries, but when her name and picture first appeared she still conformed to other values and sought to protect her privacy. It was known, however, that she was a twenty-eight-year-old scuba-diving instructor at the Newport Hotel in Miami, and very good at her job too, according to the hotel manager. "She has attracted a lot of business," he said happily.

Among the business was Clifford Irving, who showed up during his Miami trip. In January she signed on with a Miami escort service called Rent-a-Supergirl, but a month earlier Irving seems to have got her company rent-free.

Ten days after her discovery by the postal inspectors, Anne Baxter was persuaded by the *Chicago Tribune* to describe her part in the affair. Like Nina, she retained fond memories of Irving. He had told her of the Hughes autobiography and had actually let her read sections of it. "I wondered, in fact, whether it was publishable," she said, though her doubts were not so much because of the book's authenticity but because it was so outspoken and opinionated.

Anne Baxter grew very fond of Cliff, she said. "He came to me in the pool as a student during the first week of December, and from his actions I was convinced he was a gentleman." She explained that Clifford had told her that he and his wife, Edith, were separated, that they were going to be divorced, and that the only thing he cared about was his two sons. "All this made Cliff a slightly mysterious, intriguing, and adventurous comrade," she said. It also made him extremely unpopular with Edith.

Gentleman or not, Clifford Irving invited his scuba-diving instructress to St. Croix after they had known each other for only eight days; he told her he was going to meet Howard Hughes. They arrived on December 9 and registered at the King Christian Hotel in Christiansted (in separate rooms, she pointed out).

Next day they went shopping and scuba diving. "I remember thinking during that day that we might see Hughes with his graying hair, as Cliff described him, swimming up from the bottom to join us in the boat. Cliff said Hughes's agents were fantastic and would find us anywhere, even out in a boat," said Anne breathlessly. But Hughes never broke surface. On December 11, after some dune-buggy riding and more scuba diving, Irving disappeared into the sunset, bound for New York.

Anne Baxter's evidence was not so obviously damaging as Nina's, but it added to a generally held suspicion that Clifford Irving's mind was on other, arguably finer, things when he was supposed to be interviewing Howard Hughes. Her involvement also helped create a myth of Irving as a raunchy *Playboy* magazine hero—a myth that did not survive the next four weeks. But the appearance of his tall blond girl friends sucked more and more newspapermen into coverage of the story. At one point the *Los Angeles Times,* which had landed most of the scoops, had nine men on the job. There were more reporters involved covering this hoax than there were covering the war in Vietnam.

# ACT VI

## Consternation in the Marketplace

# Double Trouble

Now that everybody from the chambermaids
to Albertini has been summoned to this
ridiculous party, what I want to know is this:
why hasn't Howard Hughes been invited?

> Gerald Albertini, by telephone from Ibiza,
> February 14, 1972

A severe credibility gap yawned between Clifford Irving
and his public, following the unmasking of Edith and the
exposure of Nina and Anne. To most people in the rapt
audience the affair was reaching its climax, but for Irving's
new lawyer it was only the beginning.

Maurice Nessen did not have much time to brief himself.
Irving had been subpoenaed to appear before not one but
two grand juries the following Monday, January 31, only
four days after Nessen's appointment. One had been established by the Manhattan District Attorney, a legendary
seventy-year-old prosecutor called Frank Hogan, who had
been elected for eight successive terms to a job he first held
in 1940. The legend has tarnished slightly with time, but
it is dangerous to underrate Hogan, who remains remarkably
tough. The other grand jury had been established by the
authority of the U.S. attorney in the Southern District of
New York, Whitney North Seymour, Jr. (his father is a sub-

stantial Wall Street lawyer). Seymour is of a different generation from Hogan, having taken the post over from his prede-
cessor, Robert Morgenthau, only in 1970.

It was difficult to grasp at first why two grand juries were
sitting to investigate a similar series of offenses. There is a
legal explanation for the duplication (mail fraud is a federal
offense, while perjury and obtaining money under false pre-
tense are breaches of state law). But the legal explanation does
not tell all the story. Rivalry between state and federal prosecutors is endemic throughout the United States, and in New
York City it had been notoriously severe. Seymour, who had
tried to heal the breach between the two offices, offered to
share with Hogan the results of the federal investigation.
Hogan warily agreed, and the two announced a policy of cooperation between separate but equal grand juries.

A grand jury is a venerable democratic instrument designed to prevent arbitrary justice, and, like some other
democratic instruments, it has been declared redundant, both
in England, where it began, and in many of the states. But
New York State and the Justice Department like to adhere
to the principle that no one should be indicted for, say, a
felony without evidence against him first being heard in
secret by a jury of his peers. Besides, the grand jury is a
useful investigative tool, and the Justice Department has
been known to use grand juries for fishing expeditions in
areas where they would like to know more—such as the
publication of the Pentagon Papers.

In January 1971, Chester Davis was anxious to put the
system to work. The Hughes organization knew its value;
there was a grand jury in Miami considering a technical
breach of the law by a local detective agency which had had
the impertinence to bug Howard Hughes's room in Nassau
shortly after his arrival. Hughes Tool was anxious to find
out what had been overheard, and the jury was a possible
source of that information. Now Davis desperately wanted
to uncover the causes of McGraw-Hill's confidence in Clifford

Irving. And if Rosemont could not do it in a civil suit, maybe the grand jury could in a criminal investigation. Davis was right about the grand jury, though the process took an inconveniently long time.

After January 16, Davis had had high hopes of powerful allies within the administration itself. Since the autobiography was said to contain such unsavory memoirs as the account of Hughes's loan to Nixon's brother, surely the administration would also have a motive for exposing the book as a fake.

But politicians are not always conspiratorial or venal. In this case Chester Davis did not get very far at the Justice Department. He was told that the case did not seem serious enough to warrant a criminal investigation. And when it finally did become serious enough, it was not Davis who provoked the Justice Department into establishing a grand jury; it was his arch-enemies, McGraw-Hill and *Life*.

On Monday, January 24, the publishers trooped down to Whitney North Seymour's office in the federal courthouse in Foley Square. They told him about the episode in Zurich and commented that it looked as though all was not well. Seymour said he would consider the case. *Life* and McGraw-Hill replied that if there was anything else they could do to help, Seymour just had to ask. Then they went through a similar routine in Hogan's office in the state court building just up the street at Centre Street.

Seymour knew that the postal inspectors had been alerted, and learned shortly afterward that their investigation had already begun, so there was no need to bring in the FBI. He passed responsibility for the case to the head of his criminal division, Robert Morvillo, who had a reputation for ferocious prosecution, and to John J. Tigue, the head of the fraud section, a blander, younger lawyer. They were well matched.

At the beginning, Morvillo and Tigue did not know as much about the case as the reporters, who had at least three weeks' start on them. But it did not take the federal attorneys long to catch up—three days, in fact. It was the morning of

January 27, and the investigators were still not sure whether they could prove that Edith and Helga were indeed the same person. Morvillo decided the best way to end the speculation was to fly Frau Schaffner, the Swiss Credit cashier who dealt with Helga Hughes, to New York and see if she could identify Edith. He phoned Switzerland and offered to pay her fare over; it was another of the factors which, during that day, caused Irving's gentlemanly resolve to keep his family out of the affair to crumble. Early that evening he formally revealed to the District Attorney that Edith was Helga. Later he made the same admission to McCulloch and Goldman. Immediately he was given unbreakable appointments to appear before both federal and state grand juries on January 31. Justice had begun to take its course, and it was not always to run smooth. It started not as a torrent, but as an unsteady drip.

Maurice Nessen's first action before the grand juries on January 31 was to ask that his client be excused, to allow him to prepare his case. The request was granted. Among other things, the attorneys wanted to talk to his researcher, Richard Suskind. He was the only person claiming to have seen Clifford Irving in the company of Howard Hughes. The investigators thought that his story of meeting Hughes unexpectedly and of accepting an organic prune from him a highly suspect one; but the weak link adamantly refused to move from Majorca for questioning. So Tigue, in New York, got a subpoena. It was not binding on Suskind because he lived abroad, but he was told that if he ignored it, he might face fines of up to $5000 a day. "Most people come when they hear that," one postal inspector commented laconically. Suskind said he would be in New York on February 7.

The first grand jury witness to arouse anticipation was John Meier. Suspicion that he might well be the much-sought George Gordon Holmes had spread widely since that night at Ackerman's house when Clifford Irving had been shown his photograph and had failed to take the bait. His name had subsequently been canvassed in public, and he was still a possible suspect. But then Irving released a categorical statement which said that Meier was not Holmes; his actual appearance before the grand jury was thus something of an anticlimax. It certainly could not compete with the revelations of Nina Van Pallandt from the Bahamas.

It was a quiet first week for the twenty-three men and women on the federal jury—even quieter for the state grand jurors, who heard no witnesses at all. But the postal inspectors were hard at work. As frauds go, this was not particularly big for them; but, as frauds go, it was particularly entertaining. At one point there were thirty enthusiastic postal employees tracking clues throughout the Western Hemisphere. Eventually they were to provide the federal grand jury with a surfeit of witnesses and information.

By the end of the first week, however, the action was still taking place outside the courthouse. It was, for many fascinated observers, the high point of the affair. Only a few questions had been resolved, so speculation could flow unchecked by details of fact. An air of hilarity settled on New York City, even though it was February. Jokes started to circulate. They were mildly sardonic and rather obvious, but they were a product of their time—like the one about McGraw-Hill suffering such a financial drain because of the payments to Hughes that it was going to be taken over by Irving Trust. As if to rub salt in the wound, Irving Trust was actually to open a new branch on the first floor of the new McGraw-Hill building on Sixth Avenue, and its signs were going up under the gilded letters announcing McGraw-Hill's presence.

Then there was another about Ralph Graves having lunch at Pearl's, a fashionable Chinese restaurant much used by Time-Life writers. "Look," says a *Life* man to a companion as he enters the door, "there's Ralph over there eating alone. Let's join him." "Lord, no! Can't you see he's with Howard Hughes?" As the jokes proliferated, they got rather worse. Anyway, they could hardly compete with the humor of what was actually happening to the Irvings, the publishers, and Howard Hughes.

Clifford Irving's first appearance before the grand jury, on February 7, also turned into a joke. As soon as he arrived he began to stall. He replied to questions by pleading the Fifth Amendment. The grand jury then asked for handwriting samples from both Clifford and Edith Irving. Still pleading the Fifth Amendment, both refused; to anyone who thought about it, the request seemed rather unnecessary. It was known that Edith had countersigned at least one of the McGraw-Hill–Hughes checks, and no one thought that either of them had forged the alleged Hughes letters. But the federal attorneys persisted, and the Irvings continued to refuse. This meant that much of their time was spent in the canteen near the grand-jury room. Sitting there, sipping coffee, Irving was approached by a waitress. "Could I have your autograph?" she asked. "Certainly," said Irving. "What's your name?" "Eleanor," she told him, and he wrote: "To Eleanor, Very truly, Clifford Irving."

A judge was obliged to inform the Irvings that Fifth Amendment rights do not stretch to refusing handwriting samples, and he had to threaten them both with contempt of court to obtain what Irving had freely given Eleanor. But the threat was effective, and the next day the Irvings wrote out the text of the first three letters Clifford said he had received from Hughes, together with specimen check endorsements and signatures. The exemplars were bundled up and sent to Robert Cabanne, the most experienced handwriting expert in the Post Office's crime laboratory on Church Street, not far from Foley Square.

It was a bad day for the Irvings. Suskind had arrived in New York and been told by the federal authorities that they might forget a mail fraud charge against him if he would confess that Howard Hughes's organic prune was an indigestible figment of Irving's imagination. Faced with a choice between sticking to his unlikely story, and the chance of a reduction of the charges against him, Suskind chose the latter. It would not save him from the perjury charge Hogan could bring, but at least "mail fraud" might not be listed on his criminal record.

To make things worse, the Internal Revenue Service had put tax liens on any assets held by the Irvings and Suskind. On February 7 the IRS had gone to the county court and demanded from Clifford Irving $246,993; from Edith Irving, $243,118; and from Richard Suskind $22,446. Just like everyone else, the IRS showed no doubt about who had profited from the autobiography, even though it might not know exactly what the profits were, or how they had been distributed. (The remarkably precise demands were based on records of previous earnings and allowances.) "We wanted to be sure we were not left out of it; we wanted to be first in line for their money," said an IRS spokesman, on behalf of all the American people.

Clifford Irving still managed to look cheerful as he left the grand-jury hearings, apologizing to reporters waiting in the bitter cold for his silence, and blaming Maurice Nessen. But he had very little to be cheerful about. Not only had Suskind exploded another piece of his battered story and the IRS padlocked his assets; the Swiss wanted their day in court with Edith.

Peter Veleff, the Zurich prosecutor, had charged Edith Irving with fraud and forgery, and he insisted that she come to Zurich to stand trial. She had used a forged Swiss passport and had defrauded a Swiss bank. Those were not offenses to be taken lightly, especially when committed by a Swiss citizen, even one who lived in Ibiza. Veleff wanted extradition proceedings to begin.

On February 9, Irving and Nessen sought out Whitney North Seymour and asked him if he would make a deal. Irving said that he might cooperate with the investigation if the federal authorities could persuade the Swiss not to be so humorless and legalistic about Edith's relatively small role in the whole affair. Morvillo and Tigue were interested in the offer, but they wanted to know just how much cooperation they would get. Morvillo got Nessen to ask Irving whether he would continue to insist that he had met Howard Hughes. It was a question of more than academic importance. Unless Irving did concede that there were no meetings, the attorneys would need to get Hughes to swear that, for his part, he had never met Irving, and that was a complication they could do without.

Nessen returned and told Morvillo that Irving would admit there had been no meetings. Morvillo agreed then to fly to Zurich and test the mood of the Swiss; he had to go anyway to push his own investigation further. But before he left he warned Nessen that Irving had better not welsh on the deal. "Irving should know that we'll break his balls before the grand jury if he tells them he met with Hughes," Morvillo said roughly. Nessen could have been in no doubt that he meant it.

Morvillo did not have a strong negotiating position in Switzerland. The Zurich cantonal police were complaining at the paucity of information that was reaching them from New York. Maurice Nessen had said disgustedly that week— when news of Irving's admission that he had not met Hughes was headlined in every newspaper in the country—that the grand-jury investigation was being conducted in a goldfish bowl.

Lieutenant Willi Ulrich, head of the Zurich fraud investigation against Edith Irving, saw matters somewhat differently. "We just don't know what the blockage is along the line, but nothing is reaching us. We get the impression that the United States authorities, perhaps for procedural reasons, are not interested in helping us," Ulrich complained at the time. Since Swiss police are disinclined to believe what they read in the newspapers, he asked for formal notification of Irving's confession about Edith's being Helga. Ulrich heard nothing. The Swiss have never been partial to the kind of deals that are made every day in the clogged judicial system in New York City, but after the long silence from New York they were even less inclined toward compromise. They were determined to get Helga, and they were positively incensed at newspaper reports suggesting that Seymour had made a deal with Irving at the expense of their own case against Edith. (They were to be outraged the following week at another newspaper report stating that they, the Swiss police, had actually concluded a deal with Morvillo that would let Edith go free.)

Morvillo had troubles in his own back yard, too. They were not yet serious, but there were rumblings of the old argument between Hogan's office and Seymour's. The state investigation had been totally eclipsed by the flair and success with which the federal investigation was being conducted by Morvillo, Tigue, and the postal inspectors. The state grand jury did not even hear a witness until February 11, by which time Morvillo and Tigue had already decided to visit Switzerland.

Hogan's investigation was handled by Leonard Newman, head of the District Attorney's fraud section, and it was suffering from a severe manpower and informational deficiency. Reports from the postal inspectors were received but Newman could not personally call on federal agents or dispatch detectives to Europe. The ambitions of Hogan's office were not, however, to be dashed by the irritating shortcomings of its own investigation. It could achieve almost as much with one man as the vast postal team: all he had to do was to stand at the door of the federal courthouse and present departing witnesses with a subpoena to appear before the state grand jury nearby. Nina Van Pallandt and Anne Baxter were both bagged this way. There was another trick Hogan's office could play. If the federal authorities really were making private deals with Irving, as the newspapers suggested they were, the state could go right ahead and charge Irving with perjury then and there. It had a cast-iron case against him, with Nina and

Anne Baxter as witnesses. The plan was considered. But it horrified Morvillo. He wanted to trace everyone involved in the plot, he wanted to charge each with all the offenses they had committed and he was not satisfied that he knew enough.

Meanwhile, Clifford Irving was becoming a hot social property. When he managed to slip away from the Chelsea Hotel and his lawyer's office (which was not often) he found himself the center of attention. At a Manhattan dinner party he was asked, "How does it all feel?"

Irving said he felt like the man who jumped off the Empire State Building. Halfway down, he was engaged in conversation by an office worker who was looking out of a window. The man on the inside asked, "How do you feel?"

The falling man replied, "Okay, so far."

But even Clifford Irving had no idea of just how fast he was falling. Late on the same day that Morvillo and Tigue arrived in Europe a *deus ex machina* was about to arrive on the scene in New York. The *machina* was a Boeing 707, and it was carrying Jim Phelan from Los Angeles.

# Mr. Phelan Comes to Town

"It is hard for thee to kick against the pricks."

*The Acts of the Apostles,* Ch. 9, Verse 5

While popular attention was directed at Nina and the court-house in Foley Square, the experts were playing a more subtle game. How could one really judge the value of the "auto-biography," they argued, until more people knew what was in it? The integrity of Irving's manuscript was, after all, the last resort of those who had invested money in it and had read all or part of it. Most of them still felt that it was authentic.

Around the end of January outsiders could, for the first time, begin to judge for themselves. Portions of Irving's manuscript began to "leak." Someone on the inside delib-erately started to farm out sections of it with intent. The idea was to float some of Irving's better stories publicly and see whether they could be shot down.

For a while it seemed that this process might actually con-firm the validity of McGraw-Hill's coup. Some of the "leaks" were frivolous, like the New York *Daily News's* reproduction of Hughes's alleged memorandum of instruction about how to deploy Jane Russell's bosom in a new movie: "I want the rest of her wardrobe to be low-necked (and by that I mean as low as the law allows) so that the customers can get a look at that part of Russell which they pay to see. . . ." But others were less easily dismissed. One of the most popular leaks concerned Hughes's precautions for "hospitality liquor" during Prohibition. Hughes had become worried about the security of his supply and had asked Noah Dietrich to change the combination on his vault so that only he and Dietrich could open it. Dietrich did as he was told, but some months later, while Hughes was away in Acapulco, he tried the changed combination and it did not work. At his next meeting with his boss, Dietrich managed to clear up the mystery: Hughes had changed the combination again.

There were those who felt that this yarn in Irving's manuscript must have come from Hughes. Then it emerged that Dietrich had been dining out on the story for years as an example of Hughes's "complete confidence" in people.

On February 4, Wallace Turner of *The New York Times,* who was carving out a niche for himself as conduit-in-chief for the "leak" merchant, wrote up another story from Irving's manuscript—this time one which contained greater detail about the by now famous loan to Donald Nixon. The manuscript quoted Hughes as saying that Nixon had failed to fulfill his side of the bargain, so ". . . I leaked the details to Drew Pearson."

This phrase had a dramatic effect on Jim Phelan. His recollection of the Nixon-loan episode, which he had covered for almost a year back in 1961, was different. He remembered Hughes doing all he could to *suppress* the story and he even knew the identity of the man who had *really* leaked the story to Pearson. For the first time Phelan began to have serious doubts about Irving's manuscript.

Then, on Thursday, February 10, *The New York Times* did it again, with another Wallace Turner article. Turner noted that many of the previously "leaked" stories might have been based on imaginative use of material in newspaper and magazine files. But he had a tale from the Irving manuscript that could not be traced back to any file or even gossip. It ran as follows:

> IRVING: You must have had to carry a sack full of dimes and quarters around with you (to call your executives) wherever you went.
>
> HUGHES: I'd charge the call to my office number. Some smart guy, one of my publicity men, was visiting one of those Hollywood columnists one time—Hedda Hopper, I think it was—and I called him and told him to get out to a public phone and call me back. A few minutes later—this was Perry Lieber, a publicity man at RKO—he called. I asked him his number and he gave it to me, and right away I knew something was wrong.
>
> I checked my book, and the number he'd given me was Hedda Hopper's unlisted number.
>
> So I got back on the wire and said, "What the hell are you trying to pull, Perry? When I want you to call from a public phone I mean a public phone, because that's private. Hedda Hopper's private phone is about as public as you can get, and I mean public in the worst possible way. What are you doing?"

On finding the story, Turner had got on to Perry Lieber in Las Vegas and read it to him. Lieber, who, like every other diligent Hughes PR man, had been pouring scorn on Irving's claims, was bewildered. Turner's article quoted him as saying: "You've shaken me. I don't want to lend any credence to that book, but that story was never published. I have never used it in a speech and I cannot remember ever telling anyone. How could Irving have learned of it?" The memory of the occasion was still fresh in Lieber's mind because "it was the only time I ever lied to him [Hughes]."

Jim Phelan, just back from a tiring magazine assignment in Florida, was relaxing at his home in Long Beach, California. He plowed his way through *The New York Times* and finally came upon Turner's story on page 36. He read halfway through and then shouted, "Bingo! Eureka! *Voilà!* Jackpot!"

For Perry Lieber's memory was slightly at fault. He *had* told the story—to Jim Phelan ten years ago. But that was not all. When Phelan had started collaborating with Noah Dietrich, he had found that even Dietrich was unaware of the incident. Dietrich, however, considered it such a fetching example of Hughes's passion for secrecy that he had insisted on its inclusion in the first draft of his memoirs. Apart from Hughes himself, the only conceivable origin for the Lieber story was Phelan's unpublished draft manuscript.

"I've got it," Phelan told his wife. "That bastard Irving has stolen my manuscript."

He promptly put in calls to New York—one to Frank Mc-Culloch at *Time,* the other to Morrie Helitzer at McGraw-Hill, and went back to his files to search out his old script, which had lain untouched for ten months. Phelan was gaining a reputation as something of a busybody among the McGraw-Hill people. Since December 7 he had called them seven times with offers to scrutinize their product, and seven times the offers had been politely refused. But when he rang for the eighth time, McGraw-Hill was in a more receptive mood.

February 10 had been Black Thursday for the Publicity Department. As Faustin Jehle, the corporation counsel, was clearing his desk at the end of the day, he came across an unopened envelope. He looked up at his companion, Ted Weber, and said, "What's this? Looks like something from Osborn."

"Well, why don't you open it?"

Jehle did and experienced his worst moment of the whole affair.

"They've reneged. I just can't believe it. They've reneged and just sent the news around by messenger."

Osborn, Osborn and Osborn, the world-renowned handwriting experts, and the linchpin of McGraw-Hill's assumption that Hughes had written his autobiography, had quietly revised their opinion. Evidence for the authenticity of Hughes's letters to McGraw-Hill and Irving was no longer "overwhelming"; further investigation had revealed that the letters were "clever forgeries." The holographic chain had been broken by McGraw-Hill's own experts.

A dispirited Ted Weber arrived home at 8 p.m. and found a message from Helitzer. He called him and got his second trauma of the day: Phelan now thought that he might have the basic source material for Irving's manuscript. Weber called Phelan and asked him to hop on the next plane to New York. "About time," said Phelan. He had already found his manuscript and made the reservation.

Phelan flew through the night and arrived in New York, attired in his normal combat gear, coonskin cap and bush jacket, and ready for High Noon. He got there at 7 a.m. and paced the half-empty streets impatiently until *Time* magazine opened for business. He found Frank McCulloch already waiting for him.

Late the previous evening McCulloch had located Clifford Irving at his lawyer's office and had told him about the plan. "We've got the Phelan manuscript on its way to New York," he said. "Phelan's flying here with it, and we're going to lay it alongside your manuscript and read them together."

There was a long pause at the end of the line, and then Irving let out a long, low "Wooooooowwwwwww!!!!!!!"

"We're stupid, you and I," McCulloch told Phelan the next morning. "You told me about the Dietrich manuscript almost a year ago, and yet we never connected it to the Irving manuscript."

"How could we?" said Phelan. "You didn't know what was in my manuscript, and I didn't know what was in Irving's."

They went at once to the office of *Time*'s lawyers and discovered that the McGraw-Hill people had contrived a novel restriction to the plan. They would be happy to inspect

Phelan's manuscript, but Phelan was not to be allowed even a peep at Irving's.

Phelan dug in his heels. "Tell them, 'No way,'" he growled. "Absolutely no way. This is going to be a two-way street or no traffic."

While the lawyers discussed a compromise, McCulloch drew Phelan out into a corridor and promised him that if McGraw-Hill refused to cooperate, they would both go off and buy a black-market copy of the Irving manuscript. McCulloch said he knew where they could pick one up for $100.

At 11:30 a.m., however, Phelan was ushered up to the executive conference room on the nineteenth floor of the McGraw-Hill building. He laid his coonskin cap to one side, extracted his manuscript from its dusty manila envelope, and got straight down to business. Across the table was Robert Stewart, who had edited the manuscript. He had it neatly assembled in front of him. He was flanked by Faustin Jehle, Ted Weber, and Morrie Helitzer. The session lasted four hours and was joined at later stages by Harold McGraw and Shelton Fisher. When asked later to describe the atmosphere of the opening minutes, Phelan could only comment, "Tense."

The strategy was that Phelan should read out extracts from his manuscript, and Stewart, if he found parallels, would respond with extracts from Irving's. Weber and Helitzer acted as tally clerks. It was an eerie, muted occasion.

"Let's take some key incidents," Phelan suggested. "I assume you have the story of how Hughes hired Noah Dietrich?" Stewart nodded. Without even glancing at his manuscript, Phelan asked, "Does the incident have anything about golf? About Hughes asking Noah how the distance from a battleship to its target is computed? Anything about the principle of the internal-combustion engine?" Stewart nodded again. Phelan leafed through his manuscript, found the passage, and handed it over.

They moved along swiftly, with Phelan reciting specific

incidents from his memory, establishing that they were in the Irving version, then pulling out the passage from his own manuscript and showing it to Stewart.

"You have the Billie Dove watch story—when Hughes lost it on his yacht?"

Stewart nodded.

"Does it have the stuff about a seaman being arrested? And Hughes wouldn't prosecute? And Noah got the guy off and gave him money to get out of town? But the fellow hopped off the train and came back and tried to sue for false arrest?"

Nod, nod, nod, nod.

The clincher, from Phelan's point of view, came very early in this curious dialogue. It was the story about the private nickname for the Spruce Goose, Hughes's astonishing wooden flying boat. Among the Long Beach hangar crew, it was known as the Jesus Christ, and Phelan's manuscript related how it had come by this name:

> "When people walk in the hangar for the first time they are overwhelmed. They stand there with their mouths open and tilt their heads back until they are looking away up there at the top of the plane. Then they say, "Jeeeeeeesus Chriiiiiiist!"

When Stewart confirmed that Clifford Irving's "Hughes" had related this same story, Phelan's left eyebrow rose.

"Let me tell you gentlemen something," he said. "Not even Noah knew that story. I picked it up a few years ago from a disgruntled ex-hangar employee who had been laid off by the Hughes organization. Howard himself hasn't been down at that hangar for at least fourteen years—so how could *he* have picked it up?"

While the McGraw-Hill forces struggled with this problem, Phelan excused himself and went to an empty nearby office. He called McCulloch and brought him up to date.

The session lasted for another three and a half hours. McGraw-Hill argued that the mere coincidence of similar material appearing in Dietrich's memoirs and Irving's manuscript was not, in itself, conclusive evidence that Irving had cribbed. It could also mean, the publishers maintained, that Hughes and Dietrich merely remembered certain incidents the same way. But the pace of the meeting was quickening.

"Have you got the business about Hughes sending two lobbyists to Sacramento to kick Long Beach in the ass about the tideland oil settlement?"

Another nod and tick by the vice-presidential tally clerks.

"How about the business of Hughes sending $60,000 in cash to Maine to defeat Owen Brewster?" (Brewster was a Senator who had crossed swords with Hughes at the 1947 hearings.)

They had it—and on an impulse Phelan asked to read the Irving version. In writing this incident for Dietrich, Phelan had provided a context for the story out of his own knowledge. He had pointed out that Maine is a small state, with limited sources for political contributions, and that therefore Hughes's $60,000 had had a considerable impact on the campaign—which Brewster lost. There, in the manuscript, Irving had Hughes pointing out that Maine was a small state, with few sources of political contributions, and that therefore his cash had had considerable impact on the campaign.

In most cases Irving had diligently rewritten and rephrased the Phelan material, rather than plagiarizing it directly. But at this point he had apparently grown tired. There were one or two other places where the similarity in language was a bit too close for coincidence. For instance, Phelan's manuscript had Dietrich advising Hughes to dispose of the Spruce Goose with the following remark: "You can junk the plane now, and nobody could possibly criticize you." Irving's manuscript had Hughes recalling the same comment with uncanny accuracy: "you can junk that plane now, and nobody will criticize you."

After four hours they had covered about one-tenth of Irving's manuscript and discovered twenty-five close parallels between the two drafts. Among the twenty-five there were four incidents which could not by any stretch of the imagination have been known by Howard Hughes. One was known only by Dietrich, the other three (including the Jesus Christ story) were known only to Phelan himself.

Toward the end the nods became shrugs: McGraw-Hill was simply prolonging the autopsy for the sake of appearances. Irving's manuscript was a fine imaginative work, but it was the product of invention, old clippings, and some genuine nuggets stolen from Phelan's meticulous research. A complete fraud.

There was only one sour moment. Shelton Fisher, the company president, came in late and asked what he obviously thought was a penetrating question. "I hope I don't offend you, Mr. Phelan, but how do we know that *you* didn't lift your material from *our* manuscript?"

The other McGraw-Hill men, who had been in from the beginning, were obviously embarrassed by this display of corporate paranoia, and possibly worried that the man in the bush jacket might do their president some injury. But Phelan was under control, just. "You don't offend me, Mr. Fisher," he said. "You've been taken in by one fast-talking, persuasive con man, and I approve of your caution in wanting to be sure you're not taken in by another."

As Phelan was leaving the disconsolate McGraw-Hill brass, one of its members looked closely at his bush jacket and asked the purpose of the two brass rings that dangled from its lapels. "Those little rings? Why, that's where I hang my grenades."

Before the day was out, *Life* had declared the Irving manuscript "a hoax." McGraw-Hill, cautious to the bitter end and beyond, issued the following statement:

> As part of our continuing investigation into the Howard Hughes autobiography, McGraw-Hill has discovered [*sic*] additional information concerning a possible source of the material in that book. The new information was provided by James Phelan, an investigative reporter who was a collabo-

rator on a manuscript about Howard Hughes written by Noah Dietrich. We have informed the U.S. Attorney and the New York District Attorney of this new information.

Phelan's commentary was more succinct: "They ought to rename the Hughes autobiography 'Son of *Fake!*' "

There was one disagreeable complication before news of exactly why Irving's manuscript was a hoax could get out. All along there had been a fundamental moral justification for the corporate conduct of the publishers. They had erred on the side of trust. They had shielded an author against problems on what had seemed a difficult assignment, and then, when he was subjected to public vilification and attack, continued to accept his word until they were forced to believe his word was worthless.

They had acted, from an author's point of view, in an honorable fashion. The money expended on the Irving project was a drop in the bucket in relation to McGraw-Hill's over-all expenditures. The company could have chopped it off, without financial remorse, at the first hint of trouble from Rosemont Enterprises. The reason it did not do so was not simply because it dreamed of making huge profits, but because a number of respected people in the organization had come to believe in the project.

By the afternoon of Friday, February 11, they were forced to *disbelieve* in the project. But rather than broadcast the fact that it had been duped, McGraw-Hill made a dismal attempt at suppression. On Saturday morning *Time* magazine was hauled before State Supreme Court Judge Gerald P. Culkin by a strange array of opponents. *Time* planned to explode the whole fantasy by reproducing extracts of the Phelan and Irving manuscripts, side by side. In the plaintiff's corner, strongly resisting any such move, there were Hughes's Rosemont Corporation; Clifford Irving, represented by Maurice Nessen; and the attorney for McGraw-Hill.

Without any apparent discomfiture, McGraw-Hill set out its case for siding with an author who had consistently lied to it for thirteen months, and with a corporation with a virtually unparalleled record of legal censorship. The line-up was compelling to Judge Culkin, who ruled that Time-Life's proposal to publish sections of the Irving material was "violative of their own agreement not to publish any portion of the manuscript until the matter [of its authenticity] is finally determined. . . ."

It was less convincing to Appellate Court Justice Theodore Kupferman, who heard the case in his Manhattan apartment a few hours later. He found in favor of *Time*'s argument that the petition was "a clear case of prior restraint" and gave permission for the magazine to publish up to a thousand words of the spurious magnum opus.

So *Time* had its story on Monday morning, labeled on the front cover: "Con Man of the Year." In revenge, *Newsweek* its chief rival on the newsstands, observed that *Time*'s exposé of *Life*'s gullibility was "as pragmatic as a man discovering his wife *in flagrante* and then selling tickets at the window." But *Time*'s piece had done the job. Irving's manuscript had its public funeral.

By the time everything was over, Phelan had gone four days on four hours' sleep and was punch-drunk from role reversal. He had been interviewed exhaustively by McGraw-Hill, *Time*, the *Los Angeles Times*, *The New York Times*, his hometown newspaper, the *Long Beach Press-Telegram*, the Associated Press, NBC, CBS, ABC, and the federal investigators. En route to collapse into his bed at the Dorset Hotel, he stopped by to see an old friend, Ralph Daigh, vice-president of Fawcett Books.

"You've been shaking up the New York publishing establishment," Daigh told him.

Phelan looked at him, red-eyed and groggy with fatigue. "I've also just coined a brand-new aphorism that is going to sweep the country."

"What's that?" asked Daigh.

"It goes like this, Ralph: 'Honesty is the best policy.' "

As Phelan collapsed, his old collaborator, Noah Dietrich, revived. Over the weekend of the exposé, Dietrich had gone into the hospital for a prostate operation. On Monday he summoned the press to his bedside in the Cedars-Sinai Hospital, Los Angeles, and announced that the news had marvelously speeded his recovery. "I haven't had so much fun since I was seventy-five," he said. It was a euphoric moment, but the basis for the hoax had still not been revealed; no one knew how Irving had got the manuscript, and no one knew who the forger was. There were still a lot of surprises to come.

Howard Hughes, himself, had just experienced one of them. Just as he was beginning to savor the prospect of seeing his upstart biographer finally routed, he received a most unpleasant stab in the back.

# ACT VII

## The Monarch Flees
## His Palace

# Nicaragua, Olé!

"He can run but he can't hide."

Joe Louis, shortly before knocking out
Billy Conn in 1946

On February 14 Howard Hughes became a physical casualty of Clifford Irving's hoax. On that afternoon a group of Bahamian immigration officials arrived on the ninth floor of the Britannia Beach Hotel and demanded entrance to Hughes's sanctuary. They claimed that all they wanted was to make a routine check of the work permits of Americans on Hughes's staff, but they were turned back at the door. Hughes concluded that this was tantamount to harassment, and he decided to leave immediately.

Two days later the immigration officials went back to the Britannia Beach, armed this time with expulsion orders for three members of the staff. They were still uninvited guests, so eventually they broke down the door separating Hughes from the outside world. But, like other mortals, they were not to see the great recluse. Early on the morning of February 16, Howard Hughes slipped out of the hotel and left the Bahamas, his home for fifteen months.

The first hint that all was not well for him in Nassau had come on February 2 when the leader of the Opposition Free National Party (FNP), Cecil Wallace Whitfield, asked a number of Parliamentary questions directly inspired by the controversy over the autobiography in New York. The questions were primarily designed to embarrass the governing Progressive Liberal Party (PLP), but they were also to undermine completely Howard Hughes's own security of tenure on Paradise Island.

Whitfield asked—as was his right under British-inspired parliamentary procedure—what status Hughes had vis-à-vis the Immigration Act of 1967. He also wondered whether the attendants who ministered to him had valid work permits, and if permission had been given by the Immigration Department to any persons to be gainfully employed as bodyguards. Whitfield told the Home Affairs Minister, Arthur Hanna, that he would like the answers within a month.

There was no immediate response from the government or from the Britannia Beach, where Howard Hughes passed his life watching old movies on television or having them specially projected for him by the man hired to keep him in trim, an English physical-culture specialist called Gordon Margulis. His food was specially prepared for him and mostly consumed shortly after midnight. Besides Margulis the bodybuilder, the Hughes entourage included a barber-valet, two doctors, two aircraft pilots, the "Mormon Mafia," secretaries, accountants, and four native Bahamians, hired as guards, who had previously been employed as architect, pilot, businessman, and newspaper cartoonist.

Most of them lived in the hotel, and their presence was not the only thing that distinguished the white stucco structure on Paradise Island, a $2 toll away from the rest of Nassau. There were powerful spotlights, guards, a German shepherd dog on the roof, and a closed-circuit camera designed to deter anyone foolhardy enough to try to intrude. All his servants were people Hughes could trust, so most of them had accompanied him to Nassau from Las Vegas.

There are not many British colonies left, but the Bahamas is one, and until the late 1960s it was run in a colonial manner by a commercially oriented white minority. Nassau, the capital, was famous for the sun in winter and infamous for its complete absence of income taxes all year round. Hughes had tried to buy a large share in the Bahamas in the late 1950s. He wanted leases on some of the islands and control of the airport and telephone company. But the Bahamians wanted to negotiate personally with Hughes, who lost interest shortly after this condition was mentioned.

In the late 1960s, after a succession of financial scandals and the steady growth of black political parties, the whites were defeated in a Parliamentary election. Lynden Pindling became Prime Minister, and the Bahamas finally began to change. Pindling is hardly a rabid exponent of black power, but he represents people who believe that they have been servile for too long. The result is that Nassau is not always a happy place for "whitey"; servility has sometimes been replaced by surliness, and it is possible that Howard Hughes would not have stayed so long at the Britannia Beach if he had ever met the hotel doorman. The credentials of the island's white population are being carefully scrutinized now, and many are being told to go. In the past three years the exodus has been considerable.

Howard Hughes had never bothered about bureaucratic and legal inconveniences like immigration statutes. He had always been able to persuade the state of Nevada to bend its laws a little when he was there, and he had no reason to suppose that he could not also remain aloof from Pindling's immigration act. But he and his advisers had seriously underrated the Bahamian penchant for punctilious application of this law. In Nassau, Howard Hughes could not even claim exemption because of the quantity of his investments. Contrary to all expectations, he had not invested a dime in the Bahamas since his arrival. That removed virtually any incentive the government might have to bend the law a little.

Once Hughes's eccentricity became massively exploited in New York early in February, his attraction to the Bahamians diminished even further. The name of their capital city was becoming exclusively associated with a man whose face was now adorning T-shirts, over the words "Sincerely, H. R. Hughs" (*sic*). The price was $2, and the spelling error was deliberate, possibly as a protection against Edith Irving's copyright, but the intention was enough to bring Rosemont Enterprises into court with another suit trying to prvent the sale of the insulting T-shirts. (The manufacturers' defense was that Rosemont had not shown whether Hughes was alive or not. It did not work.)

But what could Rosemont do about a pornographic movie called *Helga and Howard* that was playing to full houses on 42nd Street? How could it stop people wearing lapel buttons reading, "Is this a genuine Howard Hughes button?" and, "Swiss bankers can't keep secrets"? Paramount Pictures re-released *The Carpetbaggers*, an undistinguished movie at best, but with a theme that was relevant; it was supposed to be about Hughes. Naturally, there were new issues of the three best-known paperback books about Hughes, by Albert Gerber, John Keats, and Omar Garrison. There was also a new book—one whose first draft had already received considerable publicity—by Noah Dietrich and Bob Thomas (with "preliminary research" by James Phelan), called *Howard: The Amazing Mr. Hughes*. Not only was the Irving affair generating a good deal of business; it had totally undermined Hughes's privacy.

Once Hughes had decided to go, Intertel had to decide just *where* he should go. Hughes's irregular movements, and the secrecy in which they were cloaked, were always planned by Intertel, which spirited him away from Las Vegas and into Nassau. It looked around frantically for a new cocoon for Hughes to inhabit. It had to be outside the United States, but not so far away as to make instant and continuous communication difficult. Then James Golden, who had worked for Intertel and now worked full time for Hughes in Las Vegas, remembered that Turner Shelton, the American Ambassador to Nicaragua, had been very helpful when Hughes went to Nassau. Golden called Shelton and asked whether Hughes would be both welcome and secluded in Managua, the Nicaraguan capital. Shelton made inquiries and discovered that Hughes would be received with rapture by the nation's President, no less. So the entourage set course for Managua.

When Hughes slipped out of the Britannia Beach he boarded a yacht anchored just 200 yards away from the hotel in Hurricane Hole, and made for Miami, where he was transferred to a chartered jet and flown to Managua. He learned on his way that there might even be profit in his flight. Intertel told him that the Nicaraguans wanted to buy some aircraft for the national airline, and Hughes happened to have a couple for sale. One was actually carrying his bags from Nassau.

Hughes was followed by an astonishing assortment of goods. The excess-baggage items loaded on board the cargo aircraft in the small hours of February 17 included a stand looking like a blood-plasma carrier, boxes of purified Poland water, a refrigerator, six television sets, boxes of films, a shredder used for destroying documents, pots and pans, office furniture, hundreds of yards of cable, mattresses, and a hospital bed. The cheapness of it all impressed the CBS television producer Don Hewitt, who was staying at the Britannia Beach and first spotted the exodus. There was a cheap-looking vinyl couch, an old electric stove and heater. "It was not rich man's stuff," he commented.

But the departure of so eccentric a rich man was creating shock-waves in Nassau. The Home Department issued a statement saying: "During the course of a routine investigation it has been discovered that several non-Bahamians allegedly employed by Mr. Hughes or organizations connected with him were in the Bahamas without proper immigration status and were escorted out of the Commonwealth by immigration officials." There was some political capital to be made out of the departure. The National Democratic Party charged the Governing PLP and the Opposition FNP with foolishness and stupidity, saying that the Bahamas had passed up millions of dollars' worth of free publicity. But Cecil Wallace Whitfield had first raised the matter because he thought the publicity was of dubious value anyway.

On Paradise Island the management of the Britannia Beach first rose and then fell in the face of the challenge. To begin with, the security director, Fenelon Richards, promised journalists present a guided tour of the Hughes quarters. It was an eagerly anticipated exercise in the bizarre, but the idea was vetoed by Richards' superiors. The hotel confined its public utterances to a statement by Jack Davis, the president of the management company, which was remarkable for its brevity and its grammar. "It is the company's policy not to comment regarding guests of our hotels or any rooms that may have been rented to guests," it said. The company's policy did not prevent reports from appearing two days later that the quarters Hughes occupied had been booked by Frank Sinatra.

On February 18 the citizens of the United States discovered Nicaragua and its capital city, Managua. It was not a nation whose presence had been burned into the American consciousness, and the discovery put a considerable strain on the American embassy in Nicaragua, which was unused to such attention. On the evening of George Washington's birthday, Wesley Stewart, the embassy's public-affairs officer, surfaced at the Intercontinental Hotel, looking quite dazed. He asked for a scotch and soda and explained to reporters that he had been on the telephone for an uninterrupted six hours during the day, taking some forty calls. He did not mind the hours so much, but a radio station in Green Bay, Wisconsin, had pushed him a bit far. They remembered a snatch from an old song about Managua and wondered if Stewart could oblige the listeners by singing it. In the service of his President, Stewart did so, and over the long-distance line floated the lyrics of a rhumba written in 1946 by Albert Gamse and Irving Fields:

Managua, Nicaragua, is a beautiful town.
You buy a hacienda for a few pesos down.
So take a trip, and on a ship
Go sailing away
Across the *agua* to Managua, Nicaragua,
*Olé.*

Hughes's arrival was greeted with a number of *olés* in Managua itself. One radio commentator enthused: "This will really put us on the map. This is as important as Nixon's trip to China."

There was talk of business deals between Hughes and the President, and there were reports of business proposals made by the Nicaraguans to visiting journalists. A cab-driver sidled up to an American reporter and asked, "You want an interview with my sister? She spent the night last night with Howard Hughes." But the journalists concluded that the old routines were the best ones. Instead of the cab-driver's promiscuous sister, they approached the assistant manager of the Intercontinental Hotel, where the Hughes entourage had taken the whole of the eighth floor and part of the seventh, and the following transpired.

REPORTER: "Why don't the elevators stop at the eighth floor?"

MANAGER: "I don't know."

REPORTER: "Is Howard Hughes up there?"

MANAGER: "I don't know."

REPORTER: "I have this letter for Mr. Hughes. Where can I leave it?"

MANAGER: "Just give it to the girl at the front desk. Those people come and pick up their mail every four hours."

REPORTER: "Then Howard Hughes is up there?"

MANAGER: "I don't know."

It may have been Managua, Nicaragua, but it was the same old scenario.

# ACT VIII

## The Jester Loses
## His Bells

# A Call to the Chelsea

Plans are all right sometimes, and sometimes
just stirring things up is right—if you're tough
enough to survive, and keep your eyes open so
you'll see what you want when it comes to
the top.

Dashiell Hammett, *Red Harvest*

After the stake had been driven through the writhing heart of the Irving manuscript, there were only two important whodunits left. One was the identity of the forger who had so brilliantly misled Osborn, Osborn and Osborn. The other was the identity of the man who had given the Phelan/Dietrich manuscript to Clifford Irving.

It was the second question that most seriously exercised Jim Phelan. He already had his short list of suspects and a powerful motivation for finding the culprit. As most of the cast of characters were in New York or expected shortly to attend the grand-jury hearings, Phelan decided to delay his return to the West Coast and stay on in Manhattan. He made one significant addition to his wardrobe—another bush jacket because, as he put it, "I ain't out of the jungle yet."

He also had an important piece of information that he had not aired publicly. It had come out by accident in the session with McGraw-Hill, and Phelan had noted it down on his scratch pad at the time. He had been able to get an occasional look at the passages in Irving's manuscript that were under comparison, but what had struck him on one occasion was a passage just below one being compared. It had a story which he recognized but which was not in his manuscript and which had never been published before. He recognized it because it was in the original *transcript* of his recorded conversations with Noah Dietrich.

The story was about a famous movie star who had given Hughes a fright when she had contracted VD. She had been his close companion not long before, and Hughes, panicking, ordered Dietrich to destroy the whole of his wardrobe. Dietrich thoughtfully took the clothes to a charity instead, and that part of the story had appeared in Phelan's manuscript, although he had omitted the name of the actress on the grounds of taste (she was still alive). Nevertheless, here it was, complete with name, in Irving's book. Phelan noted on his pad: "——— ——— and clap story (in transcript not in book)."

The importance of the note was that it narrowed the range of suspects. Phelan knew that his manuscript could have been leaked to Irving by several people at several times, but the transcript was something else. Up to the end of February 1971, he and he alone had possessed it, and he had guarded it with great care as his basic research material. So far as he knew, there were only four people who might have had access to it between late February and late June, when Irving returned to Ibiza to write (or perhaps edit) his great work. One of the four was himself; another was Noah Dietrich. Phelan knew that Dietrich was not about to donate his "last hurrah" to a hoaxer. So that left two suspects.

On the evening of Tuesday, February 22, 1972, the authors of this book were drinking with Phelan in the bar of the Dorset Hotel, discussing how he could get the number of suspects down to one. There was, of course, one man in town who could solve the whole problem without further investigation—the hoaxer himself.

Phelan thought there was no harm in trying some of the more subtle arts of persuasion on him, so he went up to his room, where he could place a call in private. He dialed the Chelsea Hotel, and we sat down to take notes on the first and only conversation between Jim Phelan and Clifford Irving. Phelan reckoned that the only way to get Irving to talk was to goad him into blowing his cool. The verbal traffic was mostly one-way.

"Hey, Cliff, is that you? Jim here, Jim Phelan. . . .

"Well, I just thought we might have a little talk. After all, we got one helluva lot of things to say to each other. We're the only two guys, Cliff, you know what I mean. You set the whole thing up, and I'm the one who blew it apart. We're the only two guys who can put the whole thing together—the real story. . . .

"What do you mean you don't want to comment? Now, come on, Cliff. Nobody asked you to comment, did they? You sure don't *have* to comment. Sure, sure. . . . I understand, I really do. But I tell you something I'd like to know. Who is calling the shots over there, you or the lawyers? Boy, if you've got the lawyers on top of you, you really have my sympathy. Get the lawyers in, and that's it.

"Cliff, you and I have a lot in common. I mean—no offense, now—I wrote the darn thing and you really used it. . . . Hell, no I'm not the kind of guy to have hard feelings. Why, I've got offers coming at me from all directions. So in a way I'm grateful to you, I really am. There's just one thing I want to find out. Just one. Who was the son of a bitch who stole my material and gave it to you? And you know what, I think I am just one-sixteenth of an inch away from finding him. One-sixteenth. . . . What's that? You'd sure like to help but . . . Jesus H. Christ, Cliff, do I ever understand your position.

"You know how it is. I guess there are three guys who are

responsible for all your problems. Well, first there's Frank McCulloch of *Time* magazine. You know Frank, of course. Well, Frank and I have been friends for years. . . . Yeah. . . . Yeah. . . . He was the guy who wrote up the similarities between my manuscript and yours. . . . You bet, that was really something. And then there's Wallace Turner, the *New York Times* guy. He wired me and Frank together. Uh-uh. Well, you know, Wally is stuck way out there on the West Coast, and Frank's off on some trip to the Caribbean, and that just leaves me, the little old country boy, in town. I had nothing much to do, so I just put in this call.

"Wow, Cliff. Did you hear about how the *Life* copy of your manuscript was returned to McGraw-Hill? . . . No? Well, I'll tell you. I was riding down in the Time-Life elevator, and there was this guy with me who's carrying a large bundle. Well, we get talking and it turns out he is on the legal staff and he is taking your manuscript back to McGraw-Hill. So he invites me to share the *Time* limousine over to McGraw's, and when we get there—I know you'll like this, Cliff—this guy lets me carry the bundle over the McGraw-Hill threshold. . . . You got it in one. I carried the corpse in.

"Jesus, Cliff, what did you do to that woman Beverly Loo? Was she something! I'm down at McGraw's and she's rushing round the corridors saying, 'You are my enemy. You are my enemy.' What did you do to that woman? . . . What's that? Why, sure as hell I met Stewart. He was right across the table from me at High Noon. . . . You wish that you had been there? . . . I just bet you do, Cliff. What would you have done, acted as umpire?

"It's a funny old world, Cliff. I have a friend who always says there are only fourteen hundred people in the world and all of them know each other. Did you know that back in the fifties I lived in Majorca for a while—wife, family, a maid . . . What's that? . . . Expensive? . . . No, I put the whole thing together for a hundred and five bucks a month. We were a pretty cultured community, too. . . . Yeah. You got it again, nobody would be seen without his beret on.

"Cliff, we really got a lot to talk about. I'm going to be in town for a couple more days and hell, why don't we just get together, have a few drinks . . . what . . . lawyers . . . grand jury. . . . I guess you're right, Cliff, that sounds like a real tough schedule you have there. . . . Yeah, when it's all over.

"Yeah . . . I can hear . . . you got the children with you right now. I sure hope I didn't make a mistake in calling you. Nice talking to you too, Cliff.

"Hey, before you go. I have to tell you there's one thing that strikes me as really ironic about the whole situation. I mean here's the li'l ol' country boy going the rounds of all those sophisticated Manhattan cocktail parties and there's you, Cliff, with no action except talking to lawyers and doing the baby-sitting. . . . Yeah. . . . Real nice talking to you. Good luck, Cliff."

When he hung up, Phelan said, "I really wasn't trying to rub salt into him. I was trying to gig him until he lost control and blew. But it didn't work. Cliff is a *very* controlled guy."

As it happened, Phelan did not need Irving's assistance. On the very next day, Wednesday, February 23, one of his last two suspects quietly selected himself before the federal grand jury. His name was Stanley Meyer.

# With Friends like This...

Let every eye negotiate for itself
And trust no agent.

William Shakespeare, *Much Ado About Nothing*

Stanley Meyer had been a suspect for some two weeks before his appearance at Foley Square. But to inquisitive press men he had told the same story. It was true, he said, that he had had access to Phelan's manuscript. It was also true that he was an old friend of Clifford Irving's and that he had met Irving again in the summer of 1971. But it was categorically *not* true that he had given Irving any of Phelan's or Dietrich's material.

Mr. Meyer was lying. In fact, as he told the grand jury under oath, he had given Clifford Irving the first draft of Dietrich's memoirs. But even this did not indicate the full extent of his services to the hoax.

It would, of course, have been disastrous for the progress of Irving's enterprise if Dietrich's memoirs had been published before Irving could mobilize McGraw-Hill behind his project. An enterprising editor at McGraw-Hill would certainly have noticed on reading Dietrich's work that many of those dazzling inside anecdotes could have had a source other than Irving's conversations with Howard Hughes.

Three basic things were necessary for the over-all success of the Irving enterprise.

1) An assurance that Dietrich's memoirs would not be published until *after* Irving's book came out.

2) The disruption of Dietrich's collaboration with Jim Phelan, after the first draft of the memoirs had been written.

3) The passage of Phelan's material over to Clifford Irving without Phelan's or Dietrich's knowledge.

Stanley Meyer was instrumental in making all these things happen. Although the mustard seed of the hoax was the semi-public conflict between Robert Maheu and Chester Davis in Las Vegas back in November 1970—this provided Irving with the Hughes handwriting samples on which to construct his forgeries—the seed would never have taken root without the secret garden prepared by Meyer. He started on its cultivation, almost by accident, at the very time that the Las Vegas power struggle was reaching its noisy climax.

At that time, Stanley Meyer's personal situation was desperate. Although his public circumstances contained no hint of real poverty, Meyer—known to some of his acquaintances as "one of the last of the big-time spenders"—was running out of funds. He had a reputation for generosity around Hollywood, and it was important to him. He was fifty-four years old and was one of those fringe personalities, on first-name terms with the Hollywood barony, who had never seemed able to find a continuing niche for his own talents. A wheeler-dealer whose deals kept coming unstuck.

He had married well—the daughter of Nate Blumberg, the former boss of Universal Pictures—and was himself the son of a highly respected Twentieth Century–Fox labor-relations chief. But Meyer's own business career had been erratic; he assaulted the commanding heights of the motion-picture industry but never quite made it up the incline. In the late 1940s he put in a bid to take over the theater side of Hughes's RKO operation. The deal fell through. A few years later he became involved with Louis B. Mayer, the dying lion, in a proxy fight to take over M-G-M. The proxy fight failed. For a time during the late 1950s Meyer achieved a modest eminence as Jack Webb's partner in promoting the successful television series *Dragnet*. But it was not enough to stanch the slow hemorrhage of his cash.

Throughout all his vicissitudes, however, Meyer maintained a buoyant image as a party-giver and bringer-together of "interesting people." His beautiful home in the San Fernando valley, Four Oaks, which had been inherited from Nate Blumberg, was the normal arena for these gatherings. One of the interesting people he met and introduced around Hollywood back in the early 1960s was a struggling young novelist called Clifford Irving. Meyer was genuinely fond of Irving and generous to him; when Irving's son Josh fell ill, Meyer paid the hospital bill. But in November 1970 thoughts of Clifford Irving appear to have been remote from his mind. Meyer had more pressing concerns. The major one was the question of his involuntary bankruptcy action.

On November 16, 1970, the United States District Court, Central District of California, opened file number 82967 at the federal courthouse in Los Angeles. It made a depressing commentary on the big spender's financial state, which he had been forced to reveal by a demand for payment on two promissory notes totaling $52,000. Meyer's status report showed that his most substantial asset was Four Oaks, its grounds and effects. This showpiece was valued at around $1,700,000, but it had been mortgaged up to the hilt. The borrowing had started back in 1966. (Meyer had even borrowed on a trust fund set up for the benefit of his four children.) He insisted that he was not bankrupt but claimed that he needed "more time" to pay on the promissory notes. His position, in short, was highly illiquid.

The shadow of this bankruptcy action was to hang over him for a full year before it was finally cleared. It is charitable to bear this in mind when examining his maneuvers in relation to Dietrich's memoirs. For they can be justified only as the actions of a desperate man.

They started in October 1970, when Meyer renewed an old acquaintance with Noah Dietrich, whom he had first met when vainly trying to take over the RKO theater operation, and who was now living in retirement in Beverly Hills, less than ten miles from Meyer's home. On this occasion Meyer asked Dietrich whether he could give him some advice, as he had a problem of refinancing on his house. Dietrich recalled that he was unable to be of much help beyond referring Meyer to a good bank, and that the conversation swung around to his own area of personal enthusiasm—progress on his book about his relations with Howard Hughes. It was coming slowly, but Dietrich had high hopes for its success. At this Meyer became extremely interested and ostensibly helpful. He told Dietrich that he had some good contacts in the publishing world who might be able to promote such a property on a grand scale. Dietrich was intrigued.

Meyer then went away and consulted another friend of his, the bestselling author Irving Wallace, who also lived in Los Angeles. Wallace suggested the name of Paul Gitlin, his own agent in New York. Gitlin, of Ernst, Cane, Berner and Gitlin, is a lawyer with a track record as a "big property" agent dealing in six- and sometimes seven-figure advances. Apart from Wallace, he also handled Harold Robbins, whose book *The Carpetbaggers* was a thinly disguised fictionalization of Howard Hughes's life. Meyer, who also knew Gitlin slightly, responded to the suggestion and passed it back to Dietrich. Dietrich was delighted. He envisioned profits in the millions from his book, and Gitlin was precisely the man to rustle them up from the publishing world.

Meyer then sent, on Dietrich's behalf, some of the material that was rolling off Phelan's typewriter to Gitlin in New York. A message from Gitlin came back on October 29, saying he had taken "a quick look" at the material and found it "quite impressive"; he would be coming out to the West Coast shortly, and they should all meet to discuss it.

This summit conference took place over lunch at the Century Plaza Hotel on November 16, with Noah Dietrich,

Jim Phelan, Paul Gitlin, and Stanley Meyer assembled together. It was a confused but euphoric occasion, and none of
the other guests picked up the slightest hint that Meyer was
facing a bankruptcy action that very day. Had they done so,
Meyer might not have been assigned such a pivotal role in
the "merchandising" of the book.

Over lunch a peculiar strategy was evolved. Phelan would
write the chapters and give them to Dietrich for correction.
Dietrich would pass them on to Meyer, who in turn would
send them on to Gitlin in New York. Meyer's anomalous
position was called that of the "referral agent." Gitlin was
to be the full agent, charged with prying a large advance out
of a publisher.

Phelan was not entirely happy with this strategy. "I remembered thinking at the time that there seemed to be too
many big egos congregated around one little book and wondering what the hell Stanley Meyer's function was." But his
basic concern was the method of delivery. Like most authors,
he was reluctant to have parts of his opus flashed around before
he had an opportunity to impart a final polish to the whole.
But Dietrich seemed happy to have Gitlin "on the team," so
in the interests of a quiet life Phelan went along with this
odd mode of delivery. It was Phelan's first and biggest mistake.

Meyer, however, seemed to take his "referral agent" role
very seriously. He even imparted some cogent literary criticism on the first chapters. In a letter to Noah Dietrich on
November 23 he wrote: "After viewing the three chapters,
extra notes and material, I think your over-all story is great,
and Jim is doing a fine job. The 'Spruce Goose' chapter was
marvelous, the 'Liquor Smuggling' fascinating and the
'Nixon' one fine, but in need of a rewrite. Now, a few con-
structive words. . . ."

The letter then outlined a nine-point plan for improving
the structure and pace of the book. The suggestions were
eminently sensible, and the conclusion was suitably defer-

ential. "Please accept this advice in the spirit it is intended, and that is to be helpful in making your 'Last Hurrah' a tremendously commercial success." Dietrich passed a copy of the letter on to Phelan with a note: "Jim—Stanley's qualifications may be subject to question but he is trying to be helpful and had been acting as a sort of intermediary with Gitlin."

What surprised Phelan was the quality of the criticism. Over lunch Meyer had not displayed any latent literary talent. Phelan was even more surprised when, fifteen months later, he found out that the criticism had in fact been written by Irving Wallace, whom Meyer had consulted and whose comments Meyer had passed on as his own without Wallace's knowledge. It was a small but significant fact.

The big one came on the same day, November 23. That morning Meyer took the three chapters that had apparently so impressed him around to the office of Gregson Bautzer on Wilshire Boulevard. Bautzer was the last man in the world that anyone hoping to see Dietrich's "Last Hurrah" get into print would consult. He had personally negotiated the "no book" contract with Dietrich back in 1959 and still had Howard Hughes as his wealthiest client.

There was no precedent for Bautzer acting as midwife at the birth of any book about Hughes. He was rather, a literary abortionist, and from Bautzer's viewpoint, there was no better candidate for suppression than Noah Dietrich's memoirs. Meyer knew Bautzer's background quite well. The only way Bautzer could make, in the words of Meyer's letter of that day, "a tremendously commercial success" out of Dietrich's book would be by getting Hughes to buy Dietrich off.

Few words were spoken on this occasion, nor were they necessary. As Bautzer recalled it, Meyer came in and laid a folder on his desk with the remark, "I think this might interest you, Greg."

Bautzer had a quick look at its contents. He remembers that his reaction was deliberately muted. "I just kind of grunted. I thought it best to adopt the position advocated in the Chinese proverb: If you don't open your mouth the flies can't get in." He did not ask any questions. But, said Bautzer, "that was maybe because I did not want to turn up the answers. I just kind of assumed that Meyer was acting on Dietrich's behalf."

The assumption was incorrect. Neither Dietrich nor Phelan had any inkling that their "referral agent" had just referred their work into the Hughes secrecy machine.

Although Bautzer's reaction was muted, it did not appear to disappoint Meyer. He went on his way, leaving the three chapters of Phelan's manuscript. (On February 4, 1971, he came around again and deposited another bundle of chapters with Bautzer. Again, Bautzer remembers himself as "continuing to adopt the Chinese position." Again the referral was made without Dietrich's and Phelan's knowledge.)

As a result of this mime in November, Meyer ensured the first basic ingredient of success for Irving's as yet unborn hoax. The raw material for the book now stood a fair chance of running into difficulties with Hughes's lawyers before publication, giving Irving time to fictionalize it.

The second ingredient—disruption of the Phelan-Dietrich relationship—was not long delayed.

Around Christmas 1970, Dietrich started to receive negative feedback on the quality of Phelan's work from both Meyer and Gitlin. The warmth of their initial reaction to Phelan's prose had apparently died, but they seemed still eager to make a success of the memoirs. In January both advised Dietrich that a new writer should be sought out after Phelan had finished his draft. As coincidence would have it, this was the very month that Irving started making his initial connections with McGraw-Hill. Some time was to pass, however, before the two slimy dramas met and enriched each other.

The idea of delivering Dietrich's manuscript chapter by chapter to New York had been originally imposed by Dietrich's desire to interest publishers at the earliest possible stage, but Gitlin did not make any move in this direction for some weeks. On January 29, Dietrich called him in New York and instructed him to submit some chapters to a publisher, but there was a division of opinion. Gitlin, who by this time had only nine chapters, argued against submitting them to a publisher, as he felt the material was not yet strong enough and should be reworked by a new writer.

Dietrich was insistent. Gitlin then promptly submitted a few sample chapters to Michael Korda, an editor at Simon and Schuster, that same afternoon. They came back four days later, having failed to excite Korda. He was not much interested in the subject matter and could not understand Gitlin's enthusiasm for it. Korda later recalled, "Gitlin was very keen on it and saw it as a really big book." But that was the end of the episode as far as Korda and Simon and Schuster were concerned.

The message that Dietrich got back, however, through his "referral agent," was that Simon and Schuster was keen on the project but not keen on Phelan. Dietrich, who had once been greatly delighted by these earlier chapters, then moved into the Meyer-Gitlin "consensus" about the need for another writer.

On February 24, Phelan came to New York with another batch of eighteen chapters and the transcript of his original conversations with Dietrich. By this time he had caught some worrying intimations of weird moves going on behind his back and was anxious to have a "second opinion." He had an appointment with the editors of *Look*, who had expressed an interest in the basic material. Before going around to *Look*, however, he checked in with Gitlin, who turned out to be adamant that Phelan should not show anything to them. "He became incoherent at the notion *Look* should have even a peek at the work in progress," Phelan recalls. "His negative ardor astonished me."

Phelan canceled his appointment at *Look* and went instead to see Gitlin. His recollection of the meeting is precise. Gitlin told him that they had a "good chance" of success with Simon and Schuster and did not want any deal "blown" by approaches to other parties. He also thought that it would help greatly if Michael Korda could be shown the whole range of material, including the tape transcript. He stressed the need for a rewrite, by Phelan, on completion of the first draft. And he sympathized with Phelan's difficulties with Dietrich, who, Gitlin fully understood, was not the easiest man to work with.

Phelan agreed to the necessity for a rewrite but was reluctant to part with the transcript. He pointed out that it was his "property" and the only transcript of the tapes in existence (Dietrich had the original tapes, and it had taken a stenographer, paid for by Phelan, three months to transcribe). Phelan did not want to let it out of his hands while so much uncertainty hung over the project. Gitlin, however, was insistent on its importance in negotiations with Simon and Schuster (which were, of course, nonexistent at that stage) and clinched his argument with the assurance, "I wouldn't screw you, Jim."

"Well, Paul," said Phelan, "I hope you don't try, because I'm a hard man to screw." He then handed over the transcript. Both men, at that point, had made a big mistake: Phelan in the short term, Gitlin in the long.

Gitlin, on receipt of the transcript, made two copies of it. He kept one for his own file and sent the other to Stanley Meyer, possibly the one man in America Phelan most wanted to keep away from his "property." Meyer acknowledged recept of the transcript of Phelan's tapes from Gitlin on March 15, 1971.

After his conference with Gitlin, Phelan wrote a long memorandum to Dietrich. He offered to revise the first draft, which was now near completion, within ninety days, and made a few observations about the difficulties he was experiencing:

> I need to be freed of the present hovering cloud of uncertainty about my position as the writer on this project. I cannot work properly while clandestine efforts or proposals are being made to remove me as the writer. I have a great deal of faith in this

project, as well as confidence that I can produce a good manuscript. I also, needless to say, have a much larger investment (in terms of time and finance) in the project than any other single person.

One further thing. I have never understood the role of Stanley Meyer in this project, nor the necessity of the present Rube Goldberg device of having me write a chapter, having it edited by you, typed without my even reading it, and then turned over to Meyer for transmittal to Gitlin. I am quite capable of seeing that the manuscript, when in acceptable form, gets to Gitlin without the intervention of Stanley Meyer.

Paul Gitlin gave the following explanation of his motives to one of the authors of this book: "How I obtained the transcript is not material. I obtained it to protect Mr. Dietrich. I was acting in his interest as he, not Mr. Phelan, was my client. Of course, the physical paper was his [Phelan's] property, but the material on it belonged to my client Mr. Dietrich. This is the legal position." Gitlin returned "the physical paper" to Phelan early in March. He sent the transcript to Stanley Meyer, since, Gitlin understood, he was conducting the search for another author and gathering all the material together on behalf of his client, Mr. Dietrich.

The ramifications of that hopeful "summit conference" at the Century Plaza four months earlier had by now a Byzantine complexity. Before going further into the maze, we should perhaps take stock. This was the situation of the four parties in late March 1970.

*Noah Dietrich:* Thought Gitlin was close to clinching a big deal with Simon and Schuster. Was awaiting the final chapters from Phelan before giving him his marching orders and, he hoped, drafting a new writer recommended by Gitlin. He did not know that Gitlin had sent Phelan's transcript to Meyer.

*Jim Phelan:* Thought that he had Gitlin's sympathetic understanding, that a deal with Simon and Schuster was in the offing and he would be invited to rewrite the material before publication. He thought his transcript was being used to whip up the publishers' interest. He did not know that Meyer had a copy, preparatory to turning it and his other material over to a new writer.

*Paul Gitlin:* Knew that Dietrich was preparing to discharge Phelan, that there was no agreement in the offing with Simon and Schuster, and that Phelan and Dietrich did not realize the coolness of the publishing house toward their project. It is difficult to say precisely what Mr. Gitlin thought.

*Stanley Meyer:* Also knew that Dietrich was preparing to dump Phelan. Knew that a lot of interesting material was coming his way. Knew that the Hughes secrecy machine had been kept well posted. It is possible that Mr. Meyer was too confused by this time to be able to think anything.

There is perhaps only one thread that can be established in this crazy quilt: the producers were experiencing a failure of communication with the agents.

In April the situation clarified itself a little. On April 7, Phelan took the final chapter of his draft to Noah Dietrich and received in exchange his written notice to quit, dated April 6. Phelan calls it the "Dear John letter." It informed him that Dietrich, acting on Gitlin's advice, deemed the manuscript "unpublishable." Phelan penned his reply the next day:

> Other than some confusing and highly contradictory statements from Gitlin regarding Simon and Schuster, I have no knowledge that *any* publisher has seen even one chapter of the manuscript.
>
> The fact that Gitlin and I agreed that the manuscript's first draft could be improved by revision does not—for God's sake—mean that the manuscript is unpublishable. Almost all books are revised before publication; many are completely rewritten, often two or three times.
>
> Even the flat rejection of a manuscript by one, four, seven, or even twelve publishers does not mean a manuscript is unpublishable.

Phelan also noted: "Five publishing houses besides Simon and Schuster had conveyed to me a lively interest in examining my manuscript." None of them had been approached.

A few days later, on April 13, Phelan tried to find out exactly what had happened with the transcript he had loaned to Paul Gitlin. "It has been more than six weeks," he wrote to Gitlin, "since I turned over to you my transcript of the Dietrich tapes, at your request, so that you could make a copy of it and submit such copy, along with the major portion of the first draft of my manuscript, to Mike Korda of Simon and Schuster." He went on to ask the outcome of that submission, the names of any other persons or publishers who had been given access to it, and the whereabouts of any copies made. With hindsight, it is clear that everyone would have been saved a lot of trouble had Gitlin given a clear and precise answer to these questions. But Gitlin chose not to reply to the letter. Mr. Gitlin, when asked about this letter by us, recalled, "It was a peremptory letter, and I had no obligation to Mr. Phelan, so I did not reply. This was ethical procedure."

The ethics of the situation, however, were by now rather difficult to discern. Phelan, in the process of negotiating suitable severance terms for his work with Dietrich, was at the same time eager to establish just how far negotiations had advanced with Simon and Schuster. When he called the publishing firm, editors had some difficulty in remembering that any project associated with Noah Dietrich had ever been submitted. But eventually they found a trace of its rejection two months earlier. Phelan passed this information on to Noah Dietrich, and it was news to him. Apparently, Gitlin had not improved his process of communication with his client. Phelan, who by this time saw no reason to burnish Gitlin's reputation, pointed out to Dietrich, "If Gitlin is prepared to screw me, he might also screw you."

In May there was a general parting of the ways. Dietrich, on one hand, negotiated settlement terms with Phelan for his work—$40,000 against royalties should the book come out on being rewritten by another writer (the agreement was signed on June 18)—and on the other hand, Dietrich disengaged with Gitlin. The circumstances of the second parting were less clear-cut and were later the subject of conflicting accounts by both sides.

Dietrich's account is as follows. After experiencing some mild confusion in getting various pieces of manuscript, memos, and other material back from Gitlin, he sent a stockbroker friend in New York around to Gitlin's office with an authorization to collect them. The stockbroker did so and sent the material on to Dietrich on the West Coast. Some weeks later Dietrich was leafing through it and found that it did not contain the transcript of the tapes, although he knew that Gitlin had made a copy of it from Phelan's original. So he called Gitlin and asked him where the transcript was. Gitlin said he had sent it to Stanley Meyer, at Meyer's specific request. Dietrich then called Meyer, who claimed he had no recollection of receiving a transcript. At this point Dietrich threatened to issue suit against Meyer if Meyer did not find the transcript somewhere, somehow.

Meyer "found" it the next day. It had apparently come in a delivery of mail that had lain unopened around his place. (It appears to have slipped his memory that in March he had acknowledged receipt of a transcript to Gitlin.)

The account Gitlin gave us of his disengagement from Dietrich is more than marginally different. He agreed on the date the stockbroker came to pick up Dietrich's stuff—May 26. But he remembers no complications in the parting. He says he put his copy of the tape transcript in with the rest of the material, and that was the end of it. He asserts, categorically, that there was no call from Dietrich asking for the transcript.

Despite the contradictions in these accounts, one thing is clear: Stanley Meyer, by early June, was in the catbird seat. Dietrich was bereft of both agent and author, but he still had Meyer to turn to as a potential recruiter of a rewrite man. And despite the contretemps over the transcript, Meyer was still ostensibly his ever-helpful self.

However, Meyer did not tell Dietrich anything about his next effort in recruitment. Having, accidentally it appears, helped to supply the first two ingredients of Irving's hoax—putting Hughes's lawyers on red alert, and fouling up the Dietrich-Phelan collaboration—he was about to supply the third and most essential ingredient of all: the transfer of Phelan's material to Clifford Irving. Again, it happened as a result of one of those coincidences that keep recurring with distressing frequency.

The story, as outlined later to a friend by Meyer himself, began and ended on June 12, which was, it will be recalled, the day on which Clifford Irving and Richard Suskind allegedly met and received an organic prune from Howard Hughes in Palm Springs, California. It was very hot in southern California on that day, and Meyer decided to take his children out of town to see their grandmother, Mrs. Blumberg. It was a longish drive, about two and a half hours, and everybody was hot and a bit sweaty by the time they arrived at Mrs. Blumberg's place in Cathedral City, near Palm Springs. When they got there, Meyer recalled, he found "Mother" Blumberg playing cards near the swimming pool with an old friend, Mrs. B.B. Hamilburg. Meyer wanted to get right into the pool with the children to cool off, but before he dived in Mrs. Hamilburg called across to him, saying, "Have *I* got a surprise for *you*, Stanley."

Mrs. Hamilburg then went off and about forty-five minutes later, just as Meyer was getting out of the pool, returned with her nephew, Clifford Irving, whom Meyer had not seen for many years. "Cliff, how are you?" said Meyer. "What are you writing these days?" Then, before Irving could answer, he tumbled out his own proposition. "I've got an idea for you. How would you like to rewrite, do a polish or a rewrite on a book Noah Dietrich has written on Howard Hughes?" He went on to tell Irving a little of the background circumstances.

Irving listened sympathetically but declined the offer. "I can't," he said, "because I have a four-book contract with

McGraw-Hill and I'm already working on a book about the four richest men in the United States, four billionaires, Howard Hughes, Richard Mellon, H.L. Hunt, and Paul Getty." Meyer tried to dissuade him, saying that the other billionaires were dull and only Hughes was interesting. But Irving was adamant. He could not help with the rewrite. Naturally, Meyer claimed, he had not shown any of Phelan's work to Irving. It was not the sort of thing he would take with him on a family outing to a relative's. And that, according to him, was the extent of his contact with Clifford Irving that summer.

But it was not, quite. Before the grand jury, Meyer told the same story about June 12, but with one significant addition. The casual setting of the poolside was the same, so was the pitch of the conversation, but now, it appeared, Irving had said that, although he could not do the rewrite job, he would like to take a look at Phelan's material. Shortly after, Irving and Richard Suskind went to Meyer's place in Encino, where they picked up Phelan's material, took it back to their hotel in Beverly Hills, and Xeroxed two copies before returning it to Meyer two days later. The copies, Irving and Meyer stated before the grand jury, were taken without Meyer's knowledge or permission.

Needless to say, at the time, Meyer told neither version of this coincidental meeting with Clifford Irving to Noah Dietrich. What Clifford Irving did with the material on Howard Hughes which he had received from Meyer is now history, but back in the summer of 1971 Meyer had not exhausted his omnidirectional helpfulness—to Dietrich, to Irving, and to Bautzer, all parties with highly conflicting interests.

Meyer did eventually recruit a new writer for Dietrich: Bob Thomas, the Associated Press Hollywood correspondent, who had written some twenty books, most of them about Hollywood figures. On June 30, Meyer brought Thomas and Dietrich together, and a fruitful relationship developed. Thomas read through Phelan's manuscript and transcript over the next week and was thrilled by its contents. "It was a bit disorganized," said Thomas later, "but I remembered saying to my wife, at the first reading, 'This is a million-dollar property.' "

Thomas went to work with a will, and since practically all the basic research had already been done, he produced copy fast. By the end of August he had effectively finished the first draft. Both he and Dietrich were delighted with it, and Thomas was grateful to Meyer for bringing them together. Sometime in September, Thomas donated a copy of his draft manuscript to Stanley Meyer, and he too appeared to share their enthusiasm.

On October 10, Meyer, without Dietrich's or Thomas's knowledge, paid another visit to the Wilshire Boulevard office of Gregson Bautzer with another bulging folder under his arm. He deposited the Thomas draft of the Dietrich memoirs with Hughes's personal lawyer. Bautzer's recollection of this visit is the same as his recollection of the earlier ones. He continued to adopt "the Chinese position," continued to assume erroneously that Meyer was somehow acting as Dietrich's agent in these deliveries, and continued to stockpile the material he had, as he put it, "been spoon-fed by Stanley." He insists that no money was paid to Meyer for his unsolicited services. If there was no pecuniary interest, there could, of course, be only one of two explanations for Meyer's dealings with Bautzer. He was just randomly playing the role of secret literary agent, or he was trying to get publication of the Thomas manuscript, like the Phelan one before it, stopped.

As it happened, it was strongly in Clifford Irving's interest, at this point in time, to see that the Thomas-Dietrich book was delayed. October was a delicate month in the progress of his hoax. He was putting pressure on McGraw-Hill for an early announcement of his book and in Zurich, on October 19, Mrs. Irving was just completing the discreet transfer of $266,000 from the H.R. Hughes account in the Swiss Credit

Bank to an account of her own. Early publication of Dietrich's book would have blown the whole thing.

Publication was indeed delayed, but not, initially, through the intervention of Hughes's lawyers. They were prepared to pounce when a publishing house actually signed a contract for the book, but not before. Luck was on Irving's side. For three crucial months the Dietrich memoirs had difficulty in locating a publisher; one of the reasons—apparent with hindsight—being that it was offered to some publishing houses that had corporate links with Dell and *Life,* and they, of course, were not in the market for a Hughes book, with the "authentic autobiography" in the pipeline.

Dietrich was deeply baffled by the difficulty of shifting his work. At one point, he rang his old collaborator Jim Phelan with the lament, "Hell, Jim, this guy Thomas is no better at writing a book than you are." Phelan, in retrospect, treasures the remark as "the ultimate compliment."

In November, Meyer experienced a happy change of circumstances. He paid off the $52,000 on the two promissory notes, and the bankruptcy proceeding was finally wound up on November 16, a year to the day after it had been initiated.

But the problems of his role in the publishing business still appeared to weigh on Meyer's mind. In mid-December, shortly after McGraw-Hill had announced their plans for the Hughes autobiography, he called his friend Irving Wallace and said a funny thing had happened; he had just heard from their old acquaintance Clifford Irving, who was now so big in the news. Wallace, naturally interested, inquired about the circumstances. Meyer told him the story of his meeting with Irving at Palm Springs back in June (the innocent version, of course), and read over the letter he had received from Clifford Irving. It was dated December 6, the day before McGraw-Hill's announcement, and came from Golden Beach, Florida.

Wallace took a note of the letter, which was cast in the form of an apology for having to mislead Mr. Meyer. Irving wrote that he was sorry that he had had to be so mysterious at their June meeting, but Meyer would soon realize that it was because he was engaged in a top-secret project with Howard Hughes. Irving assured Meyer that the material they had discussed at their summer meeting was not new to him, and concluded his letter with a request for Meyer's help in trying to fix up film rights for the book. Irving said that he had control of the book's dramatic rights and a 50-per-cent financial participation in them.

Wallace was highly intrigued by this communication. It aroused his first major suspicions about the authenticity of Irving's claims. He could not, for the life of him, imagine Howard Hughes giving away 50-per-cent rights on his life story to Clifford Irving. If there was one thing Hughes could claim it was connections with the most powerful figures in the movie industry. He did not need Clifford Irving and Stanley Meyer to hustle his film rights.

Wallace, however, did not doubt Meyer. He specifically asked whether that part of the letter which mentioned material under discussion between Irving and Meyer had involved Meyer showing Jim Phelan's work to Clifford Irving. Recalling Meyer's answer later, Wallace said, "Stanley said absolutely not, he swore to it."

While Meyer was buttressing his credibility with Irving Wallace, it was being chipped away in an entirely different area. After the public McGraw-Hill announcement, Dietrich, like Jim Phelan, became convinced that Hughes had written his autobiography. And for very much the same reason. Both assumed it was Hughes's way of pre-empting Dietrich's revelations.

On December 12, while Phelan was still making the rounds of his Hughes contacts in Las Vegas, he was surprised to find out that Perry Lieber, Hughes's hotel and casino PR man, had actually read some of his draft manuscript. Up to that point, he had no idea that anyone in the Hughes organization had seen it. On checking back, he found out that the source in the Hughes organization had been Gregson Bautzer. Phelan remembers thinking, "How the hell did *he* get his hands on it?"

He gave Dietrich this tidbit of information, and Dietrich hit the roof. He phoned Bautzer and two days later, on December 14, was informed by Hughes's lawyer of Meyer's contacts with him.

Still, neither Dietrich nor Phelan made the connection between Meyer's conduct and the Irving book. Neither of them knew that Meyer had any acquaintance with Clifford Irving.

Meanwhile, progress on publishing Dietrich's book was still slow. Nobody, of course, was going to pay big money for the property while the Hughes revelations were publicly in the offing. But the situation changed when the credibility gap in Irving's story started to open up. In mid-January, just after the Hughes telephone press conference, Dietrich obtained a good offer. Phelan actually made the initial connection with Ralph Daigh, head of Fawcett Books. Within days a contract was nailed down on the basis of a $65,000 advance —$40,000 for the book and $25,000 for serialization in *True* magazine. Fawcett received the ritual call from Hughes's lawyers requesting it not to publish as such a book would be in breach of Dietrich's contract with Howard Hughes. But by this stage their hearts did not seem to be in the suppression game; they were still desperately trying to shoot down the Hughes "autobiography." Ralph Daigh informed the Hughesmen that he was going ahead with the book. Rosemont fell back and regrouped around a new tactic—an action to attach all Noah Dietrich's royalties and Fawcett's profits.

The news that Fawcett planned to publish before March the Thomas version of Dietrich's memoirs with, as the Foreword put it, "preliminary research by James Phelan," had a peculiar effect on Stanley Meyer's activities. Anyone who knew, or had any inkling, that there might be a connection between the Dietrich and Irving oeuvres might well be expected to exhibit odd symptoms. Meyer reacted in the first week in February by broadcasting the "innocent story" of his meeting with Irving among friends and acquaintances—one of them was Bob Thomas. He received this version, and the contents of the December 6 letter that had been shown to Irving Wallace six weeks earlier. With hindsight, it seems clear that Meyer was trying to establish the "innocent version" on the public record before the bad news broke about the possible origins of Irving's book. Thomas was rather surprised that Meyer had not mentioned such an intriguing incident earlier in their relationship, but no more than that. He, like Phelan, still did not perceive any connection between his work for Dietrich and the forthcoming autobiography.

Then, on February 11, the wire services carried the news that Jim Phelan had made the connection and that, as a result, *Life* had branded Irving's book as "a hoax." Every journalist involved in the story suddenly became very interested in the history of the Dietrich memoirs, trying to find out at what stage and by what mechanism it had been subsumed into the Irving hoax.

The names of Stanley Meyer and Paul Gitlin in connection with the drama surfaced into public print for the first time. Phelan, who was tied up with *Time*'s "Con Man of the Year" issue, threw out some clues, but had no time to go into the full background. He told *The New York Times:* "I'm not pointing the finger at anybody. It passed through my hands, through Stanley Meyer's hands, through Noah's hands, and through Paul Gitlin's hands." Gitlin was quoted as saying some remarkable things, bearing in mind his complex role in the affair. On February 13 *The New York Times* carried a story in which Gitlin alleged that Phelan had showed the manuscript to the editors of *Look* before it went out of business. Asked whether Phelan might have shown it to other magazines as well, Gitlin was quoted as replying, "He probably did. He's that kind of guy." Since Phelan had not shown his manuscript to *Look* or any other magazine on Gitlin's express instructions, Phelan was intrigued by Gitlin's apparent readiness to accuse him of bad faith. He began to feel that his low opinion of Gitlin might still be too high.

Stanley Meyer was slower in getting his observations on the record. When on the evening of Friday, February 11, journalists started to ask him for comments on the connection between the two manuscripts, he fended off all inquiries with a series of "no comments." He then called Bob Thomas for advice: the journalists were making his life a misery; what should he do? Thomas made the obvious point that, in a situation like the one that had developed, a "no comment" from Stanley Meyer aroused rather than allayed suspicion. Speaking as a friend rather than a reporter, Thomas advised him to tell the true story. Thomas, at that time, of course, thought the true story was the one Meyer had privately conveyed to him a week earlier.

Meyer proceeded to answer all further press inquiries with the innocuous version of his poolside meeting with Clifford Irving. The calls started to taper off, and a few days later he rang Thomas with a thank you. "That was great advice you gave me, Bob. I told the truth and feel much better for it."

But the "truth" that emerged was so puzzling that for several days most investigators on the story did not know what to do with it. The initial problem presented to investigators by Meyer's "true story" was that it was such obvious salami that it was difficult to know where to start slicing it up. The other problem was then compounded by Meyer's sudden unavailability. From Tuesday, February 15, onward he seemed to be permanently en route to the grand-jury hearing in New York. It was perhaps as well, for the public was spared any further elaborations of his story. But for journalists trying to clear up a few obvious discrepancies it was a trying period. "How the hell is that guy coming across this country," one New York journalist asked a colleague. "By wagon train?"

Nobody, of course, was waiting more impatiently for Meyer's advent in New York than Jim Phelan. He had an arrangement with *The New York Times,* which had undertaken to check around all the main New York hotels every day for the arrival of a Mr. S. Meyer from Encino, California. Once they had tracked him down, the deal was that Phelan and a *Times* reporter would go along for the interview that would clinch the whole story.

In the interim, Phelan was making what checks he could without Meyer's assistance. During this period he found out for the first time from Simon and Schuster that Gitlin had not shown the tape transcript to the publishing house. On hearing this, he decided that it was high time he renewed acquaintance with Paul Gitlin. On Thursday, February 17, Phelan called Gitlin, and Gitlin told him why he had obtained the transcript "to protect Dietrich's interests" and furnish raw material to a new writer. "Well," said Phelan, "I'm glad you told me that, Paul, because I've just found out you were lying to me. But I'd like to get this clear. Your alibi for not giving the transcript to Irving was that you were simply double-crossing me and drafting in a new writer."

Gitlin felt that was a harsh way of construing his activities on behalf of Dietrich's book. Phelan then suggested that he, accompanied by a *New York Times* reporter, should come around the next morning and get Gitlin's story absolutely straight, for the public record. Gitlin felt this was a rather extreme thing to do. He had a better idea. Phelan should come around for a private talk in which just the two of them could clear up any "misunderstandings."

Phelan consented to those terms and arrived at Gitlin's office the following morning. He was ushered into his library alone and was greeted by Gitlin plus a colleague. Phelan saw this as yet another breach of faith by Gitlin and, thoroughly exasperated, refused the offer of Gitlin's hand with the comment, "What's that?"

"Well, Jim," replied Gitlin," if you can't shake my hand, I don't see what we can have in common."

Phelan exploded. "Listen, Paul, you had better believe we have nothing in common."

They had nothing further to discuss.

Locating Stanley Meyer proved an insuperable problem. Somehow or other he eluded all his journalistic pursuers in New York and managed to slip into the grand-jury hearing on February 23, unnoticed, with his new true story. It came out only as a "leak" from the grand jury a few days later that Meyer had admitted to passing Phelan's material to Clifford Irving, albeit unwittingly.

With nothing further to detain him in New York, Phelan returned to the West Coast to continue his pursuit of Stanley Meyer. But Meyer was always "out" to Mr. Phelan and indeed to all journalists. Phelan did, however, have some interesting conversations with Meyer's friends and acquaintances. One of them was Irving Wallace, whom Phelan had written a profile of two years before and with whom he got along well.

They had an interesting session comparing notes on their recollections of Stanley Meyer's year. At one point in the discussion, for example, Wallace asked Phelan whether he could recall his *own* comments on the early sections of the Dietrich manuscript. Phelan, who had always been suspicious of the critical talent revealed by Meyer back in November 1970, leafed out the relevant letter. As Wallace began to read his own comments from his own file, Phelan joined in with a rendition of Meyer's letter. They had a word-for-word duet, *a capella*.

The revelation that Meyer had passed on his own comments in this way was very upsetting to Irving Wallace. But then, it had been an upsetting year for many of Stanley Meyer's friends.

# Bargaining Collectively

"If you can't give me your word of honor,
will you give me your promise?"

Samuel Goldwyn

The identity of the forger was the only serious missing link in the investigation of the crime. It had always seemed likely that he was a confederate of the Irvings in Ibiza. The obvious candidate was, of course, Irving's folk hero in *Fake!*, Elmyr de Hory, and as every detective from Father Brown to Hercule Poirot knows, it is a great mistake to dismiss a suspect simply because he is the first one you thought of.

*Time* magazine had made a good joke of the forger's identity on the cover of its February 21 issue, with its strap line reading "Con Man of the Year" and a portrait of Clifford Irving by Elmyr de Hory, forger of fine paintings, hero of *Fake!* by Clifford Irving, and—the unmistakable message went—forger of the Irving-Hughes correspondence. The evidence against him was circumstantial, admittedly, but it was also overwhelming.

For a long time the Swiss police confided that de Hory came at the top of their list of suspects, and the Ibizan police were asked for every scrap of evidence concerning him. For dozens of journalists, unable actually to pin anything on him, it was a case of guilty until proved innocent. All of which distressed Elmyr very considerably, because he knew he wasn't guilty.

The very suggestion that he should be hand in glove with that *monster* Clifford Irving was enough to make Elmyr quite *weak* with anger. He despised him. He distrusted him. He was owed money by him. According to de Hory, the deal that Irving and he had made when they collaborated on *Fake!* was that any proceeds would be split fifty-fifty within fifteen days of their receipt. So far he had received nothing.

"I needed money to buy food to eat," says de Hory dramatically. "But all I got from Irving was a letter in which he wrote: 'If I met you and you were crying from hunger I would not give you a dime.' My lawyers wrote to Irving and told him: 'You are not the United States tax collector—you haven't the right to collect everything everybody has.' All that happened was that Irving presented me with a list of expenses he said he had incurred on the book, and after he had made all his deductions all that was left was $3000."

So the accusations that de Hory had collaborated with Irving a second time were doubly distasteful. "I ask you!" he exclaimed. "Would I be likely to take part in such an operation of forging documents for a man who had proved himself untrustworthy? The whole thing is ridiculous. And furthermore I don't need the money [now]. I have plenty! It's really the ultimate insult that I should be associated in this way with a man whom I despise more than anyone in the world apart from Fernand Legros!" (Legros is the art dealer with whom de Hory quarreled violently toward the end of their association in the art-forgery market.)

But nobody paid any attention. For weeks de Hory's life was a constant flow of telephone calls and visits from reporters of varying nationalities, all armed with trick questions designed to make him slip up and reveal his complicity. They simply would not listen to the piece of evidence which de Hory regarded as his trump card. He had a perfect alibi, a "star witness."

For the last three years, de Hory's constant companion has been a twenty-three-year-old American named Mark Forgey. (It is, in the circumstances, perhaps an unfortunate name.) Mark was able to verify that de Hory could not have indulged in forgery without his knowing. "One can't live with someone twenty-four hours a day and not know *anything*," points out de Hory. Referring to Mark's role in giving him an alibi, he said: "Mark is my Nina Van Pallandt." It is a role which Mark confirmed whenever he was asked about the forgeries. "If Elmyr had done anything like that," he said, "I would have been the first to know."

And so, in a way, he was. Clifford Irving had issued public statements as soon as the names of Robert Kirsch, the *Los Angeles Times* book reviewer, and John Meier, the Senatorial candidate from New Mexico, were associated with his plot, denying the involvement of either in the strongest terms. But about Elmyr, Irving said not a word.

Clifford Irving's omission helped concentrate de Hory's mind when he was questioned about the identity of the forger: if it wasn't he, who was it, then? He asked for copies of the forged letters, addressed them with an artist's eye, and quickly pointed out one or two things that had not been in the report submitted by the handwriting experts at Osborn, Osborn and Osborn to McGraw-Hill. He noted, for instance, that they showed one unusual characteristic. Some of them looked as though they had been written hesitantly, rather than with the confident, flowing action of genuine handwriting.

Who was it? Well, said de Hory, he knew one thing: Clifford Irving was adept at borrowing other people's talents. His guess was that the forger was Clifford Irving.

But no one believed him because they thought he was simply trying to divert attention from himself. Early in March the questions from the world's press had still not abated. As he finished talking to one reporter, the phone rang. It was *Paris-Match* announcing that it wanted to come and see him immediately. "Tell them I'm too tired," he said, full of self-pity, "and that I have to receive my *piqueur*."

So everyone *thought* he knew who it was, but no one had the evidence to satisfy a court. Still, that should surely not be difficult. The forgeries were of such a high quality that only a master could have done them. One of the Osborn family, Paul, was lyrical about the quality of the work which had misled himself, his brother, and his father. "The forgeries were of a startlingly excellent nature, done by a professional who must have practiced and practiced," he commented after the Osborns' rebuttal of their original report had been submitted to McGraw-Hill. He described the nine-page letter written to Harold McGraw, dated November 17, as unique. "This office has never seen or heard of such a document. I hope one day they discover who the artist is. I'd love to know where his artistry came from, and how he practiced for this."

Another handwriting expert was trying to satisfy Paul Osborn's curiosity. The problem had been passed by the postal inspectors to Robert Cabanne in their New York Crime laboratory. The Post Office prides itself on the quality of its handwriting analysis, and Cabanne was the most experienced man in the New York bureau. He had been doing the work for twenty years, and he demonstrated the essential qualities of patience and observation that had taken him to the top of his trade.

His brief was simple. The federal investigators asked him: "First: do we have a forgery? Second: do we have a forger?" The first question might have seemed redundant to anyone outside the legal process, but the attorneys wanted evidence. Cabanne's colleagues assembled the largest single collection of Howard Hughes's handwriting outside his own closed files. It had been subpoenaed from Las Vegas, Los Angeles, and the Defense Department in Washington, and brought to

New York to be laid out on a table next to the thirteen separate examples of Hughes's handwriting in the possession of McGraw-Hill. "It was unusual," remembers Cabanne, "to have so much handwriting that was suspected." Perhaps it was because he had such a multiplicity of specimens, but it did not take Cabanne as long as it had taken the Osborns to conclude that the Hughes-Irving correspondence was faked.

But there was the second question. The only clue he had was the handwriting specimens unwillingly conceded by both Clifford and Edith Irving to the grand jury on February 8. He had nothing at all from Elmyr. Demanding the Irvings' handwriting specimens had seemed like a long shot at the time. Of course, Edith had forged at least one check endorsement, but that did not mean she had forged the whole correspondence. As for Clifford Irving, it seemed to be an act of simple cussedness to demand a sample from him. He was a writer, not a forger.

The attorneys were shrewder than they knew, because Cabanne became immediately interested in the personal idiosyncrasies of Clifford Irving's handwriting. There was a dot over the i, for instance, which faded off to the right and looked, under microscopic examination, like a v placed on its side. That was also present in the letters and checks signed Howard or H. R. Hughes received by the publishers of his autobiography. Moreover, there were no similarities between Edith Irving's handwriting sample and the forged letters. After five days' work, Cabanne reached the astonishing conclusion that Clifford Irving was not only the editor of Howard Hughes's autobiography; but the forger of his correspondence and of two of his check endorsements too. It was such a startling conclusion that no one outside the government guessed it. Elmyr de Hory remained the uncontested number-one suspect long after Robert Cabanne had completed his work, for his conclusion remained a tight secret; the only clue to it was the total lack of interest by the District Attorney in de Hory's whereabouts. Everyone else whose name had been whispered in the same conversation as the Irvings' had been asked to come before the grand jury, but not Elmyr.

Robert Morvillo and James Tigue did not bother to seek him out during their trip to see their Swiss colleagues, a trip that had been slightly marred by the linguistic incompatibility between Peter Veleff, the Zurich prosecutor, and Morvillo. But the differences between them went deeper than that. In New York the extraordinary volume of crime makes justice a negotiable commodity. There is so much pressure on the courts that prosecutors are permitted to recommend a lower sentence, sometimes to a lesser crime, to a man who will plead guilty—leaving the courts free for other jury trials, and often aiding the prosecutor by supplying information about the crime. The process is called plea bargaining, and it is uncommon in Europe. Indeed, many European prosecutors, who work under immeasurably less pressure than New York district and prosecuting attorneys, have a well-developed dislike of the whole process. In Switzerland, Morvillo had suggested to Veleff that some arrangement might be discussed which would exchange a confession from Clifford Irving for a partial amnesty for Edith Irving. That proposal was one of the reasons Morvillo had gone to Zurich in the first place, but the negotiations were necessarily more delicate than they would have been in another North American city, and they broke down because, on February 14, the New York *Daily News* carried a headline saying: SWISS OK DEAL FOR IRVING'S WIFE. The Swiss were appalled. To admit that they had even discussed the matter was embarrassing; to suggest that they had made a settlement was a catastrophe. Veleff answered with an angry public statement in which he said, "We're justice authorities, not merchants."

The delicacy of the Swiss did not stop the bargaining process from continuing in New York. It merely changed the negotiating positions of both sides, and whichever way it was considered, the bargaining strength of the Irvings was diminishing each day. Shortly after his return to New York Tigue called Nessen to Foley Square and said casually, "Maury, we know who the forger is."

The news got worse on February 15 (already a bad day, since Nina Van Pallandt and Anne Baxter had been telling the grand juries what a liar Clifford Irving was). That morning the Swiss, instead of sending a message of clemency to Edith, sent a diplomatic messenger with a demand for her immediate extradition. That afternoon a warrant was sworn for her arrest, and Edith agreed to surrender the following morning. She told reporters who clamored around her for a statement, "So far nothing has been said that is frightening. You know, I'm a fatalist. Every ending is, in a way, happy."

The next day, Edith was released on a personal bond of $250,000. It was an enormous sum, though of course she did not have to pay the money in court. It was the thought that counted, since escape was not a practical proposition. As Maurice Nessen pointed out, "The Swiss government have every assurance Mrs. Irving won't leave the jurisdiction of the court. Indeed, she can't even leave her hotel without a group of newspapermen following her wherever she goes."

The bargaining process was forcing the case to its climax now; as time went by, and more witnesses were drawn into the grand-jury investigation, there was less left for the Irvings to confess. But events in the world outside Foley Square were preventing the public, which had followed the case so loyally for six or seven weeks, from savoring the approach of its denouement. When Stanley Meyer arrived to give evidence, President Nixon was walking along the Great Wall of China, and the appearance of Robert Maheu and his son Peter, for example, coincided with the President's return from Shanghai.

By then Clifford Irving had already decided to tell all; he was only holding out for the best terms. Nessen became more like a union leader than a trial lawyer, and spent hours negotiating for his three members with Morvillo, Tigue, and finally Seymour. In the end, Nessen had to tell the Irvings that the only way Edith might escape the vigorous chase that had been mounted by the Swiss was for her to plead guilty in New York to the crimes she had committed in Switzerland. There were Swiss laws that prevented a person from being charged twice for the same offense, and Nessen believed her case was covered by them. The other thing that would help, of course, was to return the money to McGraw-Hill, and the Irvings agreed to that as well.

On March 3 the confessions began to pour out when Clifford Irving spent three hours with Morvillo and Tigue; two days later Edith Irving did the same thing. Their private appearances were satisfactory enough for the prosecutors to bring them before the grand jury as witnesses. There was no question of their pleading the Fifth Amendment this time. Suddenly they were admitting that the life they had lived for a year had been a fantasy; the lies were being confessed, the punishment considered. Deceptions were being exposed, and, along with them, the Irvings—without their glamour and panache. But good fortune had not entirely deserted them.

Their first appearances before the grand juries were on March 6. Clifford went before the federal jury, and both Edith and Richard Suskind answered questions from the state grand jury. The next day the schedules were reversed. But it was all being done in undignified haste. Their confessions were being taken at face value and placed straight into the indictment because Morvillo and Tigue were also coming under pressure. The Justice Department in Washington, and Seymour's office itself, were receiving a growing volume of correspondence from anxious citizens who were not amused by the antics of the Irvings. They noted angrily that New York had a serious law-and-order problem, and that a three-quarter-of-a-million-dollar fraud against McGraw-Hill was hardly the worst of it. They demanded that the time be more usefully spent, and neither Hogan nor Seymour was inclined to deny the argument. They told their criminal divisions to get the indictments out just as quickly as possible. That was very quickly indeed. Court appearances were scheduled only thirty-six hours after Clifford Irving's appearance before the state grand jury. The last witnesses went before the federal jury less than an hour before the indictments were handed down. The juries heard and looked at Baroness Nina Van Pallandt for one last time, and only heard from David Maness of *Life*—the very last of about a hundred witnesses.

While the federal jurors were hearing them, the state grand jury was indicting the defendants in an avalanche of legal language on fourteen criminal counts in the case of *The People of the State of New York* vs. *Clifford Irving, Edith Irving, and Richard Suskind.*

Twelve of the counts accused the defendant Clifford Irving, aided and abetted by the defendants Edith Irving and Richard Suskind, of Criminal Possession of a Forged Instrument in the Second Degree. Each letter and forged check was listed, and each time the defendants were accused of "knowing the same to be forged and with intent to defraud, deceive and injure another, uttering a falsely made and completely written instrument, the same being and purporting to be and calculated to become an instrument which did and may evidence, create, transfer and otherwise effect a legal right, interest and obligation."

The fifth count "further accused the said defendants of the crime of Grand Larceny in the Second Degree committed as follows: "The said defendants in the County of New York, from, on or about March 12, 1971, to December 2, 1971, stole certain property owned by McGraw-Hill, Inc., having an aggregate value of $750,000, to wit, checks."

The fourteenth, and last, count of the comprehensive state indictment charged the Irvings and Suskind of the crime of Conspiracy in the Third Degree. There were two further counts of Perjury in the Second Degree against Irving and Suskind based on the demonstrable falsehoods in their affidavits. Having digested that, the three defendants went to hear the second installment of the charges against them at the federal court, in the courtroom of Judge John Cannella. It was, linguistically, at least, less of an ordeal.

In the case of *The United States of America* vs. *Clifford and Edith Irving* the indictment charged two counts of mail fraud. Richard Suskind was named as a co-conspirator but not charged, despite the fact that the indictment observed quite specifically that Suskind had posted the nine-page letter which Harold McGraw had received on November 22. Irving was bailed on his own bond of $100,000; Edith was already on bail; and Suskind, in county court, had given his word that he would not run away. They were given a long weekend to decide how to plead.

On Monday, March 13, Federal Judge John Cannella's spacious, paneled courtroom was appreciably more crowded than usual; twenty minutes before the start, the illustrators for the television news programs, whose presence invests any legal occasion with importance, were already in their seats. The clerks came in, chattering, like orchestral instruments being tuned before a concert, and it was not immediately easy to register that the man and woman sitting in the front row were not a married couple mildly interested in the course of justice, but Clifford and Edith Irving, whose interest in the proceedings was very keen indeed.

They sat, silent and puffy-eyed, looking as though the party was over and had ended only a few hours earlier. Journalists left them alone at last and crowded instead around Maurice Nessen, who appeared to be enjoying the affair rather more than his clients. In the front row there was a class of sixth-grade students about to get a dubious lesson in citizenship.

When Judge Cannella swept in, Clifford Irving stood up and buttoned his jacket as though he were being introduced to his elders. He was asked to come forward and with a slightly overdeliberate appearance of deference followed Edith into the pit in front of the judge's rostrum.

Judge Cannella is no magisterial symbol of the law, rather

a chatty pillar of it. "I was driving in down East River Drive this morning, listening to the radio, and they were saying that the defendants here are going to plead guilty. I was wondering whether I should bother to come here at all. You don't seem to need me," he began cheerfully. He then asked Irving whether the reports were true.

"My client pleads guilty on the first count of this indictment, also Mrs. Irving," said Nessen.

The judge then explained that he must satisfy himself that the defendants fully understood the meaning of their plea. Cannella agreed that everybody and his brother knew what the charges were; all the same, he had to ask Irving what he had done wrong. "It was that I conspired to convince the McGraw-Hill Book Company that I was in communication with Howard Hughes when, in fact, I was not," Irving confessed. Then the judge began a rapid examination: How old? forty-one; education? Cornell; ever taken drugs? no; good health? yes; did he know the scope of the punishment? yes, Irving replied diffidently, looking over at Nessen, who prompted him to reply that the maximum was five years and $10,000 on each count.

Then Judge Cannella turned to the prosecutor, Robert Morvillo, and asked him if he had anything to add to what he had already said on television. "The record should reflect that we have made two commitments to the Irvings," Morvillo replied in a monotone. "We have committed ourselves to calling to your attention the defendants' cooperation, and also calling to your attention discussions we have had with the Swiss government with regard to Mrs. Irving's status."

The judge then asked Irving if there were any other promises. "Yes," replied Irving smartly, "that I will be allowed to plead guilty on the first count and that the government will dismiss the second count on a motion." There was a flurry of embarrassed lawyers telling Irving to shut up, and the judge said he would ignore what Irving had said, the import of which was that the possible penalty he might face had been halved since he was pleading guilty on one, not two, counts, after private negotiation.

John Tigue then explained to the judge that Irving had confessed orally to the forgeries, and that his confession had been backed by independent handwriting testimony. Irving admitted to writing all the letters and two of the three check endorsements. At this Judge Cannella said that he had heard enough and concluded that Irving had acted voluntarily, and he formally allowed Irving to plead guilty.

Then Nessen leaped urgently to his feet. "About probation: both sides have agreed that the maximum of ninety days for the preparation of a report should apply in this case."

"OK," said the judge and asked the clerk to give him a date for sentencing in ninety days' time. The clerk dutifully announced May 19, and Nessen and Morvillo nodded automatically, until a strangled cry issued from Clifford Irving. "That's only sixty days," he said in the voice of a writer whose deadline has suddenly had thirty days chopped off it. The date was finally set for June 16, 1972, by which time the Probation Department would have prepared reports on the characters of the defendants.

Next the judge turned to Edith Irving. How old? thirty-six; OK, we don't need the Youth Correction Act. Edith didn't look especially pleased at that, refused an interpreter, confirmed that her health was good and that she never took drugs. She explained that her crime had been to travel with forged documents, to open bank accounts with forged documents, to have known that it was all a hoax, and to have realized that hoaxing people was wrong. Judge Cannella concluded that she too was acting voluntarily, accepted her plea, and adjourned his court. The Irvings left for another court, and so did the spectators, well pleased at having observed a civilized and amusing legal exercise.

The three walked out of the courtroom into the unnatural glare of the television lights. They suffered some momentary discomfort from the jostling cameramen, but it was going to happen only once more—on June 16, when they were sentenced. There would be no interminable days of trial in which their plot was picked apart piece by piece. But the privacy of the Irvings' conspiracy was not preserved. Paragraph 6 of the federal indictment contained seventy-six subparagraphs revealing all the significant episodes of the hoax; a five-page description of the conspiracy in the state indictment described its conception. Posterity was not going to have to rely solely on Clifford Irving's book for an intimate account of the hoax.

# How They Did It

But if he does really think that there is no distinction between virtue and vice, why, Sir, when he leaves our houses let us count our spoons.

Samuel Johnson, July 14, 1763

Clifford Irving is fond of using metaphors to describe the way his mind works. "A lightbulb has exploded in my head," he writes, or, "some wheels are beginning to turn in my brain," as if his decisions were sparked off not by a rational process of thought, but by the sudden impulse of some alien mechanism. Like most of his explanations, it is a bit too complicated. But it would certainly be true to say that he is more disposed to the quick flash of inspiration than to the diligent pursuit of logic.

The idea of perpetrating a hoax was not a difficult one for him to accept. For one thing, the dividing line between right and wrong, between exaggeration and plain lying, had always been somewhat blurred as far as he was concerned, and he had crisscrossed it often during his life; for another, the Elmyr de Hory affair had taught him that fraud is far easier than one might believe, provided it is carried out with sufficient panache and on a suitably grandiose scale.

When news about Howard Hughes in Las Vegas reached Ibiza in early December 1970, the lightbulb began to glow gently, and the wheels to revolve in a mind that was already well disposed to grasp the possibilities. Irving was embarking on the busiest year of his life, and it was to end with an announcement that he had pulled off something that better writers had tried and failed to do. The year is described in outline in the federal and state indictments. There are gaps and small errors in them, partly because they were drawn up so hurriedly that the confessions could not be completely checked. But they are an excellent record of an active year, and they begin to explain the most intriguing question of the whole affair: how the Irvings thought they would get away with their prodigious hoax.

The newspapers are usually at least a day late by the time they reach Ibiza airport, and the American magazines take even longer to arrive. It was not until the middle of December 1970 that it even became clear that Howard Hughes had left Las Vegas for Nassau. But by this time Irving had had two important thoughts. The first was not unique: A book about Hughes that contained enough inside information to solve the mystery would make money. The second idea was also pretty common: The chances of getting that information were negligible. From here to a third, more unusual, not to say delicate concept—the manufacture of an authorized biography—was a mere pirouette from reality to fantasy for a mind as agile as that of Clifford Irving.

On December 21, when *Newsweek* ran an extended article on Howard Hughes's departure from Las Vegas and the machinations within his empire that lay behind it, carrying with it a tiny, four-by-three-inch reproduction of the last page of a letter signed by Hughes himself, it gave Irving that extra dimension which his idea needed to become real. Elmyr had also taught him that confidence is the forger's best friend and that a flowing hand will conceal the occasional error far better than a slavish attention to detail, so he never

worried about his own ability to imitate Hughes's handwriting.

But there was another consideration. To be convincing,
the biography would need to contain a wealth of information
on Hughes's background, his past life, his ideas and outlook.
Irving had no idea how good the sources were on Hughes,
but he realized that it would take a lot of tenacious research
to dig up sufficient material and to write it into a form that
would begin to interest a publisher. That kind of work did
not appeal to him, and, even if it did, it was probably too
much for one man. He needed a researcher. Irving joined
the Christmas shoppers on the plane to Palma.

Richard Suskind was a receptive listener. He was interested
in serious money and a big book, and the way Irving described it, the plan sounded fun, too. He would be required
to do the kind of work he was used to—searching out the
facts—and he would receive a generous 25 per cent of the
proceeds.

They sat down together and began to work out the snags.
The most obvious was: What if Hughes came out and denied
that the biography was authorized? But it was still not clear
where Hughes was, or what condition he was in. He had not
been seen in public for fifteen years and no longer communi-
cated with anyone outside his tiny clique; it seemed probable
that he was incapacitated, perhaps even dead, all of which
suggested that he would be unlikely to denounce the book
personally. A denial from any of his lieutenants would also
be suspect, since the Vegas incident had demonstrated that
nobody really knew who was speaking for Hughes and who
wasn't. But the first things to do were to test the market and
to get to work copying Hughes's handwriting. Early in January Irving sent off his first letter to Beverly Loo.

At this stage neither Irving nor Suskind had thought the
hoax out any further, but there was one problem that had to
be catered for immediately. McGraw-Hill would pay an
enormous sum for the property if it was convinced that it

was authorized, but it would expect most of the money to go to Hughes himself. Even if the publishers could be persuaded to hand it all over to Irving so he could give it to Hughes, he would have to make sure no one knew where it went. The first place they thought of for absolute secrecy was, of course, Switzerland, and since neither of them could speak German well enough to remain unobtrusive, they had to find someone who did, and who could be trusted. Naturally they turned to Edith, and she agreed to help. From that moment they were vulnerable to detection. Their story could not withstand the revelation that H. R. Hughes was a woman called Helga. Bob Peloquin of Intertel, who first learned of the sex of Swiss Credit's client insists: "If they could have found a man to go instead of a woman, it wouldn't have mattered, even if he'd been a dwarf." Analysis of Howard Hughes's physical condition is rarely influenced by facts, but no one has yet suggested a change of sex.

On January 30, when Irving sent his second letter to Beverly Loo, announcing that Hughes had shown interest in a biography written by him, it was not a risky commitment. One of the early joys of the plot was Hughes's reputation for unreliability. If, at any stage, things looked like going wrong, or the hoaxers began to get cold feet, they could pull out by simply announcing that Hughes had called the book off. The plan was beginning ridiculously risk-free.

Late in January, Irving began to work on the forged Hughes letters. He was still using the tiny reproduction in *Newsweek* as his basic inspiration. It was small, but he was sure that it was enough. It contained the Hughes signature, and that was the most important thing of all. He had to write three letters to show to McGraw-Hill, and the wording of them was as important as the writing. He had by now read Albert Gerber's book, *Bashful Billionaire,* and that gave him enough authentic Howard Hughes material to copy.

Irving decided early that his "Hughes" would have to travel. It would be far too risky for him to hang around the

Britannia Beach Hotel in Nassau, for weeks, maybe, attracting the attention of the palace guard, so an itinerary was mapped out which would have the added advantage of producing hotel bills and plane tickets to show that Irving had been in the right places at the right times. But again, no final commitment had been made.

On February 10 Irving took the first serious plunge, when he walked into the offices of McGraw-Hill to see if he had sufficient *chutzpah* to put the whole idea over to a set of hard-nosed publishers. One of the things working for Irving was, of course, the relative softness of the noses at McGraw-Hill. The first hurdle was cleared with such ease that Irving felt able to add the first little elaboration of the many he was to invent later to add conviction to his story. He invited Beverly Loo around with him to see if Howard Hughes had kept his word and sent him the plane ticket for their first rendezvous. He pretended to be as surprised and delighted as she was to find it waiting for him at the offices of American Express, where he had himself ordered it a few hours before.

But Irving was not prepared merely to sit in a hotel room pretending to talk to Howard Hughes for the sake of a verisimilitude which he considered unnecessary. If he was going to have to travel around he might as well mix business with pleasure. He decided that neither of his co-conspirators needed to know that, instead of pretending to see Howard Hughes, he was advancing his relationship with Nina Van Pallandt. He had taken the precaution of asking her whether she would like to go to the Bahamas with him. Now he suggested they might go instead to Mexico. He was sure that he could rely on her discretion. . . .

When, on February 17, Irving returned to McGraw-Hill, he was approaching the point of no return: money was going to be discussed and contracts were to be drawn up. He sensed the kind of money involved. Half a million dollars would make the whole thing worth the risk, and anything much below that might raise suspicions. Everyone knew that

Howard Hughes liked making money, and Irving was able to insist that Hughes was certainly not willing to make an exception for his biography. On March 2 Irving checked into the El San Juan Hotel, San Juan, and once again forged Hughes's signature, this time on the bottom of the contract.

It was a skilled job, not only because he was by now fairly well practiced, but because on arriving in New York he had discovered an infinitely superior model from which to work. *Life* magazine's issue of January 22 had contained a full-color reproduction of the entire "Dear Chester and Bill" letter, and, as he read it, Irving realized how desperately amateurish his own forgeries had been. They might convince the McGraw-Hill executives to whom he had shown them, but they were not good enough for experts. If the letters were subjected to any outside test they would be laughed out of court. Irving simply began all over again and produced a new and superior version of the letters. Even these, he was to conclude at a later stage, were inadequate; eventually he produced yet a further set, which was the one which convinced Messrs. Osborn, Osborn and Osborn.

The hoax received another jolt on March 23, when the contract was finally executed. The major installments due to Hughes, McGraw-Hill insisted, would have to be made out *in Hughes's name.* It was standard procedure. The stipulation was undoubtedly a setback, but it was not entirely unexpected and by no means disastrous. Provided checks were made out to a person of indeterminate sex they could still be collected by Edith and lie undetected in a Swiss bank. Irving had already taken the precaution of signing his first three letters from Hughes "H. R. Hughes" with this thought in mind, although he had no reason to believe that Hughes had ever used this form. (In fact, he did so at least once to sign documents at a Senate hearing.)

After three months the hoax was not only intact, it appeared to be growing stronger every day, and the confidence of the master mind was burgeoning. He decided that the time had come for Richard Suskind to get down to work.

On April 13 Suskind came to New York and set to work at the Public Library, where, in the imposing reading room of that institution, he began sifting through the available documents. They were probably less helpful, however, than the books he read—the only three which have managed to slip past the Hughes censors: John Keats's *Biography of Howard Hughes, Howard Hughes in Las Vegas* by Omar Garrison, and, of course, Alfred Gerber's *Bashful Billionaire,* which they had already consulted. They provided an invaluable skeleton of information, and they were backed by the articles, both scurrilous and laudatory, which every magazine from *Esquire* to *Fortune* has carried at regular intervals over the years.

Meanwhile, Irving was engaged on the more glamorous part of the operation: meeting Ralph Graves and discussing the publication of excerpts from the biography in *Life,* and receiving from McGraw-Hill the first real fruits of the enterprise, a check for $97,500, all of it made out to him, the biggest installment on the advance he had been given until then. Half of this first $100,000 was intended for Howard Hughes himself. (Later, of course, it would be made out directly to H. R. Hughes.) Two days later Irving went through the motions of transmitting the money to Hughes by buying check no. 016561 made out for $50,000 and payable to "H. R. Hughes" from the Bankers Trust Company of New York. But instead of dispatching it to the Britannia Beach Hotel, he kept it in his own wallet. Next day, April 16, he joined Suskind.

Irving's first plunge into research was at the Library of Congress in Washington, a vast neoclassical building across from the Capitol, which contains, among many other things, an exhaustive collection of political records. Irving went to one of the alcoves off the main reading room and asked if he could see the records of Howard Hughes's appearance before the 1947 Senate subcommittee. The assistant informed him that he would have to obtain a pass, but there would be no problem about that. It would not, however, be possible for him to take the volume he required out of the library. Only members of Congress, the press, other libraries, and, by an ancient ruling, members of the clergy, were allowed that privilege. If he had known about that, Irving would probably have gone into the library wearing a dog-collar, but as it was, he was faced with a difficult decision.

To copy the 1500 pages of the volume he needed would take at least two weeks, and he simply could not afford to wait that long. But to read it in the library and take notes was far too laborious for him. That was Suskind's job. He spent the first day taking notes, working out how easy it would be to smuggle the volume out. He returned next morning, wearing an overcoat. The same assistant showed him into the documents room, and, after waiting a respectable time, Irving slipped the 2½-inch-thick volume under his coat and walked past the guard at the door. A minor case of larceny had now been added to the growing list of crimes perpetrated by the hoaxers.

Irving spent one more day in Washington, doing a tiresome round of government reference libraries, including those of the Atomic Energy Commission, the Civil Aeronautics Board, and the Defense Department, picking up a few official references to Hughes's dealings with the government, and then returned to New York, where he was able to witness yet another firm step toward total acceptance—the signing of the contract between McGraw-Hill and *Life*. Once again he impressed on all concerned the importance of preserving absolute secrecy. More meetings with Hughes were scheduled, but the old man would be certain to throw the whole thing over if he thought for one moment that there might be a breach of security, or that his movements were being checked. Irving was able to note that everyone involved appeared to accept this without reserve. There were still no obvious flaws.

His next move, however, would have proved fatal if he had carried it through. On April 3 he had written to the Hughes Medical Institute in Miami, Florida, on headed paper bearing the name of William Heinemann, Irving's London publishers. He had taken the precaution of "borrowing" a batch last time he had visited their offices, and it now served a useful purpose. The message he had typed out read:

> To whom it may concern:
> This letter will introduce *Mr. Clifford Irving,* one of our most distinguished authors.
> Mr. Irving has been commissioned by us to write a book, as well as a series of articles for The London *Sunday Times,* on the subject of American Medical Foundations: their origins, activities, and links with American business organisations.
> We would deeply appreciate any help that you may be able to afford him in his research. Thank you very much.

The signature at the bottom, that of Mr. Dwye Evans, Heinemann's chairman, was a very poor forgery, done from memory, but no one, Irving reasoned, was going to check up on that. (Nor did anyone check with the *Sunday Times,* which had not commissioned Irving to write about medical foundations, or anything else, not even Howard Hughes.) Having dispatched the letter, he telephoned Kenneth Wright at the institute and fixed an appointment for lunch on April 27.

But at the last moment he decided not to go and sent a cable canceling the meeting. He may have reasoned that a visit to the Institute would be too close an approach to the Hughes organization for comfort. Word might reach the Hughes entourage and they would be alerted. It was the nearest either Irving or Suskind got to seeing any of the Hughes employees.

Instead, he went to Nassau with Edith. There is no record of Irving's using his stay there to pay a visit to the Britannia Beach Hotel, but it would seem unlikely that he did not at least go to gaze upward at the ninth floor and wonder what the man behind the shutters was really like. The Irvings stayed at the Montagu Beach Hotel, where he pretended to carry out another series of extended interviews.

In his affidavit nine months later Irving referred jokingly to the fact that because of them Edith was forced to spend many an evening doing the rounds of the local nightclubs and even had to spend a night on the beach. But there are no reports extant of a lone female patrolling the streets and beaches of Nassau around this time.

Richard Suskind was more profitably employed. He was in Las Vegas, and though he was keeping well away from any channels that might lead back to Hughes himself, he had lunch with a senior official of the Atomic Energy Commission (from whom he got absolutely nothing), visited the County Assessor's office (where he took notes from twenty-six cards listing Hughes's properties in Las Vegas), and the cuttings library of the *Las Vegas Sun* for a detailed rundown on Hughes's gambling interests. There was also a ready availability in the town of back numbers of the *Nevada Post,* which had reproduced many of Hughes's handwritten memoranda to Robert Maheu. They were part of the "fallout" of Hughesiana after the explosive power struggle in Vegas back in December 1970.

Next he went to Hughes's home town, Houston, and visited the public library—another gold mine. The Texas Room at Houston Library not only contains an extensive scrapbook with cuttings about the activities of Hughes, but is stacked with social directories, out-of-town newspapers, pictures of the young Hughes, and details about him unavailable elsewhere. Suskind certainly found it good enough to stay six days, taking copious notes. Assistants at the library remember him as a reticent and industrious visitor, well able to look after himself but impatient if his requests for information were not immediately answered.

Meanwhile, the third conspirator was about to make a

debut. Edith Irving had the most dangerous assignment any of the three had so far undertaken. She was to go to Zurich with a forged passport, on her own, wearing a disguise, and open an account in the name of a stranger who did not exist. The passport had been Clifford's work. He had carefully altered the number 1640396-390 on Edith's old passport, which she had previously reported lost, to 1640898-398, effecting the easiest changes, in the first "three," the second "six," and the last "zero." He had taken off the old photograph and inserted a new one, which he had taken of Edith wearing a black wig and hornrimmed glasses.

On May 12, Edith, now back in Ibiza, dressed up in clothes she had not worn in many a year—a smart suit, stockings, sensible shoes. To anyone who met her on the way to the airport she intended to explain that she was going to visit her former husband in Germany—who, as everyone knew, was so stuffy and respectable. As a matter of fact, the explanation was also true. She caught a plane to Zurich and checked into the Hotel Glarnischhof, using a name with which she, and the world, was to become extremely familiar—Helga R. Hughes. Next day she walked into the main banking hall in the Swiss Credit Bank and sought instructions for opening an account. There were, as we have seen, no problems in depositing the first check for $50,000. She had spent many an hour, under her husband's expert guidance, copying the H. R. Hughes signature, and although she never became quite as proficient as he did (perhaps lacking his complete confidence), her effort was satisfactory.

From Zurich she went to Wuppertal in Germany, where she spent a weekend with her former husband, Dieter Rosenkranz, and his new wife, Hanne, whose hospitality she repaid by stealing Hanne's identification card. A quick switch of photographs, and Edith was able to check into the Gotthard Hotel in Zurich on May 27—as Frau Hanne Rosenkranz. The object was to find out how easy it would be to open another account, perhaps more than one, into which the Swiss Credit money could be paid. If McGraw-Hill did manage to check up on the money, it would find that the trail had gone cold.

Edith opened Account No. 312,627 that same day at the Swiss Banking Corporation across the road and deposited a small sum of 5000 Swiss francs. She stayed on in Zurich long enough to draw $46,500 from Swiss Credit, and then returned to Ibiza with the money. It had all gone more smoothly than any of them had dared to hope. The second phase of the hoax was over.

They were able to take stock now. They had the fullest confidence of both McGraw-Hill and *Life,* who were sworn to secrecy and had no reason to disbelieve that Irving was enjoying the most intimate of conversations with Howard Hughes. They had the first installment of the money safely locked away in a Swiss bank, with most of it still intact—if the worst came to worst, they would at least be able to pay it back. And they had the beginnings of a collection of material on every phase of Hughes's life, except, perhaps, the last fifteen years.

But the research material was flat. There was nothing that infused life into the personality of Hughes. Suskind and Irving returned to America for some more intensive reading. It was to be a period during which two pieces of amazing luck transformed the whole operation from a run-of-the-mill fraud into a literary hoax of historic dimension.

On June 2 Clifford Irving had a working lunch with Ralph Graves. They discussed the progress of the biography, and Irving was able to say that the interviews with Hughes were going extremely well, but that of course they were still heavily engaged on the additional research that any decent biography requires. He wondered whether the Time-Life files on Hughes might be worth examining.

Graves saw no reason why not. When they returned to the

office he summoned David Maness, who was meeting Irving
for the first time. Graves explained Irving's position and
asked Maness to give him some help.

Normal procedures at Time-Life impose one limitation
on library files being used by non-staff writers. The file in
question must first be looked at by a *Time* or *Life* editor,
who removes any confidential material which might embarrass the corporation. Maness arranged to meet Irving at
ten the next morning, June 3, went back to his office, and
called for the Howard Hughes file from the library. He inspected it, and then removed six or seven confidential items
from it.

What remained was material from the 1930s—Hughes as
a film-maker and flier; in the 1940s and 1950s there was fine
material on Hughes as an independent businessman thumb-
ing his nose at Senator Brewster; in the 1960s, the file concentrated on Las Vegas. But what differentiates a Time-Life
file from those in, say, *The New York Times,* or even the
newspaper collection at the New York Public Library, is
that correspondents' reports are kept. *Time* magazine has a
voracious appetite for words, and demands many more than
it actually prints. The best of the unused reports, including
records of off-the-record conversations, are filed along with
the brief published stories. This makes the Time-Life library
files rather more time-consuming than any others in the city.
They are more than a day's work for anyone who is not looking for a specific item.

Maness had wanted to have a chat with Irving before
joining an editorial meeting at 10:30. But Irving did not
arrive until 10:25, carrying with him a large Spanish straw
bag. Maness was hurrying by then; he introduced Irving
to his secretary, pointed out the files on his sofa, opened the
door to Room 2902, where Irving could work without interruption, mentioned the photo-copying machine outside, and
said that he would see him later. When he looked in at lunch-
time, Irving had gone to lunch, and when Maness reappeared

at 4:30, Irving had gone for good. "He didn't seem to think much of our files," Maness's secretary commented.

But Irving, on the contrary, thought a great deal of them. So much so, in fact, that he photographed between 350 and 400 of the documents in the Time-Life library file. The camera had been hidden in his Spanish straw bag.

Irving was later to tell the federal investigators that the file had been the single most important source for his Hughes book. But he was exaggerating. His reasons for claiming this are fairly obvious: It must have appealed to him greatly to suggest that Time-Life, an organization which he was hoaxing, had provided the bulk of the material with which it had been hoaxed, and the allegation certainly caught Time-Life on the raw. Frank McCulloch, when he read the indictment, slapped the document in anger and said, "So that's why Irving was able to reproduce my conversations with Hughes so accurately." A vigorous, occasionally bad-tempered debate about who was to blame began in the Time-Life offices.

But evidence proving Irving's assertion is thin. For one thing, Maness insisted that there was nothing really confidential in the files he finally handed over to Irving, and he is the only other person who knows; for another, the *Life* researchers who checked the sources of Irving's information in the 30,000 words the magazine was proposing to serialize found outside sources for every bit of information they came across, and they had gone through 90 per cent of it by the time the project was condemned; and finally, though Irving may have found some useful guidelines in the file, they had little to do with the wholly convincing tone which the final manuscript achieved.

On June 7 both Suskind and Irving went to Texas and worked for three days at the public library and the offices of the *Houston Chronicle* and the *Houston Post*. Both papers contain a wealth of background material on Howard Hughes. At the *Chronicle* Irving had to exert all his charm to per-

suade an assistant to bend the rules and copy twenty-six clippings on the 3-M machine instead of the six to which most
readers are restricted. Then they went to Los Angeles and
called on Dr. David Hatfield of the Northrop Institute of
Technology, where there are more files on Hughes's career
as an aviator than anywhere else. It was typical of the Irving-
Suskind division of labor that Irving should engage Hatfield
in conversation while Suskind was dispatched to do the serious work on the files. But on this occasion the interview was
more profitable than the hard research. Dr. Hatfield had
known Hughes in the late 1920s and 1930s and was able to
tell some stories that only he knew. But he was not impressed
by Irving's knowledge of the subject. "When the book was
announced I assumed it was a fake," he said later. "They
wouldn't have been here if they had had original material."

Hatfield was also useful in putting them onto Charles
Lajotte, the man who taught Hughes to fly, and it may well
have been he who was able to impart at least some of the astonishing grasp of aviation detail which is one of Howard
Hughes's main characteristics, and which Irving succeeded
in introducing into the book:

"I taught Hughes to fly," recalls Lajotte. "That's right. I
remember the day: it was August 15, 1927. We went up in a
Waco 9 and later in a Waco 10. It was powered by an OX 5
engine, 90 HP, water-cooled. It was what the United States
Army used for training during the First World War. The
school had just started—the American Air Flying School at
Santa Monica, where the Douglas Aviation plant is. It was
the Lindbergh year. Everyone wanted to get into the act.
'Charlie,' he said to me the last time we went up, 'I want to
make another tailspin.' Up we went. We took a couple of
tailspins. Then he took off and made *Hell's Angels*. The
Waco 9 sold at that time for $3500. Very reasonable. It was
made in Troy, Ohio, and we couldn't get them fast enough."

It might have been Howard Hughes himself talking, which
could be what Clifford Irving thought as he scribbled down

the details. Next they visited the Academy of Motion Picture Arts and Sciences, where details about each of Howard Hughes's films are available, together with an 11-inch file of newspaper and magazine clippings. They also arranged for a private showing of Hughes's movie *Hell's Angels*.

In Hollywood they managed to acquire some rather more intimate details of Hughes's life than are generally available in a public library. One evening, a Hollywood lady who had once known Hughes received a phone call from Clifford Irving. He introduced himself as a friend of Robert Kirsch, who, he knew, was a friend of hers. Would she care to join Kirsch and himself for dinner? It was a somewhat convoluted invitation, but since she was doing nothing on that particular evening, and since she had not seen Kirsch for some time, she agreed to come.

She was more than a little surprised, on arriving, to find that there was no sign of Kirsch. Irving, apologizing profusely, explained that Kirsch had been taken suddenly ill. Champagne was served, and the evening became a relaxed and pleasant occasion with much cheerful badinage. The conversation moved inexorably around to the subject of Howard Hughes, and the Hollywood lady began to recount some of her richer stories about his relations with women. There is no lack of such stories around Hollywood, and most of them have doubtless improved with age, but on this occasion the audience was more intent than usual. The lady in question confesses that she found the evening enjoyable, though not particularly memorable, and she realized its full significance only when the name of Clifford Irving became a household word six months later.

Altogether the West Coast was proving extremely useful— just how useful, Irving and Suskind were about to find out. On June 12 Clifford Irving renewed his acquaintance with Stanley Meyer and acquired from him a property of limitless potential.

It is hard to exaggerate the importance to the hoaxers of

the Phelan manuscript and the accompanying transcript of his interviews with Noah Dietrich. The material gave them two vital elements which were sorely lacking so far from the biography, and which were to prove decisive in persuading the publishers to back the book through thick and thin.

The first was a series of anecdotes, descriptions, and details about Howard Hughes's private life which only a man with an intimate acquaintance of him would have known.

The second was even more important: a flavor and tone for their book about Hughes which they could never have invented. Not having met Hughes, they would have had to construct a *persona* for him out of their own heads. Noah Dietrich supplied them one ready-made. Dietrich's style, the way he talks and tells his stories, is rough and ready, spattered with crude and salty phrases, uninhibited, irreverent. Brusque, rude, and impatient, he is many things that Howard Hughes is not. But he had also been, for most of his working life, Howard Hughes's public stand-in. What the outside world had seen and known of Hughes had mostly come via Noah Dietrich. He had interpreted Hughes, compensated for him, kept quiet for him when it seemed best to do so. Where Hughes was incapable of making decisions, Dietrich made them fast—sometimes before there was even a problem. Where Hughes was constantly bogged down in detail, Dietrich saw the broad and gaudy brushstrokes. Where Hughes was shy and retiring, Dietrich was bullish and open-handed. And when Dietrich was finally forced to back out of Hughes's life and stop helping run it, Hughes retired from sight shortly after, never again to present himself in public.

Noah Dietrich was, therefore, much better raw material for a book than the less colorful Hughes. All Clifford Irving needed to do was to put the thoughts of Noah Dietrich into the mouth of Howard Hughes (as Noah had done for so many years), and he had the material for a rich, literary property.

That, of course, is precisely what he did, and that is why McGraw-Hill editors were so delighted when they finally saw his manuscript. For the one thing they had been dreading all along was that, when they emerged, the memoirs of Howard Hughes would be *dull*. Irving's end-product was anything but dull—and it owed much of its richness to Noah Dietrich. Even the question-and-answer form was borrowed from his transcripts.

Phelan's manuscript and the accompanying transcripts made further research superfluous. Irving and Suskind set off for Ibiza to congratulate themselves. Their expectations had been wildly exceeded. Not only did they have a solid body of background material, assembled by Suskind, covering every part of Hughes's life, they had numerous unpublished anecdotes from people who had actually met Hughes, a revealing file from the magazine that had written most about Hughes, and, finally, the memoirs of the man who knew him best—authentic, racy, and unpublished. It would make a sensational book, authorized or not.

In the Ibizan summer of 1971, from July 1 to August 27, Clifford Irving and Richard Suskind acted out a daily charade designed to persuade McGraw-Hill that a Hughes biography had been metamorphosed into the autobiography of Howard Hughes. Anyone overhearing their conversation—and no one was—would have been convinced that the Mediterranean sun had addled two expatriates' minds. They were interviewing each other and recording the conversation as they did so. They took turns being Howard Hughes, though no attempt was made to imitate Howard Hughes's accent. No one was going to hear the tapes; they were for transcription only. The idea had two advantages, both obtained from reading the Phelan-Dietrich transcripts: it made the interviews sound real, peppered as they were with ums, ahs, hesitations, and repetitions. And second, since conversation consumes more words than prose, it gave the book the epic length it would require. Irving was to claim that he had held a hundred hours of conversation with Hughes (exactly the same amount of time Phelan had spent talking out Dietrich's memories).

The resulting mound of paper would have to be big enough to back that up.

The wealth of research material they brought back from the United States was not enough on its own: there was, after all, a limit to the amount even Clifford Irving could plunder from another man's manuscript. Their method contained the solution: Since their imaginations were already at work putting much of the research material in question-and-answer form, the natural thing was to let that imagination run riot and just make the stuff up.

Maybe as much as a quarter of the transcribed conversations between Irving and Suskind that summer had no basis in fact at all; they were the dreams of a dreamer. Two long meetings between Howard Hughes and Ernest Hemingway, a writer much admired by Clifford Irving, are described at length. On another occasion Hughes takes a trip through the African jungle to meet Albert Schweitzer in Lambarene. Then there is an account of a non-existent trip to Ethiopia. There was, as might be expected, a good deal more rhetoric than fact in these sections, and that prevented their being scrutinized too carefully before publication. Irving's luck was bolstered by the lack of interest shown by Graves and Maness in this make-believe. Had they decided to use these excerpts, the facts would have been checked and found to be non-existent. And *Life*'s suspicions would have been aroused earlier.

By the end of August, Irving and Suskind thought they knew enough about Hughes to realize that their product would seem rather more like the real thing than the ghostly figure on the ninth floor of the Britannia Beach Hotel. They must have felt that they had done Hughes a considerable service. They decided to up the ante to one million dollars.

A million was a slight misjudgment, but Irving claimed credit for bringing the demand down to $850,000. And even before anyone from McGraw-Hill and *Life* had read the

transcribed tapes, he was confident enough to bring a check
for $100,000 with him to New York in September and tell
McGraw-Hill officials they could have the money back
if they preferred it to the manuscript. McGraw-Hill was
mildly embarrassed, though nowhere near as embarrassed as
Clifford Irving would have been, had his offer been accepted.
At that moment there was exactly $1500 in the H. R. Hughes
account at the Swiss Credit Bank, on which the check had
been drawn. Clifford Irving's behavior in September was an
echo of his master. Elmyr de Hory always told him that the
more outrageous a hoaxer's behavior was, the more easily he
was believed.

After the enthusiastic reception of the manuscript, the
problems must have seemed very small indeed. Edith was
paying checks made out to H.R. Hughes into the Swiss
Credit Bank, taking the money out again, and paying a large
part of it into the Swiss Banking Corporation. Some she took
back with her to Ibiza, where Irving and Suskind were confidently preparing their great literary scoop for the printer
and calculating the profits.

The money from the coup was beginning to circulate
nicely through the Swiss monetary system. Edith Irving had
become a regular traveler on the flight from Barcelona to
Zurich. In September, in October, and again in December
she performed a complex series of financial transactions in
the offices of the Swiss Credit Bank and the Swiss Banking
Corporation. It was at the Swiss Banking Corporation that
she opened an account under the name of Hanne Rosenkranz.
The indictment takes up the story.

> At that time the defendant Edith Irving was informed that
> the real Hanne Rosenkranz had recently opened a trust ac-
> count with the Swiss Banking Corporation. Defendant Edith
> Irving was informed that since she was a good customer her
> forgeries would be remedied by having the forged account
> transferred to another branch of the Swiss Banking Corpo-
> ration.

It is, in the circumstances, a provocative allegation—an apparently gratuitous sideswipe at Swiss banks, and all they stand for. It is also legally questionable. As it appeared to the manager of the Swiss Banking Corporation's Zurich branch, all Edith Irving had done was use another person's name to open a bank account into which money was then transferred. He had no knowledge that Hanne Rosenkranz's identity card was being used to promote a fraud, which would have made Edith's signatures forgeries. The allegation has, incidentally, been denied categorically by the bank officials concerned and by the Swiss prosecutor, Peter Veleff, who questioned them.

The Swiss banks, which have been gradually becoming more amenable to bending their secrecy law, are unlikely to look kindly on future requests for information from America, in the light of this allegation. It is even possible they will become secure enough again to accommodate another Clifford Irving.

The luck of the Irvings and Richard Suskind held firm right through the twelve months from conception to announcement of the autobiography. And luck begat confidence. The last episodes in the private relationship between McGraw-Hill and Irving were to characterize it perfectly.

In November, McGraw-Hill wanted Irving to contact Hughes and have him deny the authenticity of Eaton's book. Irving said he would, but by now he was in no mood merely just to take out his yellow legal notepad, write a single sentence, and sign it "Howard Hughes." The only problem for the plotters in Ibiza was to get the letter to Nassau, since it had to carry a Bahamian or a Florida postmark. It was a nuisance, particularly as it meant using another false passport, but Richard Suskind bought an air ticket for Nassau and went there on November 16 to post the letter himself. There was no one else they could trust.

The last trick was in Florida. Irving said he was meeting Hughes in December to deliver his last check, and he would ask him to sanction a press release then.

He telephoned Albert Leventhal, who was dealing with the momentous announcement, and told him there was only one change Hughes wanted. It was in the last sentence, which originally read: "The amount paid to Mr. Hughes by Mc-Graw-Hill will not be divulged." Irving said that Hughes would like his name taken out of the sentence, which ought to read: "The amount paid by McGraw-Hill will not be divulged." For the first time in the year of the hoax, Clifford Irving had leaned toward the side of honesty.

# Epilogue

"I would feel better if Irving had not used
the friends who had trusted him; he just
punched them up to the front line."

Martin S. Ackerman, former attorney to Clifford Irving

The comedy was rated a success. The production had been a
trifle undisciplined, perhaps, and there had been moments
when one or two of the subplots had threatened to topple
over into low farce, but the action had been well sustained
and there was an absence of that tiresome search for deeper
significance which ruins so many of the genre. Above all, it
had been brief. No sooner were the guilty characters appre-
hended than the curtain was firmly rung down. For some
members of the audience it was lowered with suspicious
speed. Amongst the Howard Hughes party, for instance, there
were loud cries of "You've forgotten the last act!"

Chester Davis in New York, Dick Hannah in Los Angeles,
and Intertel in Washington were still hard at work on the
case, convinced that there was far more to it than had
emerged in public. Specifically, they could not believe that
their arch-enemy, Robert Maheu, was not somehow involved,
and their disappointment at his omission from the federal
case can be compared to that of a James Bond addict who
realizes toward the end of the latest Ian Fleming that Ernst
Blofeld is not going to make an appearance.

Their thesis ran roughly as follows: Robert Maheu would

give anything to flush Howard Hughes into the open so that he could finally confront him with his case for wrongful dismissal. None of his attempts so far had succeeded, and he was growing desperate. He knew that this sort of ploy was one of the few things that might really catch Hughes on the raw and finally force him to come out in public, and he was demonstrably endowed with a mind sufficiently devious to think up the plot. Clifford Irving, on the other hand, was an unknown hick—he was just the tool.

The main burden of their evidence for this conspiracy rested on a claim that there was one section of Irving's manuscript whose source had not been established. It concerned the TWA case, and it could have come only from somebody inside the Hughes organization or somebody who had recently been inside it. It had been contained in the original draft of the autobiography, but then had been mysteriously dropped, so that the federal investigators would not pursue it.

Unfortunately they were saddled with a complete dearth of solid proof. The TWA material does indeed exist, but there is nothing to show that Maheu, who was called to testify to the grand jury, was involved in passing it on. It could have come from a number of other sources. Nevertheless, the Irving docket still occupies the top drawer of Robert Peloquin's desk at Intertel's offices.

McGraw-Hill simply wanted to forget all about it. But, far from ending, the nightmare became worse. Once the pattern of McGraw-Hill and hoaxes had become established, journalists began looking for stories to fit it. They did succeed in unearthing a serious case of plagiarism. The *Memoirs of Chief Red Fox*—an account, among other things, of the massacre at Wounded Knee—was a McGraw-Hill bestseller. Alas, the account turned out to have been drawn not from the chief's memory, but from a book by an Indian expert called James McGregor published in 1940. McGraw-Hill and Chief Red Fox, taken together, evoke Lady Bracknell, in Oscar Wilde's *The Importance of Being Ernest:* "To lose one parent, Mr. Worthing, may be regarded as a misfortune; to lose both looks like carelessness." The charges seemed to be rather more serious than carelessness, however, when Robert Sussman Stewart, editor of the Irving book, was accused of accepting a loan from two authors which amounted to exactly 10 per cent of their advance—the same percentage as most literary agents' fees. Stewart was summarily demoted from his post as chief editor in March. But Ted Weber, the company's spokesman, thought a lesson had been learned from it all: "If someone walked in with an Autobiography of Paul Getty," he said, cheerfully, "we'd do a hell of a lot more checking." Still, the affair seemed to have done the company no harm financially: Irving had to promise that he would return as much of the money as possible himself, and the balance was expected to come from insurance.

Another reputation—that of Messrs. Osborn, Osborn and Osborn—had been dealt an even more savage blow. It would undoubtedly be a long time before they were called as witnesses for the defense without provoking a torrent of scornful rhetoric from the prosecuting attorney. Indeed, the whole art of handwriting analysis has suffered a setback to its status as reliable evidence—which is, perhaps, no bad thing for everyone apart from handwriting analysts.

Meanwhile, in Ibiza, the camp-followers were acting true to form. Everybody, naturally, felt that the Irvings had been grossly misjudged, hounded by the cruel and unsympathetic forces of law, order, and the press. The idea that they had committed a real crime was hard to believe, so most Ibizans concluded that the whole thing was a put-up job, a plot by the outside world to do down two nice, harmless people. An anthology of their comments reflects an astonishing eagerness to achieve some sort of rationale:

"They were charming people and awfully kind to each other and their friends. . . . You could trust your life to Cliff. . . . Edith is absolutely wonderful. She's only got caught up in this thing because she's fond of him. . . . No one who knows Cliff and Edith is going to say anything but good about them. . . . I can't believe they intended anyone any harm, though they certainly intended themselves a lot of good. . . . What they were doing was quite legitimate as far as I can see. . . . There was no criminal intent in what they did. . . . I can't help feeling that Cliff still has an ace in his hand to play. . . . Of course, Cliff knows a lot more than he's told. . . . Howard Hughes doesn't really exist, but that's off the record, old boy. . . . The man who's running the Hughes empire is a member of the Mafia, but don't quote me. . . ."

When it was gently pointed out that the Irvings had actually pleaded guilty and confessed, amongst other things, to forgery, one Ibizan became positively incensed. "If I were you I'd be very careful about saying that in public," he warned, "or you may find yourself in serious trouble." There was much gossip, too, about the arrival on the island of Edith Irving's lawyer, Philip Lorber, who strode about in sneakers and windbreaker. His role was to drum up support for Edith among the islanders in the form of letters attesting to the Irvings' personal integrity. There was no lack of these, and small "signing" parties were thrown at which guests were asked to write fulsome tributes.

The affair, however, had one unfortunate side effect on Ibiza. Gerry Albertini's house, raided at one stage by the police, was found to conceal two unlicensed pistols, one loaded. In Spain that can be a serious crime, though the arms in question seem to have been only of the decorative variety. It was the second serious mishap that had befallen Albertini. Roaming the streets of New York after his grand-jury appearance, he was mugged on Madison Avenue. Mr. Albertini's friendship for Clifford Irving is believed to be undergoing considerable strain.

For the Baroness Nina Van Pallandt, however, it had been

a turning point of quite a different kind. As a direct result of four days of illicit romance with a minor novelist, Nina Van Pallandt, singer, found herself fixed up with: two appearances on the Dick Cavett Show, two appearances on the Mike Douglas Show, two appearances on the David Frost Show, one on the Johnny Carson Show, one on the *Today* show, and a television special. She had a three-week engagement at the St. Regis Hotel in New York—which was a critical triumph—engagements booked in San Juan, San Francisco, Dallas, and Miami. There are even plans for a book about her. As her manager put it, "Listen, the publicity was worth five hit records and an Academy Award."

Jim Phelan by this time had established an uncharacteristic relationship with a previously hostile organization. After years of regarding Phelan as a major irritant, the Hughes empire was now obliged to consider him some kind of improbable ally. He had, after all, effected something that the highly paid legions of Hughes detectives and lawyers had failed to achieve—the final annihilation of Clifford Irving's manuscript.

He was told by many a faithful Hughesman that Howard Hughes himself was grateful for what he had done. There was, however, one snag. The Rosemont action against Noah Dietrich had halted distribution of his book royalties until the case could be litigated, and Phelan was owed $40,000 from his settlement with Dietrich. He had collected just half this amount when Rosemont took up its hostile stance at the cashier's window. Davis gently explained the position to Phelan: Dietrich was the target, and Phelan should realize that no personal ingratitude to him was intended.

"I realize that," Phelan said, sighing, "but if you're ever talking to Howard, please tell him I hope he never gets grateful to me again."

The whole affair, it is true, reflected many of the less attractive traits in American society, but it also provided evidence of qualities that are enviable anywhere. Both Jim Phelan and

Frank McCulloch felt compelled to pursue the truth even when it led into areas which were wounding to their own pride and which involved the admission that their professional judgment had been at fault. But it was the dedication, not the errors, that was important. The final credit for exploding the hoax was deservedly theirs, and we think of them as the authentic heroes of our story.

And what of the principals?

Clifford Irving slipped from the peak of manic euphoria which he had touched when the case, and his fame, were at their height, through strain to exhaustion, and finally depression. But he could not entirely suppress the old bumptiousness. Looking back over the affair with a reporter in Westport, Connecticut, he railed against his treatment in the newspapers, particularly *The New York Times,* where he had once seen "news that was being edited, slanted, and news that was unfavorable to the paper's policies being chopped out of correspondents' reports." Coming from a man who had just spent fifteen months living out a lie which had involved a daily stream of deception, distortion, dishonesty, betrayal, slanted stories, edited facts, theft of original ideas, forgeries, and suppression of the truth, this was rich indeed.

Irving left New York after pleading guilty and rented a house in Westport, with a lease thoughtfully constructed to expire on June 15—the day before sentencing. The Connecticut suburbs were a poor substitute for St. Moritz, where he had hoped to spend the winter, and Java, which he had planned to visit in the spring. But he was trapped now not just by his plea of guilty, but by the need to earn as much money as he could. He had to pay off McGraw-Hill and Maurice Nessen, let alone the cost of housekeeping in New York. Irving calculated that his debts amounted to $1,500,000, but this was, like many of his calculations, a ridiculous exaggeration; $350,000 was closer to the mark. So the autobiographer of Howard Hughes turned to his own memoirs—to be entitled "The Book about the Book."

As for Howard Hughes, he remains . . . Howard Hughes. One of his lieutenants, looking back on the Irving affair commented, "You know this could be the best thing that ever happened to Hughes. If it succeeds in jolting him back into some semblance of normal life, it will all have been worth while." So far, however, there has been little evidence of its doing any such thing. One month after arriving in Nicaragua, Hughes left secretly again and ended up in Vancouver, where he is once more, at the time of writing, sealed off from the world, this time on the top two floors of the Bayshore Inn. Still flitting around the perimeters of the United States, he has not so far, as he promised in his telephone interview, returned to Las Vegas or Los Angeles.

Even the situation vis-à-vis the Nevada Gaming Commission, which was reaching a climax when Irving's book was first announced, has reverted to the status quo. It is again trying to get Hughes to appear in person, and Hughes is just as resolutely declining the invitation. But there are signs of a new humility amongst his employees. One of them told a reporter that he had secret knowledge of the way the commission's latest vote on the Hughes application had gone. "It was five to zero against us," he confided, "but they did give us forty-eight hours' warning."

In the end the striking thing about the hoaxer and the hoaxed is not the gulf which separates them, but the similarities between them. Both are egocentric men, deeply absorbed in their personae; both are manipulators, using other people for the cultivation of an image of themselves; both are willing to sacrifice friends and acquaintances in a crisis. Hughes would never have been hoaxed if he had not, during the upheavals in Las Vegas, behaved with such imperious disregard for other people's lives. For his part Irving used his friends so ruthlessly to make his hoax work that when he really needed their support he found that it was spent.

It is difficult to avoid the conclusion that Howard Hughes and Clifford Irving deserved each other.

# Postscript

In writing this book we were always confronted by a basic problem. Our estimate of Clifford Irving was that he had a certain glib talent but that he was incapable of formulating by himself an idea as original as the hoaxing of Howard Hughes.

Twenty-four hours before going to press we uncovered evidence that goes some way toward resolving this contradiction. It suggests that Irving's confession of guilt, as revealed in the indictments, does *not* tell the whole truth.

The evidence is contained in a conversation which took place during a dinner party in late November 1970, in New York. Present: Clifford and Edith Irving, Mike Hamilburg (Clifford's cousin), and Mrs. Hamilburg. During the course of the dinner Edith revealed that Clifford was contemplating "a proposition" that could be worth upward of $500,000. It would, she said, be a dangerous one to undertake, since it concerned people "who would stop at nothing to achieve their own ends—even murder." She did not elaborate on the nature of the project, but she suggested that because of the risks involved they might well turn it down. It is interesting that the phrase she used about the men "who stop at nothing" is almost identical to that used by the Irvings more than a year later to describe the Hughes organization. But it is rather more significant that the conversation predates *by one month* the official birth of the hoax as outlined in Clifford Irving's testimony to the grand jury. It suggests that the idea of writing a Hughes biography was prompted by more than the chance reading of a magazine article.

The Manhattan publishing world is a small gossipy one,

with which Clifford Irving is familiar. It now seems evident that in November 1970 he picked up intimations of the fact that the first part of Noah Dietrich's memoirs was becoming a "literary property." He may also have learned of the basic marketing problem it presented: too much Noah Dietrich and not enough Howard Hughes.

This, of course, was precisely the problem that he was able to resolve.